텝스의 기술 RC

텝스의 기술 RC(개정판)

초　　판 1쇄 발행일 2014년 1월 27일
개정2판 1쇄 발행일 2020년 1월 6일
개정3판 1쇄 발행일 2024년 4월 3일

지은이 송승호 외 6인
펴낸이 양옥매
디자인 송다희 임흥순

펴낸곳 도서출판 책과나무
출판등록 제2012-000376
주소 서울특별시 마포구 방울내로 79 이노빌딩 302호
대표전화 02.372.1537 **팩스** 02.372.1538
이메일 booknamu2007@naver.com
홈페이지 www.booknamu.com
ISBN 979-11-6752-462-1 (13740)

뉴텝스 독해 기본서

텝스의 기술 RC

송승호 지음

책과나무

Author's Note

"텝스의 기술"은 2013년 초판 1쇄로 세상에 공식 출판되었으며, 지금까지 50,000명이 넘는 수험생들의 텝스 학습을 책임져 왔습니다. 교재가 전국 출판된 이후로 최근 몇 년간 대형 어학원에서의 영입 제의들도 모두 거절해가며 오로지 TEPS 연구에만 몰두했습니다. 그리고 새롭게 출간되는 이 교재는 뉴텝스의 트렌드를 반영한 최신 개정판입니다. 수년 간 TEPS 기출문제 분석을 통해 도출한 시험의 모든 유형을 집대성하였으며, 학습자의 유형 별 학습이 가능하도록 단원들을 세분화하였습니다.

저는 텝스 때문에 3년을 고생했습니다. 생애 첫 텝스 시험을 보던 날 정신없이 몰아치는 문제들과 시간적 압박 속에 당황하여 "도대체 이건 뭐 하는 시험이지?" 라고 생각했던 기억이 납니다. 그리고 집에 돌아가서 텝스와 관련된 전략을 찾기 위해 인터넷을 엄청나게 뒤졌지만, 도움되는 내용은 찾을 수가 없었습니다. 그래서 텝스 시험에 적합한 전략을 세우기 위해 스스로 시험을 분석하기 시작했습니다. 텝스와 관련된 모든 전략, 점수대별 공부 방법부터 문제풀이 전략, 문제풀이 기술, 독해 문제 풀이 루틴, 오답을 발견해내는 기술 등과 같은 텝스 점수 향상에 필요한 시험의 모든 패턴들을 집대성했습니다.

그 결과, 수많은 시행착오와 고생 끝에 이론이 완성되었고, 회차 전국 11등에 이어 텝스 만점(600/600)을 달성하였습니다. 이후로 주위 사람들에게 이 이론을 전달하며 그들의 성적이 폭발적으로 상승하는 것을 경험하게 되었습니다. 이후로도 수많은 성적 역전 사례, 2년 연속 연간 최고득점자를 배출하는 등 이론의 타당성을 끊임없이 증명해왔습니다.

"텝스의 기술"은 단순 요령이나 꼼수를 가르치지 않습니다. 텝스19 수강생들이 매년 전국 최상위 성적을 차지하는 이유는, 텝스의 출제 원리에 기반한 시험 패턴을 집대성 해놓았기 때문입니다. "텝스의 기술"이 텝스 수험생들에게 올바른 접근법을 확립해 줄 것이라고 자신합니다.

기출문제에 기반한 텝스 독해 필독서의 힘을 느껴보세요.
이제는 여러분의 차례입니다.

텝스는 역전의 기회가 되어야 합니다.
모든 독자들의 성적 상승 기적을 기원하겠습니다.

– 송승호 드림

교재 활용법

텝스 시험 성적을 올리는 가장 효율적인 공부 방법은 무엇일까?
시험을 해부하여 각 요소별 출제 패턴을 익히는 것이 가장 효율적인 방식이다. 시험의 모든 패턴들을 분석하여 제시해주는 것이 수험서의 역할인데, "수학의 정석", "국어의 기술" 등을 필두로 유명 수험서들은 각 시험 문제들의 패턴을 정확하게 분석하여 열거하고 있다.
〈텝스의 기술 독해편〉은 업계 최초로 TEPS 독해 3 요소의 패턴들을 집대성하였다. TEPS 독해의 필수 3요소는, (1) 지문 (2) 질문(3) 선택지 이다.

While the so-called "dumb" phones are disappearing quickly, some other electronic gadgets are disappearing even faster. Digital cameras, portable gaming console, PDAs and mp3 players have almost disappeared off the market since 2010, and they may become completely obsolete by the next few years. The leading factor contributing to their demise is the sheer multi-functionality of smart phones. With their phones becoming more versatile and compact than ever, people are no longer feeling the need for bulky separate devices.	지문 ➡	19가지
Q. What is the passage mainly about?	질문 ➡	7가지
(a) The inconvenience of using separate devices (b) The demise of numerous electronic devices. (c) The disappearance of dumb phones from the market (d) The versatility and compactness of smartphones	선택지 ➡	7가지

첫째 [지문 구조]의 19가지 패턴 -1부

TEPS 지문은 19가지 전개 패턴 내에서 반복적인 출제가 이루어지기 때문에, 미리 그 구조를 파악할 수 있다면 속도와 정확도 모두 향상된다. 단순 주제별 학습이 아닌, 지문 구조의 패턴별로 정리된 수험서는 "텝스의 기술" 뿐이다.

둘째 [질문 유형]의 7가지 패턴 -2부

주제찾기, 빈칸채우기, 등 다양한 형태의 질문들이 출제되는데, 각 유형의 출제 의도에 따라 문제풀이 전략을 달리해야 한다.

셋째 [오답/선택지]의 7가지 패턴 -3부

TEPS가 즐겨 출제하는 오답의 7가지 유형을 학습해야만 선택지에서 시간 낭비를 줄이고 정확도를 극대화 할 수 있다.

위와 같은 패턴별 접근법은 "텝스의 기술"이 수년간 연구해온 내용들이다. 수 많은 수강생들이 패턴별 학습으로 최단기 성적 상승을 달성할 수 있었다.

뜬구름 잡는 식의 학습은 그만두고, 하루라도 빨리 시험의 패턴별 접근으로 텝스를 졸업하자!

CONTENTS

제1부 지문의 19가지 유형

제2부 문제의 7가지 유형

제3부 오답의 7가지 유형

제4부 실전 모의고사

제1부

지문의 19가지 유형

텝스의 지문 구조는 정해져 있다

제 1부에서는, TEPS19가 집대성한 텝스 지문의 19가지 패턴을 모두 학습하게 된다. 독해 시 지문의 전개 방식을 미리 판단하는 힘을 기르게 될 것이고, 문제풀이 시 정확도는 향상되는데 속도는 현저히 줄어드는 것을 경험할 것이다.

각 패턴 별 단서들을 사전에 학습하고, 지문을 훑어보면서 해당 지문이 19가지 중 어떤 패턴에 속하는지 미리 파악할 수 있고, 정보 단서가 높은 구역 위주로 강약조절하며 읽어내면 속도와 정확성 둘 다 잡을 수 있다. 지문 구조 패턴 적중률은 실제 기출문제집에서 95%를 보인다.

결국 19가지의 지문 구조는 매 시험 반복 출제가 되고 있기 때문에, 이를 미리 학습하고 시험장에 가면 해석이나 어휘 때문에 막히는 일이 현저히 떨어져 점수 극대화가 가능하다.

이것이 어떻게 가능할까? 바로 TEPS 지문의 전개 패턴들이 정형화되어 있기 때문이다.

패턴 학습

Would you like to save a bundle on computers? Build one yourself instead of buying the more expensive brand-manufactured ones. A price comparison between finished product computers and the sum of its parts showed that building a computer yourself can save up to 40% of your budget. A research that took place for over three years in local computer rental shops also proved that brand-name computers maintenance costs at only 5 dollars less per year. That's not tha and considering how quickly people buy new computers the building a computer yourself is a much better bargain.

Q: What is the main idea of the passage?
(a) Research on computer maintenance cost was performed at PC cafes
(b) Manufactured computers tend to last longer than built-at-home computers
(c) Considering various factors, it is more economical to build a computer than to buy one
(d) A research has proven that computers built at home incur less maintenance cost over time

패턴 반영

기출 문제

Want an insider tip that could save you a bundle on diapers? Switch to generic store brands instead of the pricier name-brand ones. Research performed at three local daycares—involving several thousand diaper changes—shows that you probably won't detect any difference. With ge ic store brands doing their best to duplicate the improvements nd-name counterparts are incorporating into their diapers, ually nothing to distinguish one brand from the other.

Q What is the main idea of the passage?
(a) Research on diapers was done at individual homes.
(b) Little difference in quality exists among diaper brands.
(c) Brand-name diapers have recently come down in price.
(d) Store brand diapers are better than brand-name diapers.

텝스 독해 시험에는 19가지 지문 전개 패턴이 있다. 어디에서도 이러한 기준을 설명해주지 않지만, 텝스 20년 역사 동안의 기출 문제들을 관통하는 19가지의 지문 전개 패턴은 분명 존재한다. 뉴텝스에서도 적중률이 그대로 유지되고 있는 만큼, 패턴 학습은 모든 수험생들에게 필수라고 할 수 있겠다.

제1부에서는

19가지 패턴을 모두 학습 후, 실제 시험장에서 이 패턴들이 재림하는 것을 직접 경험해보길 바란다.

참고 패턴 학습법 vs. 주제 학습법

많은 수험생들이 무의식적으로 택하는 공부법은 주제(내용)별 접근일 것이다. 지문의 "내용"에 초점을 두고 학습을 하는 것은, 그 내용이 실제 시험에서 반복 출제될 가능성이 매우 희미하기 때문에 TEPS 시험 대비에는 큰 도움이 되지 않는다. (cf. 비즈니스 영어를 평가하는 토익 시험은 동일 소재들이 반복 출제되기 때문에 주제별 학습이 중요하다.)

그리고 재차 강조하지만, 이 교재는 '요령'을 가르치는 책이 절대 아니다. 요령이라는 것은 불확실성을 수반하기 마련이기에 단순 꼼수들로는 최상위권까지 올라갈 수 없다. 하지만 텝스19 전략을 믿고 따르면 누구나 최단기 성적 상승이 가능하며, 최상위권에 도달할 수도 있다. 오로지 요령만을 가르쳐왔다면 수많은 상위권 학생들을 배출할 수 있었을까?

"본 교재는 '요령'을 가르치지 않는다.
'원리 원칙'을 기반으로 한 문제 풀이 전략 및 점수 극대화 방법을 강의하는 것이다."

쏘아보기

텝스 독해 지문들의 정형화된 패턴들을 학습하기 전에 익혀야 할 중요한 문제풀이 습관이 있다.
이는 바로 "쏘아보기"이며, 문제 풀이 직전에 지문을 3~5초 간 쓱 훑는 것을 의미한다. 사전에 각 지문 전개 유형 별 핵심 단서들을 미리 학습한 뒤 지문을 쏘아보면, 지문의 구조를 미리 파악해둔 상태에서 독해를 시작할 수 있다. 큰 틀을 미리 파악한 뒤 문제 풀이에 임하기 때문에 정확도와 속도 모두 잡을 수 있는 전략이다.
이번 '쏘아보기'는 제 1부에서 가장 중요한 단원이다. 모든 지문 유형에 필수 적용되어야 하는 것이 "쏘아보기"이기 때문이다.

일반적으로 우리는 지문 독해 시 정신없이 첫 문장부터 차례대로 읽고 문제 풀이로 넘어간다. 하지만, 큰 그림(대의)를 미리 파악해야하는 경우(ex. 주제문, 빈칸채우기), 쏘아보기를 통해 보다 더 효율적인 문제풀이가 가능하다.

쏘아보기란?

독해 지문이 주어지면 지문을 5초 동안 빠르게 훑는 것이다. 그 5초 동안 "쏘아보기 단서"들에 동그라미 표시를 하면, 그 단서들을 바탕으로 지문에서 가장 중요한 문장들을 파악할 수 있으며, 가장 중요한 문장들 위주로 독해하고 문제를 풀어낼 수 있다.

- 지문 전체를 읽는 것보다 더 정확하다 ┐
- 지문 전체를 읽는 것보다 더 신속하다 ┘ 속도 & 정확도
- 구체적인 "쏘아보기 단서"들은 19단원들에서 익히게 될 것이다

5초 [지문을 읽는 것이 아니라 훑는 것]

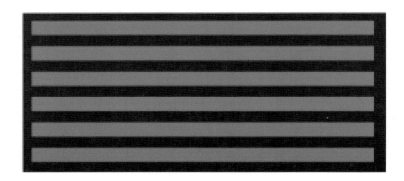

결국, 5초를 투자해서 5초 동안 지문을 읽기보단 지문을 빠르게 훑고(스키밍 X), 표시된 단서를 바탕으로 강약 조절하며 독해를 해나가는 것이다. 5초 투자로 그 이상의 시간과 정확도를 얻을 수 있다

1~19단원 각 단원 학습 시 유형 별 쏘아보기 단서를 학습하게 되니, 이를 총체적으로 학습하여 지문 구조 파악이 수월할 수 있도록 하자.

지문 패턴#1
연결어 2개

제1부
지문의 19가지 유형

BASIC 지문 구조 ▷

PATTERN 1 연결어 2개

지금까지 텝스 독해를 할 때는 지문의 내용을 읽고 이해한 후 그 내용을 떠올리며 가장 중요한 부분을 찾아 문제를 풀려고 했을 것이다. 빈칸 채우기 유형과 주제 찾기 유형에서 이러한 독해 방법은 어리석은 것이다. 왜냐하면, 결국 이 문제들에서는 항상 주제에 대한 이해도만 평가하기 때문이다. 1단원에선 연결어 두 개를 바탕으로 전체 지문에서 주요 문장에만 집중하고 문제를 푸는 방법을 소개한다. 1단원 지문을 발견하면 30초 안에 풀 수 있어야 한다.

쏘아보기 단서

연결어(연결어 뒤에 쉼표로 구분)
EX) However, ~~~~ . In addition, ~~~~~.
※ but은 연결어에서 제외.

원리 설명

텝스 지문의 길이는 정해져 있다. 이 속에서, 연결어는 칸막이 역할을 한다고 생각하면 된다. 칸막이, 즉, 연결어가 두 개면 칸은 3개가 생기게 되고, 우리는 이 3개의 칸에 우선순위를 메길 수 있다.
예를 들어, However, Additionally 연결어 두 개를 쏘아보기 시 발견했다면, 가장 중요한 부분은 however 뒤, 그다음 중요한 부분은 additionally 뒤, 그리고 우선순위 3순위는 however 앞부분이 된다.

첫 문장	3	However	1	In addition	2

문제 풀이

조건 쏘아보기에서 연결어가 2개 이상 있다면 그 두 개의 연결어를 기준으로 지문 단락 간의 우선순위를 메긴다. 그리고 3개의 칸 중 1순위 부분이 어디인지 확실히 파악한다.

풀이 지문의 "첫 문장"과 우선순위 "일 순위 문장"을 읽고 선택지로 내려간다면 문제는 풀린다. 이런 원리가 적용되는 이유는 바로 빈칸 채우기 문제와 주제 찾기 문제의 특성 때문이다. 핵심 단서만 파악한다면 모두 풀 수 있는 것이 빈칸 채우기와 주제 찾기 문제다.

※ 지문에 however가 한 개 보인다고 however 뒤부터 바로 보는 것은 무모한 것이다.
지문 속에 연결어 2개 이상이 있을 때에만 우선순위에 따라 문장을 읽는다.

연습문제

우선 30~40초동안 문제를 먼저 풀어보세요

1. Through the last two decades, the number of animals used in scientific experiments and product testing has more than quadrupled. These animals, more than five million of which are used every year, are mostly rodents like mice, guinea pigs, hamsters and squirrels. While human trials and experiments are becoming more and more expensive and politically sensitive, these animals provide a cost-effective and reasonably human-like alternative to humans. However, increased awareness of animal rights has recently made it much more troublesome to perform testing on animals. Furthermore, the increased demand for rodents as pets caused the animals' prices to rise, making it a much less attractive choice.

Q : What is the topic of the passage?
(a) The problems of testing with animals like rodents
(b) The decreased incentive to use animals like rodents as test subjects
(c) A new legislation concerning scientific testing on animals like rodents
(d) The dangers of human testing and its potential political inconveniences

1. Through the last two decades, the number of animals used in scientific experiments and product testing has more than quadrupled. These animals, more than five million of which are used every year, are mostly rodents like mice, guinea pigs, hamsters and squirrels. While human trials and experiments are becoming more and more expensive and politically sensitive, these animals provide a cost-effective and reasonably human-like alternative to humans. However, increased awareness of animal rights has recently made it much more troublesome to perform testing on animals. Furthermore, the increased demand for rodents as pets caused the animals' prices to rise, making it a much less attractive choice.

Q: What is the topic of the passage?
(a) The problems of testing with animals like rodents
(b) The decreased incentive to use animals like rodents as test subjects
(c) A new legislation concerning scientific testing on animals like rodents
(d) The dangers of human testing and its potential political inconveniences

2. During the decline of Köln Freistadt, the city officials mainly concentrated on law enforcement instead of reviving the city's withering commerce. It was their belief that restoring public order would help the city regain its former prosperity and effectively counter the impending collapse. However, the resulting harsh surveillance and restrictions only caused the city's economy to stagnate even further, since many merchants and craftsmen saw a sharp decrease in floating population, and thus, less profit. Moreover, corruption was rampant among the overly empowered police force, eating away even more of the city's commercial vigor. Therefore, ____________________ only accelerated the demise of Köln Freistadt.

(a) the commercial inactivity of the merchants and craftsmen
(b) the restoration of public order that put the city back on track
(c) the public order policies imposed to revitalize the city
(d) the corruption of the law enforcement civil workers

2. During the decline of Köln Freistadt, the city officials mainly concentrated on law enforcement instead of reviving the city's withering commerce. It was their belief that restoring public order would help the city regain its former prosperity and effectively counter the impending collapse. However, the resulting harsh surveillance and restrictions only caused the city's economy to stagnate even further, since many merchants and craftsmen saw a sharp decrease in floating population, and thus, less profit. Moreover, corruption was rampant among the overly empowered police force, eating away even more of the city's commercial vigor. Therefore, ____________________ only accelerated the demise of Köln Freistadt.

(a) the commercial inactivity of the merchants and craftsmen
(b) the restoration of public order that put the city back on track
(c) the public order policies imposed to revitalize the city
(d) the corruption of the law enforcement civil workers

3. The radioactive isotope Tepsium-19 is an uncommon by-product of spontaneous nuclear fission in stars. It is a useful substance which is essential for the operation of the most common types of nuclear fission plants across the world, but is unfortunately extremely rare on Earth. Thus, several powerful nations vied to take a larger share when an abundant reserve of Tepsium-19 was reported to have been discovered on the surface of the Moon in 1969. In addition, global energy conglomerates started lobbying their governments, each competing for an exclusive contract and mining rights. All this fuss subsided, however, when subsequent trips to the moon proved that the alleged Tepsium-19 reserve was found out to be Toefleum-19, which had a similar emission spectrum indistinguishable by existing technologies.

Q: What is the main topic of the passage?
(a) The usefulness of the radioactive isotope Tepsium-19
(b) A disputed rare resource reserve on the surface of the Moon
(c) A worldwide competition for a rare resource
(d) A historical power struggle between nations and corporate powers

3. The radioactive isotope Tepsium-19 is an uncommon by-product of spontaneous nuclear fission in stars. It is a useful substance which is essential for the operation of the most common types of nuclear fission plants across the world, but is unfortunately extremely rare on Earth. Thus, several powerful nations vied to take a larger share when an abundant reserve of Tepsium-19 was reported to have been discovered on the surface of the Moon in 1969. In addition, global energy conglomerates started lobbying their governments, each competing for an exclusive contract and mining rights. All this fuss subsided, however, when subsequent trips to the moon proved that the alleged Tepsium-19 reserve was found out to be Toefleum-19, which had a similar emission spectrum indistinguishable by existing technologies.

Q: What is the main topic of the passage?
(a) The usefulness of the radioactive isotope Tepsium-19
(b) A disputed rare resource reserve on the surface of the Moon
(c) A worldwide competition for a rare resource
(d) A historical power struggle between nations and corporate powers

4. Excessive intake of alcohol is very harmful to the human body and can even be lethal in extreme cases. Alcohol in large doses can severely impair vital internal organs such as the liver or the heart. In the pancreas, alcohol causes the production of toxic substances that can lead to pancreatitis, a critical inflammation of blood vessels that prevents proper digestion. There have been, however, studies that suggest moderate consumption of alcohol can be healthy. Small doses of red wine, for instance, ______________________.

(a) can be a contributing factor to heart failures
(b) may protect healthy adults from developing coronary heart disease
(c) have been found to increase the risk of developing certain cancers
(d) may release red toxins into the bloodstream

4. Excessive intake of alcohol is very harmful to the human body and can even be lethal in extreme cases. Alcohol in large doses can severely impair vital internal organs such as the liver or the heart. In the pancreas, alcohol causes the production of toxic substances that can lead to pancreatitis, a critical inflammation of blood vessels that prevents proper digestion. There have been, however, studies that suggest moderate consumption of alcohol can be healthy. Small doses of red wine, for instance, ______________________.

(a) can be a contributing factor to heart failures
(b) may protect healthy adults from developing coronary heart disease
(c) have been found to increase the risk of developing certain cancers
(d) may release red toxins into the bloodstream

5. Herpes simplex virus accesses human cells, homes on the nucleus and then directs itself into the DNA using high pressure stimulated from a nanometer-scale protein shell known as the capsid propel. This virus is known to cause infections such as influenza and HIV. However, the Herpes simplex virus is becoming resistant to medicines that aim at the viral proteins, which can instantaneously convert themselves and develop resistance to anti-viral drugs due to genetic mutation. Scientists, thus, are hoping to create a potent drug to reduce the resistance level. So far, they have experimented on mice to create an adequate drug. This could help ______________________.

(a) detect the reason behind the genetic mutation
(b) keep the virus from seeking other viral proteins
(c) develop a new treatment to attack the influenza
(d) prevent the virus from remaining resistant to the drug

5. Herpes simplex virus accesses human cells, homes on the nucleus and then directs itself into the DNA using high pressure stimulated from a nanometer-scale protein shell known as the capsid propel. This virus is known to cause infections such as influenza and HIV. However, the Herpes simplex virus is becoming resistant to medicines that aim at the viral proteins, which can instantaneously convert themselves and develop resistance to anti-viral drugs due to genetic mutation. Scientists, thus, are hoping to create a potent drug to reduce the resistance level. So far, they have experimented on mice to create an adequate drug. This could help ______________________.

(a) detect the reason behind the genetic mutation
(b) keep the virus from seeking other viral proteins
(c) develop a new treatment to attack the influenza
(d) prevent the virus from remaining resistant to the drug

지문 패턴#2
통념 뒤집기

제1부
지문의 19가지 유형

BASIC 지문 구조 ▷

PATTERN 2 통념 뒤집기

텝스 독해에 굉장히 자주 등장하는 유형이 바로 기존 통념을 뒤집으며 새로운 통념을 제시하는 식의 반전 글이다.
예를 들면 이런 글이다. [예전 사람들은 지구가 납작하다고 생각했다. 하지만 콜럼버스는 지구가 둥글다는 것을 밝혀냈다.] 이런 유형들을 발견한다면 30초 안에 풀 수 있어야 한다.

쏘아보기 단서

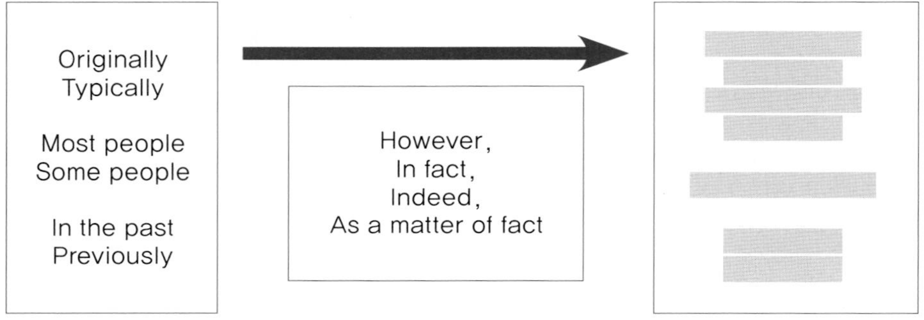

원리 설명

통념 뒤집기는 텝스에서 크게 두 가지 중 하나로 나타난다.
첫째는 ______________________________ 방식이고,
둘째는 ______________________________ 방식의 글이다.
둘 중에 무엇이든지 간에 결국 통념 뒤집기가 파악된 순간, "새로 제시되는 통념"만 파악한다면 정답을 맞힐 수 있다.
"새로 제시되는 통념"은 위에서 다룬 쏘아보기 단서 중 B part에 나온 단서들 뒤에 나온다.
[예전 사람들은 지구가 납작하다고 생각했다. 하지만 콜럼버스는 "지구가 둥글다."는 것을 밝혀냈다.] 이 예시에서는 "지구가 둥글다" 만 파악 한다면 정답을 고를 수 있을 것이다. 또한, 이 예시는 시간을 기준으로 통념 뒤집기이기도 하고 (예전, 이제) 대중의 잘못된 통념과 전문가의 의견제시이기도 하다(사람들, 콜럼버스).

(+) However, In fact, Indeed가 두 번째 문장에 나온다면 ______________________

문제 푸는 방법

주제 찾기 유형 지문 2번째 문장에 통념 뒤집기 관련 내용이 나온다면 그것이 주제일 확률이 높다. 예를 들어 in fact가 두 번째 문장에 나오면, 첫 번째 문장과 두 번째 문만 읽고 문제를 풀 수 있는 것이다.

빈칸 채우기 문제 ______________________

연습문제

우선 30~40초동안 문제를 먼저 풀어보세요

1. Recent studies indicate that wiggling one's toes may be much more effective an exercise than previously thought. They claim that just wiggling one's toes for 30 minutes a day can make you lose weight and help prevent diabetes, arthritis and even penile atrophy. A thorough test on 300 individuals of diverse physical conditions proved that an average of 100kcal was lost when they wiggled their toes for 60 minutes, and that it removed about 603mg of harmful chemicals like Tepsium from the body. These astounding numbers exceed even that of weightlifting and jogging. This is an exciting new discovery for those fitness-seekers as no other exercises that can be done on-the-go have been proven to have more efficacy than toe wiggling.

Q: What is the best title for this passage?
(a) The Horrifying Effects of Diabetes, Arthritis and Penile Atrophy
(b) Toe-wiggling Exercise Extremely Helpful for Preventing Various Diseases
(c) A Complete Guide to Burning Fat and Getting Rid of Harmful Chemicals
(d) A New Form of Exercise Found to Have Considerable Effectiveness for Fitness

1. Recent studies indicate that wiggling one's toes may be much more effective an exercise than previously thought. They claim that just wiggling one's toes for 30 minutes a day can make you lose weight and help prevent diabetes, arthritis and even penile atrophy. A thorough test on 300 individuals of diverse physical conditions proved that an average of 100kcal was lost when they wiggled their toes for 60 minutes, and that it removed about 603mg of harmful chemicals like Tepsium from the body. These astounding numbers exceed even that of weightlifting and jogging. This is an exciting new discovery for those fitness-seekers as no other exercises that can be done on-the-go have been proven to have more efficacy than toe wiggling.

Q: What is the best title for this passage?
(a) The Horrifying Effects of Diabetes, Arthritis and Penile Atrophy
(b) Toe-wiggling Exercise Extremely Helpful for Preventing Various Diseases
(c) A Complete Guide to Burning Fat and Getting Rid of Harmful Chemicals
(d) A New Form of Exercise Found to Have Considerable Effectiveness for Fitness

2. It is only recently that people started eating broccoli as food. In fact, the cap of the plant was historically a natural scrub with which the medieval peasants cleaned their latrines. It is very common for archaeologists to come across broccoli residue in medieval ruins, very often together with fecal matter. Their image as a sanitary device was so well recognized among the peasants that no one dared to try eating it. Similarly, ______________________________. A 1304 court document in Köln Freistadt describing broccoli chose words like vile, filthy and cursed, indicating even the aristocrats had an aversion for broccoli.

(a) a very negative image of broccoli prevailed among the aristocrats
(b) other organic materials like sea sponge was used for sanitary purposes
(c) aristocrats did have some different thoughts about broccoli and its tastes
(d) broccoli began to be considered somewhat edible from the 14th century onwards

2. It is only recently that people started eating broccoli as food. In fact, the cap of the plant was historically a natural scrub with which the medieval peasants cleaned their latrines. It is very common for archaeologists to come across broccoli residue in medieval ruins, very often together with fecal matter. Their image as a sanitary device was so well recognized among the peasants that no one dared to try eating it. Similarly, ______________________________. A 1304 court document in Köln Freistadt describing broccoli chose words like vile, filthy and cursed, indicating even the aristocrats had an aversion for broccoli.

(a) a very negative image of broccoli prevailed among the aristocrats
(b) other organic materials like sea sponge was used for sanitary purposes
(c) aristocrats did have some different thoughts about broccoli and its tastes
(d) broccoli began to be considered somewhat edible from the 14th century onwards

3. Many people, when they picture the Tasty Mango Islands, think of an island country full of romance and breathtaking scenery. However, this is quite contrary to reality. The island has been dealing with an extreme overpopulation crisis since it was first established. In fact, the problem has penetrated the island to such an extent that it has become acceptable and even recommended to walk on people's shoulders when one becomes immobilized in an overcrowded place. The Tasty Mango Island government has been coming up with various measures to fight the problem, but so far none of them has effectively alleviated the problem. The truth is, the island is a stifling pack of tourists and residents with nothing but people's head to see.

Q: What is the main topic of the passage?
(a) The Tasty Mango Island government's policies to counter the overpopulation
(b) The reality of Tasty Mango Islands contrasted to a common misconception
(c) Reasons that the Tasty Mango Islands is no longer what people used to know
(d) Customs that the Island residents have developed adapting to their environment

3. Many people, when they picture the Tasty Mango Islands, think of an island country full of romance and breathtaking scenery. However, this is quite contrary to reality. The island has been dealing with an extreme overpopulation crisis since it was first established. In fact, the problem has penetrated the island to such an extent that it has become acceptable and even recommended to walk on people's shoulders when one becomes immobilized in an overcrowded place. The Tasty Mango Island government has been coming up with various measures to fight the problem, but so far none of them has effectively alleviated the problem. The truth is, the island is a stifling pack of tourists and residents with nothing but people's head to see.

Q: What is the main topic of the passage?
(a) The Tasty Mango Island government's policies to counter the overpopulation
(b) The reality of Tasty Mango Islands contrasted to a common misconception
(c) Reasons that the Tasty Mango Islands is no longer what people used to know
(d) Customs that the Island residents have developed adapting to their environment

4. Prior to 1879, when the light bulb was invented by the famous Thomas Edison, activities that might seem ordinary to us were practically impossible to perform at night. With the great modern marvel, the light bulb, which provided much needed light in the darkness of night, people were able to go out for dinner, sleep at a later period, and enjoy other leisure activities that were previously impossible. People were enthralled at the fact that light bulbs ________________________________.

(a) allowed daily routines to be performed at nighttime
(b) could be modified to the more effective fluorescent bulbs
(c) could finally enhance the quality of movies
(d) were released at cheap prices

4. Prior to 1879, when the light bulb was invented by the famous Thomas Edison, activities that might seem ordinary to us were practically impossible to perform at night. With the great modern marvel, the light bulb, which provided much needed light in the darkness of night, people were able to go out for dinner, sleep at a later period, and enjoy other leisure activities that were previously impossible. People were enthralled at the fact that light bulbs ________________________________.

(a) allowed daily routines to be performed at nighttime
(b) could be modified to the more effective fluorescent bulbs
(c) could finally enhance the quality of movies
(d) were released at cheap prices

5. When one tries to hatch a baby chick at home, using a Styrofoam box can be an effective solution. However, individuals should still keep in mind that Styrofoam boxes are not the same as ordinary cardboard boxes, and so should be avoided during certain hours. This is because Styrofoam boxes impede the proper flow of air. The inside of the box gets heated during the morning hours, which might negatively influence the egg condition for hatching. Therefore, the Styrofoam box should ________________________.

(a) be used at night when the temperature is relatively low
(b) determine the optimal temperature of the day
(c) be used at all times when hatching a baby chick at home
(d) be cut into pieces of equal size

5. When one tries to hatch a baby chick at home, using a Styrofoam box can be an effective solution. However, individuals should still keep in mind that Styrofoam boxes are not the same as ordinary cardboard boxes, and so should be avoided during certain hours. This is because Styrofoam boxes impede the proper flow of air. The inside of the box gets heated during the morning hours, which might negatively influence the egg condition for hatching. Therefore, the Styrofoam box should ________________________.

(a) be used at night when the temperature is relatively low
(b) determine the optimal temperature of the day
(c) be used at all times when hatching a baby chick at home
(d) be cut into pieces of equal size

제1부
지문의 19가지 유형

지문 패턴#3
예시, 나열

BASIC 지문 구조 ▷

PATTERN 3 예시, 나열

이번 단원에서 다루게 될 내용은 크게 3가지다.
첫째는 지문에 등장하는 예시와 관련된 글, 둘째는 지문에 등장하는 나열과 관련된 글, 그리고 마지막으로는 such라는 단어가 등장하는 글. 이렇게 3가지와 관련된 접근법을 익힐 것이다. 이번 단원 또한 상당히 많이 출제되는 유형인 만큼 확실히 숙지하도록 한다.

쏘아보기 단서

❶ For example, for instance
❷ ____________________
❸ Such, such as

원리 설명

1. For example과 for instance는 지문에서 핵심 내용에 대한 예시가 나타났음을 암시한다. 다시 말해 for example이 지문 중간에 등장하면 for example 아래로는 중요하지 않은 내용이고, 결국 for example의 앞 1~2문장이 중요해지는 것이다. 텝스 독해 지문의 한정된 공간을 예시까지 들어가며 하는 것은 그만큼 중요하다는 것이다.

2. 나열된다는 것은 어떠한 범주에 있는 대상들을 늘어서 설명하고 있다. 문제를 푸는 데 필요한 것은 그 범주가 무엇인지 뿐이지, 범주 안에 속하는 내용물 하나하나 다 볼 필요가 없다.

3. Such라는 것은 용도는 두 가지가 있다.
   (1) such : ____________________
   (2) such as : ____________________

문제 푸는 방법

1. For example, For instance. 쏘아보기 시 발견된다면 단서 바로 앞 문장이 주제문이다. 단, 예외가 하나 있는데, for example 앞 문장이 This로 시작하는 경우다. (꼬리의 꼬리물기 단원 참고) [첫 문장 + for example 앞 문장] ··· 문제풀이

2. ____

3. Such가 발견된다면 as가 있는지 없는지 파악해야 한다. Such as가 보이면 __________을 봐야 하고 such가 있다면 __________에 집중하자.

연습문제

우선 30~40초동안 문제를 먼저 풀어보세요

1. Iberian Stone Axes of the Paleolithic were made by chipping and cracking rocks by whatever means possible, until the desired shape was achieved. However, a closer inspection reveals that, despite the crude crafting method, the craftsmen who made these axes were masterfully in control of their methods. Just about all of them found within one region seem to share surprisingly identical shapes, suggesting the crafting process was not all that chaotic. For example, the Altamira Axes, excavated in the Altamira Cave in Spain, have a common shape which is shared across all 455 axe heads which comprised the collection, with all of them having identical cuts and chipped-off sections of practically the same shape. The truth is that Paleolithic craf tsmen ____________________.

(a) were not far behind the Neolithic tool-crafting techniques
(b) were in fairly good control of their crafting techniques
(c) created advanced cutting tools just by chipping and cracking
(d) were the most advanced in the Iberian peninsula, like in the Altamira

1. Iberian Stone Axes of the Paleolithic were made by chipping and cracking rocks by whatever means possible, until the desired shape was achieved. However, a closer inspection reveals that, despite the crude crafting method, the craftsmen who made these axes were masterfully in control of their methods. Just about all of them found within one region seem to share surprisingly identical shapes, suggesting the crafting process was not all that chaotic. For example, the Altamira Axes, excavated in the Altamira Cave in Spain, have a common shape which is shared across all 455 axe heads which comprised the collection, with all of them having identical cuts and chipped-off sections of practically the same shape. The truth is that Paleolithic craf tsmen ____________________.

(a) were not far behind the Neolithic tool-crafting techniques
(b) were in fairly good control of their crafting techniques
(c) created advanced cutting tools just by chipping and cracking
(d) were the most advanced in the Iberian peninsula, like in the Altamira

2. Köln Freistadt was the primary commercial center of northeastern Europe from the 11th century to its fall in 1405. Although the city had only 520 permanent residents, there remains the ruins of three large cathedrals, seven minor chapels, two plazas and numerous commercial and residential structures(houses, stores, stables, etc.), ninety-seven inns and hotels, seven guard barracks and 40km of city walls and a massive government building, all of which is speculated to have accommodated over 300,000 merchants from all over Europe who supported the city's economy. As a result, the city is considered to ______________ out of all known cities either in history or in the contemporary times.

(a) have been the most commerce-dependent city
(b) have had the most lucrative commercial goods
(c) a dream for archaeologists seeking fame and fortune
(d) have been by far the most populous city

2. Köln Freistadt was the primary commercial center of northeastern Europe from the 11th century to its fall in 1405. Although the city had only 520 permanent residents, there remains the ruins of three large cathedrals, seven minor chapels, two plazas and numerous commercial and residential structures(houses, stores, stables, etc.), ninety-seven inns and hotels, seven guard barracks and 40km of city walls and a massive government building, all of which is speculated to have accommodated over 300,000 merchants from all over Europe who supported the city's economy. As a result, the city is considered to ______________ out of all known cities either in history or in the contemporary times.

(a) have been the most commerce-dependent city
(b) have had the most lucrative commercial goods
(c) a dream for archaeologists seeking fame and fortune
(d) have been by far the most populous city

3. During the colonial period of America, Puritans, a group of Christians promoting an austere lifestyle, were predominant. Whenever its members would not follow in their footsteps, the Puritan leaders either banished or publicly punished them. For example, if an individual was to involve oneself with gluttony-excessive eating and drinking-he or she would be forced to suffer public punishment in the form of a scaffold, which humiliated the offender in front of his or her peers. These types of punish ments ______________________.

(a) led to the early demise of the Puritanism
(b) encouraged rebellious behaviors among citizens
(c) were against the ideals of Puritan leaders
(d) helped sustain a strict Puritan ideology

3. During the colonial period of America, Puritans, a group of Christians promoting an austere lifestyle, were predominant. Whenever its members would not follow in their footsteps, the Puritan leaders either banished or publicly punished them. For example, if an individual was to involve oneself with gluttony-excessive eating and drinking-he or she would be forced to suffer public punishment in the form of a scaffold, which humiliated the offender in front of his or her peers. These types of punish ments ______________________.

(a) led to the early demise of the Puritanism
(b) encouraged rebellious behaviors among citizens
(c) were against the ideals of Puritan leaders
(d) helped sustain a strict Puritan ideology

4. Joanna Carroll has just published a novel that ____. This book completely reveals the malicious torture tactics that were used upon the women who had been suspected of being witches and being related to witchcraft. Women of the 17th century who were charged of witchcraft were forced to suffer from humiliation and excruciating pain of burning or ripping of the skin. The book's depiction of such preposterous behavior is extremely graphic, enabling the readers to almost feel the pain from the torture.

(a) vividly sheds light on ludicrous behaviors conducted during witch trials
(b) somehow justifies the conducts of torture during the 17th century
(c) gives attention to different types of torture present in history
(d) tries to understand the underlying meaning of the charges of witchcraft

4. Joanna Carroll has just published a novel that ____. This book completely reveals the malicious torture tactics that were used upon the women who had been suspected of being witches and being related to witchcraft. Women of the 17th century who were charged of witchcraft were forced to suffer from humiliation and excruciating pain of burning or ripping of the skin. The book's depiction of such preposterous behavior is extremely graphic, enabling the readers to almost feel the pain from the torture.

(a) vividly sheds light on ludicrous behaviors conducted during witch trials
(b) somehow justifies the conducts of torture during the 17th century
(c) gives attention to different types of torture present in history
(d) tries to understand the underlying meaning of the charges of witchcraft

5. Chlorophyll, a pigment found in the chloroplasts of plant cells, gives plants their green color. It is where photosynthesis takes place, gathering all the sunlight and dioxide, which is crucial for the health of a plant. Similar to chlorophyll are different colored-pigments, such as xanthophylls and carotenoids, which reflect the color of the plant. These pigments are used in photosynthesis as well although they appear in lesser quantities than green chlorophylls. For example, a leaf prevented from receiving sunlight would not be green due to the lack of chlorophyll for photosynthesis.

Q: What is the main topic of the passage?
(a) The process of photosynthesis
(b) Why leaves reflect colors of different pigments
(c) The elements that make plants green
(d) The effects of chlorophyll on plants

5. Chlorophyll, a pigment found in the chloroplasts of plant cells, gives plants their green color. It is where photosynthesis takes place, gathering all the sunlight and dioxide, which is crucial for the health of a plant. Similar to chlorophyll are different colored-pigments, such as xanthophylls and carotenoids, which reflect the color of the plant. These pigments are used in photosynthesis as well although they appear in lesser quantities than green chlorophylls. For example, a leaf prevented from receiving sunlight would not be green due to the lack of chlorophyll for photosynthesis.

Q: What is the main topic of the passage?
(a) The process of photosynthesis
(b) Why leaves reflect colors of different pigments
(c) The elements that make plants green
(d) The effects of chlorophyll on plants

지문 패턴# 4
빈칸 위치 접근법

제1부
지문의 19가지 유형

BASIC 지문 구조 ▷

PATTERN

4 빈칸 위치 접근법

빈칸 채우기 문제와 주제 찾기는 공통점이 있다.
두 유형 모두 문제를 풀기 위해선 결정적 단서 딱 하나가 필요한데, 그것은 바로 핵심 문장이다. 그렇다면, 빈칸 채우기 유형의 빈칸에 들어가는 내용 또한 중요한 내용이 들어가는 것이다. 텝스 시험에서 빈칸의 위치는 어떻게 중요한지 생각해보자.

쏘아보기 단서

빈칸의 위치는 크게 3가지로 나뉜다.

❶ 첫 문장에 위치한 빈칸
❷ 중간에 위치한 빈칸
❸ 마지막 문장에 위치한 빈칸

여기서 중요한 것이 있는데, 텝스 시험에서 "2. 중간에 위치한 빈칸" 는 시험에 나오질 않는다. 시험에서 정말 가끔가다 나오는 경우가 한가지 있는데, 빈칸이 뒤에서 두 번째 문장에 있는 경우다(6개월이 1문제 꼴로 출제됨). 그래서 빈칸의 위치는 다시 3가지로 재분류할 수 있겠다.

❶ 첫 문장에 위치한 빈칸
❷ 뒤에서 두 번째 문장에 위치한 빈칸
❸ 마지막 문장에 위치한 빈칸

원리 설명

들어가기에 앞서 기본 전제가 하나 있다. 빈칸에 들어가는 내용은 아무 문장이나 들어가는 것이 아니라, 주제와 깊은 관련이 있는 중요한 문장에 빈칸을 뚫어놓는 것이다.
즉, 빈칸의 위치가 어디 있든지 간에, 빈칸에 들어가는 내용은 지문 속 핵심 문장이다.

1. 첫 문장의 역할은 크게 두 개 중 하나다. 첫째는 도입식 내용이고, 두 번째는 주제문 제시다. 앞서 다룬 빈칸에 들어가는 내용에 대한 전제를 살펴보면 빈칸이 첫 문장에 위치할 때 빈칸의 내용이 도입식 내용이 될 수 없다. 따라서 빈칸이 첫 문장에 위치하면 첫 번째 문장이 무조건 주제문이다.

2. 빈칸이 뒤에서 두 번째에 있을 때엔 문제가 굉장히 어려울 확률이 높다.
그리고 이 모든 경우엔 ______________________에 문제 풀이를 위한 핵심 단서가 들어간다.

3. 빈칸이 마지막에 있을 때엔 가장 마지막 문장의 역할을 확실히 파악하기 어렵다. 그래서 포괄적인 접근법이 필요하다.

문제 풀이 방법

1~8번 문제를 풀기 시작할 땐 문제마다 빈칸에 체크를 해야 한다. 빈칸 채우기 문제를 풀 땐 빈칸에 체크 표시를 하는 습관을 들이자.

1. 첫 문장에 위치한 빈칸

____

2. 뒤에서 두 번째 문장에 위치한 빈칸

____

3. 마지막 문장에 위치한 빈칸

____

연습문제

우선 30~40초동안 문제를 먼저 풀어보세요

1. Dear Andy,

I am writing to update you on the admission process for the last spot at Benjamin Franklin Academy. So far, the number of candidates remaining has been reduced to three. The academic qualities of you and the other two candidates are outstanding and would be more than befitting for the school. As the number of students that can be admitted is very limited, we unfortunately will be selecting only one candidate. Regardless of the result, please remember that all of you are ____________ ____________. The finalized decision will be announced next Monday.

Regards, Justin Blake
Admission Administrator, Benjamin Franklin Academy

(a) students whose schools are going to miss
(b) very likely to become the dearest members of our faculty
(c) wonderful candidates who will be accepted with scholarships
(d) exceptional applicants who would be valuable additions to the school

1. Dear Andy,

I am writing to update you on the admission process for the last spot at Benjamin Franklin Academy. So far, the number of candidates remaining has been reduced to three. The academic qualities of you and the other two candidates are outstanding and would be more than befitting for the school. As the number of students that can be admitted is very limited, we unfortunately will be selecting only one candidate. Regardless of the result, please remember that all of you are ____________ ____________. The finalized decision will be announced next Monday.

Regards, Justin Blake
Admission Administrator, Benjamin Franklin Academy

(a) students whose schools are going to miss
(b) very likely to become the dearest members of our faculty
(c) wonderful candidates who will be accepted with scholarships
(d) exceptional applicants who would be valuable additions to the school

2. ________________________ is utterly natural for most scientists now and then, but it was not a concern for Marie Curie and her husband. Soon after Marie Curie finally succeeded in creating the decigram of pure radium, the treatment to cancer using this matter was newly discovered. A boom of industries using radium exhilarated the price of Curie's finding. However, she and her husband published the process on extracting radium for the public quoting that the radium belonged to the people. Her insistence on free accessibility to radium brought about developments in creating cures to cancer.

(a) Funding research for adequate experiments
(b) Requesting for intellectual rights for monetary reasons
(c) Patenting scientific discoveries
(d) Delivering the results through publications

2. ________________________ is utterly natural for most scientists now and then, but it was not a concern for Marie Curie and her husband. Soon after Marie Curie finally succeeded in creating the decigram of pure radium, the treatment to cancer using this matter was newly discovered. A boom of industries using radium exhilarated the price of Curie's finding. However, she and her husband published the process on extracting radium for the public quoting that the radium belonged to the people. Her insistence on free accessibility to radium brought about developments in creating cures to cancer.

(a) Funding research for adequate experiments
(b) Requesting for intellectual rights for monetary reasons
(c) Patenting scientific discoveries
(d) Delivering the results through publications

3. ______________________________ has not been confirmed by anyone. A number of people, however, claim that they started in the early 20th century, when an ice cream stand owner in Coney Island, New York, was selling ice cream at the State Fair. Around noon, when the sun was scorching hot, he ran out of paper cups to serve his ice cream. Not knowing what to do, the ice cream salesman went next door to a waffle salesman and asked him to make cups made of waffles. The ice cream salesman started serving his ice cream in the new cup, and surprisingly, people fell in love with the new "Waffle Cone," and therefore, a new way of serving ice cream was invented.

(a) Why Waffle Cones taste so delicious
(b) Why paper cups were so ineffective
(c) How Waffle Cones came into existence
(d) The negative effects of Waffle Cones

3. ______________________________ has not been confirmed by anyone. A number of people, however, claim that they started in the early 20th century, when an ice cream stand owner in Coney Island, New York, was selling ice cream at the State Fair. Around noon, when the sun was scorching hot, he ran out of paper cups to serve his ice cream. Not knowing what to do, the ice cream salesman went next door to a waffle salesman and asked him to make cups made of waffles. The ice cream salesman started serving his ice cream in the new cup, and surprisingly, people fell in love with the new "Waffle Cone," and therefore, a new way of serving ice cream was invented.

(a) Why Waffle Cones taste so delicious
(b) Why paper cups were so ineffective
(c) How Waffle Cones came into existence
(d) The negative effects of Waffle Cones

4. When consumers go to grocery stores to buy their beef for a family dinner, they may be upset that the price of the beef is too high. At the same time, when farmers bring beef to the market, they wish that price of the beef was even higher. These views are not surprising: buyers always want to pay less, but sellers ______________________. Could a "right price" exist for beef from the standpoint of society as a whole?

(a) want more beef
(b) want less beef
(c) always want to be paid more
(d) always want to be paid less

4. When consumers go to grocery stores to buy their beef for a family dinner, they may be upset that the price of the beef is too high. At the same time, when farmers bring beef to the market, they wish that price of the beef was even higher. These views are not surprising: buyers always want to pay less, but sellers ______________________. Could a "right price" exist for beef from the standpoint of society as a whole?

(a) want more beef
(b) want less beef
(c) always want to be paid more
(d) always want to be paid less

5. The human rights committee is in agreement to the liberation of political prisoners from China during the 1950s. Continuing to hold the politicians captive, who were forcefully arrested without a fair trial, only diminishes the significance of human rights and exudes a notorious reputation among the international society. On the other hand, discharging these prisoners may prompt wreckage in social order. Maintaining strong governmental control will become even harder. However, the committee remains firm that the state should ______________________.

(a) proceed with the movement to free political prisoners
(b) allow the argument between the government and civilians
(c) reward participants in undertaking the human rights plan
(d) substantially decrease governmental power

5. The human rights committee is in agreement to the liberation of political prisoners from China during the 1950s. Continuing to hold the politicians captive, who were forcefully arrested without a fair trial, only diminishes the significance of human rights and exudes a notorious reputation among the international society. On the other hand, discharging these prisoners may prompt wreckage in social order. Maintaining strong governmental control will become even harder. However, the committee remains firm that the state should ______________________.

(a) proceed with the movement to free political prisoners
(b) allow the argument between the government and civilians
(c) reward participants in undertaking the human rights plan
(d) substantially decrease governmental power

지문 패턴# 5
구인글

제1부
지문의 19가지 유형

BASIC 지문 구조 ▷

PATTERN 5 구인글

텝스에 종종 출제되는 문제 유형이 바로 구인글이다. 주로 회사의 구인 공고문이 출제가 되며, 정보 단서들이 매우 많다. 개별 정보 단서들이 넘치는 만큼 효율적인 문제풀이가 필요하며, 별다른 훈련 없이 시험장에 들어서게 되면, 불필요한 시간 낭비를 하게 될 가능성이 높다. 5단원 지문 유형은 구인글로 대표되나, 개별 정보 단서가 많은 모든 지문에 적용된다.
해당 유형은 세트 문제로 출제가 되는 경우가 많다. 지문의 길이는 더욱 길어지기에, 문제 풀이에 꼭 신경써서 해야 한다. 정오답으로 출제될 만한 단서 유의를 하는 것이 핵심적이며, 사전에 대비 가능한 부분들이 많으니 사전 대비가 필수다.

쏘아보기 단서

- Required, Must, Needed
- Preferred, Plus, include
- Small font size, italics, *

문제풀이

지문

해당 유형은 주제 파악은 쏘아보기만으로 지문 독해 시작 전에 이미 파악이 가능하다. 각 문단의 역할을 파악하는 것이 매우 중요하며, 세부 독해 시 '의무 vs 권장 사항'과 지문에서 명시되는 '예외 사항'에 집중해서 독해를 한다.

문제 유형

제2 부 코렉트 유형 문제 풀이법이 적용된다.

오답

제3부 오답의 7 유형과 꼭 연계되어 출제된다. 지문과 선택지 독해 시 예외가 있는 문장과 예외가 존재할 수 없는 문장을 구분하며 읽어야 한다.

연습문제

우선 30~40초동안 문제를 먼저 풀어보세요

1.

Seeking a PART TIME possible full-time experienced BOOKKEEPER

We are a local construction company located in the Van Nuys area, currently seeking for a part time accounting professional/full cycle bookkeeper with the potential of becoming full time employment. Candidate should have solid QuickBooks knowledge and accounting principles, but candidates with real estate backgrounds are exempt from such requirements. Previous construction, property management and real estate development experience preferred.

RESPONSIBILITIES INCLUDE:
- Prepare deposits
- Process mail daily; pick-up, open, date, and stamp when required

SKILLS AND EDUCATION:
- Knowledge of Microsoft Word, Excel and Power Point a plus
- Must have strong problem-solving skills
- Must be organized and able to work in a fast pace environment
- Property Management and Construction Experience a plus but not required

Q: Which of the following is correct according to the passage?
(a) Applicants must have concrete knowledge of accounting principles.
(b) Preparing deposits is one of the 2 responsibilities of a bookkeeper.
(c) Applicants with a great problem-solving skillset will become a full-time employee.
(d) Someone with no experience in construction or power point may apply.

2.

Dronefleet.com is an innovative and exciting place to work for tech geeks and drone nerds. We love learning about new technologies and helping our customers find the perfect solution to fit their needs. Over the past four years we have been recognized as a top DJI and FLIR Dealer and are still growing very rapidly! We believe our success is fueled by the bright and talented people who have joined our team to create a culture of hard work and fun.

Please, check out our website at www.dronefleet.com before applying!

JOB DESCRIPTION & RESPONSIBILITIES

Drone Fleet Supervisor position is responsible for leading the drone repair and service team.

- Managing the team of repair technicians
- Oversee order fulfillment process
- Schedule priorities for repair team

JOB REQUIREMENTS

- Minimum 3 years of management experience
- Enthusiastic and articulate professional who wishes to pursue a long-term career in technical drone repair
- Extremely tech savvy with hands-on experience with advanced electronic gadgets
- Experience in a technology repair environment (cell phones, computers, etc.)
- Any experience with drones or thermal imaging a huge plus.
- Any experience growing a startup or small business is a huge plus.

Q: Which of the following is correct according to the passage?

(a) Drone Fleet requires at most 3 years of management experience.

(b) Candidates need to have experience with repairing cell phones.

(c) Drone Fleet is currently looking to hire a supervisor.

(d) Drone fleet is a thermal imaging company.

3. We are a small Los Angeles based firm which has an immediate opening for a full-time Immigration Attorney. Duties include extensive court appearances for master hearings, merits hearings, drafting motions to reopen and appeals before BIA and AAO. Travel required. Some experience is preferred, but new admittees are also encouraged to apply. Position is available immediately. California bar license not required. This is a remote position.

Q.: Which of the following is required of the attorney?

(a) Court appearances.

(b) Experience in the work field.

(c) Immediate participation.

(d) Bar license of any state.

3. We are a small Los Angeles based firm which has an immediate opening for a full-time Immigration Attorney. Duties include extensive court appearances for master hearings, merits hearings, drafting motions to reopen and appeals before BIA and AAO. Travel required. Some experience is preferred, but new admittees are also encouraged to apply. Position is available immediately. California bar license not required. This is a remote position.

Q.: Which of the following is required of the attorney?

(a) Court appearances.

(b) Experience in the work field.

(c) Immediate participation.

(d) Bar license of any state.

4.

We are Globe Insurance Company, a Fortune 500 company. Our rapidly expanding Internet group in Culver City is seeking to hire a senior analyst to help manage our Internet Marketing Direct Response campaigns.

The right candidate will have excellent analytical & Excel skills accompanied by an interest in learning how to manage and analyze multi-million dollar digital marketing campaigns. This is a fast-paced office so we have high expectations. However, we are also a small and close-knit office with a great culture. The benefits are generous and include a Pension Plan, 401K and health/dental insurance.

Please send a detailed cover letter describing your qualifications and be sure to include your salary requirements

Q.: Which of the following is correct according to the passage?

(a) The marketing direct response campaign is fast-paced.

(b) The senior analyst will possess an adequate analytical skillset

(c) The group is small and has stable growth.

(d) Applicants can choose between a pension plan and a 401k.

지문 패턴# 6
편지글

제1부
지문의 19가지 유형

BASIC 지문 구조 ▷

PATTERN 6 편지글

[5단원] 구인글, [6단원] 편지글, [7단원] 광고글은 내용 별로 나눠서 정리된 단원들이다. 이 두 가지 유형 외엔 따로 내용적인 부분에 초점을 맞출 필요가 없지만, [5~7단원]은 따로 정리해 둘 필요가 있다. 또한, 이 세 가지 유형은 전체 시험에서 비중이 30% 정도가 되는 만큼 확실히 정리해 둔다면 빠른 시간 내에 문제를 풀어나갈 수 있을 것이다.

쏘아보기 단서

부정 However, ____________, ____________

긍정 Therefore, So, In particular

부탁 ______________________________

공지글 Announce, Please, Thank you

기타

원리설명

편지글에는 입에 발린 소리가 등장하는 경우가 많다. 편지글의 핵심, 그리고 문제를 풀기 위해서 필요한 부분은 입에 발린 소리가 절대 아니다. 주제와 관련 없는 부분은 바로 건너뛸 수 있어야 한다. 그래서 위에 나와 있는 쏘아보기 단서들을 눈여겨 봐야 하는 것이다. 위에 명시된 단서들이 형식적인 이야기에서 편지의 핵심 내용으로 건너가는 중요한 단서들이다.

문제 풀이

편지글이라는 것을 파악한 순간 쏘아보기 단서들을 잡아야 한다. 쏘아보기 단서들을 기준으로 글의 성격을 예측하고, 단서가 들어가는 문장을 읽어야 한다.
예를 들어 쏘아보기 중에 지문 중간에 therefore이 나왔다는 것은 편지의 내용 자체가 긍정적인 내용일 것이라는 것이고, therefore이 등장하는 문장이 핵심 문장일 것이다.

제1부
제2부
제3부
제4부

연습문제

 우선 30~40초동안 문제를 먼저 풀어보세요

1. Dear Ms. Clementz,

The University of St. Glenzow ______________________. We wish to inform you that your application was exceptional, and therefore will be accepting you to our exchange student program. Please send us your student visa and the confirmation application from your school. If you require more information, or wish to change your plans for the exchange program, email us via our university website st.glenzow@edu.org

(a) is excited to invite you to its annual summer camp
(b) would like to welcome you to a new semester
(c) wants to hear more from you
(d) will be recruiting new professors

1. Dear Ms. Clementz,

The University of St. Glenzow ______________________. We wish to inform you that your application was exceptional, and therefore will be accepting you to our exchange student program. Please send us your student visa and the confirmation application from your school. If you require more information, or wish to change your plans for the exchange program, email us via our university website st.glenzow@edu.org

(a) is excited to invite you to its annual summer camp
(b) would like to welcome you to a new semester
(c) wants to hear more from you
(d) will be recruiting new professors

2.

To all Jamestown residents

Sightings of a mentally ill man holding a rifle has been reported several times over the last few days. It is not yet clear who the man may be and how he gained access to his rifle, but it is suspected that he is the man who escaped from the mental asylum last week. The police say they are currently searching for this crazy man, and the situation is under control. Fortunately, there have not been any shootings or accidents, but the police warns that his rifle is apparently loaded and cocked, and the mental asylum records show that he is a retired veteran army officer with a condition of paranoia. Please stay indoors and keep your doors locked until the madman is captured and arrested by the local police.

Q: What is the purpose of the announcement?

(a) To collect more evidence for tracking down an insane man.

(b) To warn people not to leave their houses because of a danger.

(c) To ask people to cooperate with the police's search mission.

(d) To investigate where the insane man obtained his rifle.

2.

To all Jamestown residents

Sightings of a mentally ill man holding a rifle has been reported several times over the last few days. It is not yet clear who the man may be and how he gained access to his rifle, but it is suspected that he is the man who escaped from the mental asylum last week. The police say they are currently searching for this crazy man, and the situation is under control. Fortunately, there have not been any shootings or accidents, but the police warns that his rifle is apparently loaded and cocked, and the mental asylum records show that he is a retired veteran army officer with a condition of paranoia. Please stay indoors and keep your doors locked until the madman is captured and arrested by the local police.

Q: What is the purpose of the announcement?

(a) To collect more evidence for tracking down an insane man.

(b) To warn people not to leave their houses because of a danger.

(c) To ask people to cooperate with the police's search mission.

(d) To investigate where the insane man obtained his rifle.

3.

To: US Army Station Camp Henry Logistics Team

I have realized today that the number of rifles that was relocated to our base was different from what the documents say. My men and I have rechecked the numbers several times, but it seems clear that 7 of the M16A3 rifles we were supposed to receive have gone missing. I am afraid that it may have been taken by hijackers, while the cargo was passing by Jamestown. Sources suggest that ________________, which enabled this to happen despite very strict protocols. I request that you alert the military police immediately, before this matter becomes any more serious.

Regards,

Lieutenant Commander Michael Foucault

(a) the hijackers may have access to resources that the authorities are not aware of

(b) the hijackers are headed to the military police department

(c) the military police has not yet been informed about the incident

(d) the press may know something about this incident already

3.

To: US Army Station Camp Henry Logistics Team

I have realized today that the number of rifles that was relocated to our base was different from what the documents say. My men and I have rechecked the numbers several times, but it seems clear that 7 of the M16A3 rifles we were supposed to receive have gone missing. I am afraid that it may have been taken by hijackers, while the cargo was passing by Jamestown. Sources suggest that ________________, which enabled this to happen despite very strict protocols. I request that you alert the military police immediately, before this matter becomes any more serious.

Regards,

Lieutenant Commander Michael Foucault

(a) the hijackers may have access to resources that the authorities are not aware of

(b) the hijackers are headed to the military police department

(c) the military police has not yet been informed about the incident

(d) the press may know something about this incident already

4. Dear Student

We would first like to congratulate you on being selected to this year's student of the year. Your academic achievements and philanthropic spirit is no doubt exemplar for all of our students. Therefore, we are delighted to invite you to the 2013 Jamestown-Surley Dinner Party, where you will meet, dine and talk with renowned academics from diverse fields. Furthermore, you will be asked to give the starting speech for the event, which is an honor rarely given to students. Please do not miss this precious life opportunity; we assure you that it will become one of the most unforgettable moments in your entire life.

Frederick Paritzche

Professor, California Institute of Technology

Q: What is the main idea of the letter?

(a) The student has been nominated for the student of the year award

(b) The college will be holding a meeting between famous academics this year

(c) The student in question has been invited to a very special event

(d) The 2013 Jamestown College Dinner Party will be very memorable

4. Dear Student

We would first like to congratulate you on being selected to this year's student of the year. Your academic achievements and philanthropic spirit is no doubt exemplar for all of our students. Therefore, we are delighted to invite you to the 2013 Jamestown-Surley Dinner Party, where you will meet, dine and talk with renowned academics from diverse fields. Furthermore, you will be asked to give the starting speech for the event, which is an honor rarely given to students. Please do not miss this precious life opportunity; we assure you that it will become one of the most unforgettable moments in your entire life.

Frederick Paritzche

Professor, California Institute of Technology

Q: What is the main idea of the letter?

(a) The student has been nominated for the student of the year award

(b) The college will be holding a meeting between famous academics this year

(c) The student in question has been invited to a very special event

(d) The 2013 Jamestown College Dinner Party will be very memorable

5. All class-4 personnel contaminated by the microorganism SCP-9983 must consult the facility quarantine officer before leaving the premises. Under the facility quarantine protocol, all associated individuals will undergo a decontamination procedure free of charge, and will be provided with a week's dose of antibacterial tablets. The quarantine department assures you that none of the crew will suffer permanent illness due to the microorganism, and promises insurance for those whose symptoms persist. Please note, however, anyone who violates the protocol will be eliminated.

Q: What is the announcement mainly about?

(a) The actions that will be taken against those who violate the protocol.
(b) Reasons why the facility quarantine protocol should be adhered to.
(c) The medication that is to be issued to contaminated personnel.
(d) A mandatory quarantine protocol for associated staff

5. All class-4 personnel contaminated by the microorganism SCP-9983 must consult the facility quarantine officer before leaving the premises. Under the facility quarantine protocol, all associated individuals will undergo a decontamination procedure free of charge, and will be provided with a week's dose of antibacterial tablets. The quarantine department assures you that none of the crew will suffer permanent illness due to the microorganism, and promises insurance for those whose symptoms persist. Please note, however, anyone who violates the protocol will be eliminated.

Q: What is the announcement mainly about?

(a) The actions that will be taken against those who violate the protocol.
(b) Reasons why the facility quarantine protocol should be adhered to.
(c) The medication that is to be issued to contaminated personnel.
(d) A mandatory quarantine protocol for associated staff

지문 패턴#7
광고글

제1부
지문의 19가지 유형

BASIC 지문 구조 ▷

PATTERN 7 광고글

[5단원], [6단원]과 함께 형식이 정해져 있는 단원이다. 형식이 정해져 있는 만큼 정답의 기준도 명확하다. 절대로 고민하는 일이 있어서는 안 되는 글의 유형이 바로 광고글 유형이다. "제품 광고니까 당연히 이것도 정답이 될 수 있고 저것도 답이 될 수 있지 않나?"라는 생각을 하며 문제 풀이 시간이 길어진 경험이 있다면, 이 단원에서 확실한 기준을 확립하는 것이 중요할 것이다.

쏘아보기 단서

We, Our product

원리설명

광고글은 크게 세 가지로 나뉜다고 생각하면 된다.
X. 광고하는 제품/서비스, Y. 그 제품/서비스의 장점, Z. 광고성 멘트
X는 그 제품이 무엇인지 설명하는 부분으로, Samsung Galaxy S 라는 제품을 홍보하는 것이라면, "Samsung Galaxy S"가 아닌, "휴대폰"으로 생각하면 된다.
Y는 중요한 부분인데, 지문 중간에 장점이 나열된다. 여러 장점이 나열되는 것이 아니라 정확히 하나의 장점만 제시되는 형태다. 그리고 마지막 문장에 Z 광고성 멘트가 등장한다.

문제 풀이

문제를 풀 때 X (광고되고 있는 제품)이 무엇인지, 그리고 Y (장점 1개)를 파악하면 된다. 1번을 파악하자마자 지문 전체를 나열[3단원] 부분 읽듯이 빠르게 훑으며 장점만 파악하면 된다.
광고성 문제의 특징은 정답 또한 X 혹은 Y에서 나온다는 것이다. 만약 광고글 중에 고민 되는 보기가 있다면 그 땐 다시 광고글 기준을 떠올려 본다면 정답을 고를 수 있을 것이다.

연습문제

우선 30~40초동안 문제를 먼저 풀어보세요

1. Do you hate having to choose what to wear every day? Would you rather prefer 5 more minutes of sleep than having to decide what to wear? Then just call ClothesFit today for a 7-day free trial of preselected clothes every morning. We offer competitive monthly expenses, discounts for high schoolers, and trustworthy courteous service. Sign a monthly contract with us before January 6th and get 15% off. Don't ______________________________, just call ClothesFit at 466-0542!

(a) lose 5 minutes of your sleep
(b) give your clothes selection another thought
(c) hesitate any longer
(d) worry about the trendiness of the style selection

1. Do you hate having to choose what to wear every day? Would you rather prefer 5 more minutes of sleep than having to decide what to wear? Then just call ClothesFit today for a 7-day free trial of preselected clothes every morning. We offer competitive monthly expenses, discounts for high schoolers, and trustworthy courteous service. Sign a monthly contract with us before January 6th and get 15% off. Don't ______________________________, just call ClothesFit at 466-0542!

(a) lose 5 minutes of your sleep
(b) give your clothes selection another thought
(c) hesitate any longer
(d) worry about the trendiness of the style selection

2. Looking for ____________________? You should come to see the Boston Celtics play at the TD Garden located in downtown Boston! Ticket prices range from 50 dollars to 3000 dollars. Every seat is provided with an adequate amount of beer for you and snacks for you and your kids. The exciting atmosphere will be a great experience for the kids and you will be able to blow off some steam. Visit www.tdgarden.co.kr for more information.

(a) an exciting experience for you and your kids
(b) something to do on the weekend
(c) a place to eat beer and watch basketball
(d) a nice treat for your wife

2. Looking for ____________________? You should come to see the Boston Celtics play at the TD Garden located in downtown Boston! Ticket prices range from 50 dollars to 3000 dollars. Every seat is provided with an adequate amount of beer for you and snacks for you and your kids. The exciting atmosphere will be a great experience for the kids and you will be able to blow off some steam. Visit www.tdgarden.co.kr for more information.

(a) an exciting experience for you and your kids
(b) something to do on the weekend
(c) a place to eat beer and watch basketball
(d) a nice treat for your wife

3. With turnitin.com ______________________________. We digitalize the classroom so that the students can submit their assignments through the internet and also get feedback in a fast and efficient manner. We also provide a state of the art plagiarism prevention system: providing the exact percentage of how much a certain paper matches the words of others. With this system, professors and teachers can have a much easier time picking out the dishonest students in the classroom.

(a) students can have fun learning
(b) teachers have a more important role than before
(c) virtual schools can replace actual schools
(d) education from the teaching perspective becomes efficient

3. With turnitin.com ______________________________. We digitalize the classroom so that the students can submit their assignments through the internet and also get feedback in a fast and efficient manner. We also provide a state of the art plagiarism prevention system: providing the exact percentage of how much a certain paper matches the words of others. With this system, professors and teachers can have a much easier time picking out the dishonest students in the classroom.

(a) students can have fun learning
(b) teachers have a more important role than before
(c) virtual schools can replace actual schools
(d) education from the teaching perspective becomes efficient

4. Interested in working in the most comfortable working environment for you? Work-at-home jobs provide you with a convenient working environment, freedom of attire, and many more advantages. HomeWork will arrange you with companies with working home opportunities according to your career. As soon as you receive our service, you will be discovering yourself free from the intense working atmosphere. Simply leave it to HomeWork and we will bring your work to your home.

Q: What is the advertisement mainly about?
(a) An opportunity to work at home
(b) How to balance out the pros and cons of working at home
(c) A company that introduces work-at-home jobs
(d) A service that provides positions at a prestigious corporations

4. Interested in working in the most comfortable working environment for you? Work-at-home jobs provide you with a convenient working environment, freedom of attire, and many more advantages. HomeWork will arrange you with companies with working home opportunities according to your career. As soon as you receive our service, you will be discovering yourself free from the intense working atmosphere. Simply leave it to HomeWork and we will bring your work to your home.

Q: What is the advertisement mainly about?
(a) An opportunity to work at home
(b) How to balance out the pros and cons of working at home
(c) A company that introduces work-at-home jobs
(d) A service that provides positions at a prestigious corporations

5. With the service at Heckscher, you are completely free from the pain of termites. You simply make a call and relax for a while as our trained professionals eradicate even the miniscule trace of termites with FDA approved chemicals and high quality equipment. Extra services are available for 30 days within the previous session and other options, including the type of chemicals or quick-call service without additional cost, are also available. There are no better options for termite treatments than Heckschers! Call us at 602-4529-0016 right now. Free yourself from the unnecessary pain.

Q: What is mainly being advertised?
(a) A chemical engineering company
(b) A service center that augments the problem of termites
(c) An insect controlling company
(d) A family business run by the Heckschers

5. With the service at Heckscher, you are completely free from the pain of termites. You simply make a call and relax for a while as our trained professionals eradicate even the miniscule trace of termites with FDA approved chemicals and high quality equipment. Extra services are available for 30 days within the previous session and other options, including the type of chemicals or quick-call service without additional cost, are also available. There are no better options for termite treatments than Heckschers! Call us at 602-4529-0016 right now. Free yourself from the unnecessary pain.

Q: What is mainly being advertised?
(a) A chemical engineering company
(b) A service center that augments the problem of termites
(c) An insect controlling company
(d) A family business run by the Heckschers

지문 패턴#8
문장 기호

PATTERN 8 문장 기호

문장 기호라는 것은 독자에게 글 읽기를, 화자에게 글쓰기를 편하게 만들어 주는 도구로써 효과적인 의사소통을 돕는다. 문장 기호 속엔 여러 가지 강조점들과 유의점들이 암시되어 있는데, 시험마다 이 문장 기호의 사용을 통일시켜 사용한다. 토플에도 문장 기호로 유추할 수 있는 부분이 있고, 토익도 그러한 부분이 많고, 텝스에도 많은 문장 기호들이 전체 지문의 전개 방향을 보여주기 때문에 쏘아보기 시 발견된다면 내용을 어느 정도 예측할 수 있을 것이다.

쏘아보기 단서

?

!

:

,

“ ”

( )

italics

원리 설명 및 문제풀이 방법

? 물음표

개수가 하나인지 두 개 이상인지 에 따라서 접근법이 나뉜다.

물음표가 하나 있을 때엔 속으로, ______________________라고 외쳐야 한다.

물음표가 2개 이상이면, 물음이 들어가는 문장들은 ______________________

! 느낌표

중요한 부분을 강조하기 위해 사용될 때도 있지만 광고글이나 편지글에서 자신의 의견을 전할 때 사용되는 경우도 있다. 느낌표가 나온다면 느낌표가 등장하는 그 문장을 가볍게 한번 읽어보는 것이 좋다.

: 콜론

꽤 중요한 문장 기호 중 하나다. 콜론 뒤에 등장하는 부분을 ______________________________

※ 예외: 콜론 뒤에 나열이 돼 있는 경우만 특별히 예외다.

" " 따옴표

따옴표의 역할은 두 개 중 하나다. _____과 _____가 있다. _____은 예시의 용도로 사용된다고 생각하면 된다. 는 단어 1~3개 정도를 강조하기 위해 사용되는 것이며 주로 "생소개념(0단원 참고)"이 따옴표 속에 강조된다. 따옴표가 인용 하고 있다면 인용되는 부분은 읽지 않고 그 앞에 부분을 자세히 보도록 하고, 따옴표가 강조의 역할을 하고 있다면 강조되고 있는 단어가 무엇인지 확인할 필요가 있다.

, 쉼표

____

이탈릭체

텝스에서 이탈릭체는 서적 제목을 나타낼 때가 가장 많다. 쏘아보기에서 이탈릭체엔 별다른 의미를 둘 필요는 없지만, _______________ 할 때 이탈릭체는 중요하다.

연습문제

 우선 30~40초동안 문제를 먼저 풀어보세요

1. Have you ever wondered how they can tell the speed of a car right after it moves through the speed gun? Radar guns are positioned on the road, which send out waves or signals at fixed frequencies towards the car when it is moving towards the target. These signals hit the car and bounce back to the radar detector. These guns work on a principle known as the Doppler Effect. The Doppler Effect describes the change in the frequency of a wave that occurs when the source and receiver are in relative motion. The frequency of the wave increases as the source and receiver approach each other. The radar gun measures the shift in the frequency of a wave to calculate the velocity.

Q: What is the main idea of the passage?
(a) A radar gun records the changes in the frequency of a wave
(b) Speeding cars are able to calculate the speed of waves.
(c) The Doppler Effect takes relative motion into consideration.
(d) Speed measurement makes use of the Doppler Effect

1. Have you ever wondered how they can tell the speed of a car right after it moves through the speed gun? Radar guns are positioned on the road, which send out waves or signals at fixed frequencies towards the car when it is moving towards the target. These signals hit the car and bounce back to the radar detector. These guns work on a principle known as the Doppler Effect. The Doppler Effect describes the change in the frequency of a wave that occurs when the source and receiver are in relative motion. The frequency of the wave increases as the source and receiver approach each other. The radar gun measures the shift in the frequency of a wave to calculate the velocity.

Q: What is the main idea of the passage?
(a) A radar gun records the changes in the frequency of a wave
(b) Speeding cars are able to calculate the speed of waves.
(c) The Doppler Effect takes relative motion into consideration.
(d) Speed measurement makes use of the Doppler Effec

2. Don't you think it would be fascinating to ______________________? In fact, this is actually possible if you visit our website, freetrips.org. Starting today, we will post information that would require customer opinion about travel journeys: just take 2 minutes to fill out the form, and you will be given 2 free tickets to Hawaii! Make your wish come true by visiting our website. This is your ultimate opportunity to gain an experience that you would never be able to have elsewhere.

(a) play games all day
(b) go on a special vacation for free
(c) share your hobby online
(d) study abroad

2. Don't you think it would be fascinating to ______________________? In fact, this is actually possible if you visit our website, freetrips.org. Starting today, we will post information that would require customer opinion about travel journeys: just take 2 minutes to fill out the form, and you will be given 2 free tickets to Hawaii! Make your wish come true by visiting our website. This is your ultimate opportunity to gain an experience that you would never be able to have elsewhere.

(a) play games all day
(b) go on a special vacation for free
(c) share your hobby online
(d) study abroad

3. When consumers go to grocery stores to buy their beef for a family dinner, they may be upset that the price of the beef is too high. At the same time, when farmers bring beef to the market, they wish that price of the beef was even higher. These views are not surprising: buyers always want to pay less, but sellers ________________. Could a "right price" exist for beef from the standpoint of society as a whole?

(a) want more beef
(b) want less beef
(c) always want to be paid more
(d) always want to be paid less

3. When consumers go to grocery stores to buy their beef for a family dinner, they may be upset that the price of the beef is too high. At the same time, when farmers bring beef to the market, they wish that price of the beef was even higher. These views are not surprising: buyers always want to pay less, but sellers ________________. Could a "right price" exist for beef from the standpoint of society as a whole?

(a) want more beef
(b) want less beef
(c) always want to be paid more
(d) always want to be paid less

4. The SAT scores of the students in my school were all ranked within the top one percent of the nation. Beneath that, however, the desires of the higher group were not much different from those of the lower 99 percent. These overachieving students, whose daily routines never allowed for any significant pastimes, had piles of magazines and game CDs under their beds, Justin Hoover, Starcraft and Playboy were all a part of their hidden treasures. It was as if, despite having no time or apparent desire whatsoever for these mediocre hobbies, they were driven by the same instinct as any other student: to seek something fun.

Q: What is the passage mainly about?
(a) A prestigious school that the writer attended
(b) A reason why we seek fun things even when we are busy
(c) A surprising similarity between the top students and the rest
(d) The hidden treasures of overachieving students within the top one percent

4. The SAT scores of the students in my school were all ranked within the top one percent of the nation. Beneath that, however, the desires of the higher group were not much different from those of the lower 99 percent. These overachieving students, whose daily routines never allowed for any significant pastimes, had piles of magazines and game CDs under their beds, Justin Hoover, Starcraft and Playboy were all a part of their hidden treasures. It was as if, despite having no time or apparent desire whatsoever for these mediocre hobbies, they were driven by the same instinct as any other student: to seek something fun.

Q: What is the passage mainly about?
(a) A prestigious school that the writer attended
(b) A reason why we seek fun things even when we are busy
(c) A surprising similarity between the top students and the rest
(d) The hidden treasures of overachieving students within the top one percent

5. Statistics provided by UN Development Program reveal that while the United States has always been a capitalist country, the ______________________________. Over several decades, the situation exacerbated. By 2007, the average after-tax income of the top 1 percent had reached $1.3 million, but that of the bottom 20 percent amounted to only $17,800. The richest 20 percent earns in total after tax more than the bottom 80 percent combined. These outcomes challenge the general perception we have of the United States as the "Land of Equal Opportunity".

(a) everyone receives equal opportunity
(b) extent of inequality in society actually expanded
(c) democratic notions of peace were settled deeply in society
(d) country was reluctant in caring about the environment

5. Statistics provided by UN Development Program reveal that while the United States has always been a capitalist country, the ______________________________. Over several decades, the situation exacerbated. By 2007, the average after-tax income of the top 1 percent had reached $1.3 million, but that of the bottom 20 percent amounted to only $17,800. The richest 20 percent earns in total after tax more than the bottom 80 percent combined. These outcomes challenge the general perception we have of the United States as the "Land of Equal Opportunity".

(a) everyone receives equal opportunity
(b) extent of inequality in society actually expanded
(c) democratic notions of peace were settled deeply in society
(d) country was reluctant in caring about the environment

지문 패턴# 9

양괄식

제1부
지문의 19가지 유형

INTERMEDIATE 지문 구조 ▷

PATTERN 9 양괄식

[9단원]은 의외로 굉장히 단순한 단원이다. 이미 양괄식 구조에 대해 들어 온 학생들도 많을 것이지만 그만큼 중요한 단원이기 때문에 추가하였다. 또한, 양괄식에 대한 정확한 개념을 알고 있는 학생은 많지 않기 때문에, 다시 정리해보는 단원이다. 양괄식 구조를 쏘아보기 단계에서 잘 맞춰보고, 기준에 들어맞지 않을 때는 양괄식 구조라고 생각하면 안 된다.

쏘아보기 단서

마지막 빈칸, So, Therefore, Thus (마지막 문장)

원리설명

양괄식 구조는 글의 중심 내용이 첫머리와 끝 부분에 반복하여 나타나는 문단 구성 방식이다.
하지만 9단원에서 양괄식이라는 개념을 재 정의 하겠다.
텝스의 기술에서 말하는 양괄식 구조란, "문제를 풀기 위해 첫 문장과 마지막 문장이 필요한 구조" 다. 이런 구조를 발견만 할 수 있다면 첫 문장과 마지막만 읽고 문제를 풀면 되는 것이다.

문제 풀이

1. 첫문장이 도입식 문장이 아니고

2. 빈칸이 마지막 문장에 있는데 (선택)

3. ______________로 시작하고

4. 지문 중간에 ______________가 따로 없을 때

지문은 "양괄식 구조"로 분류된다.
이런 조건에 맞는 문제가 있다면 무조건 첫 문장과 마지막 문장을 읽는다.

연습문제

우선 30~40초동안 문제를 먼저 풀어보세요

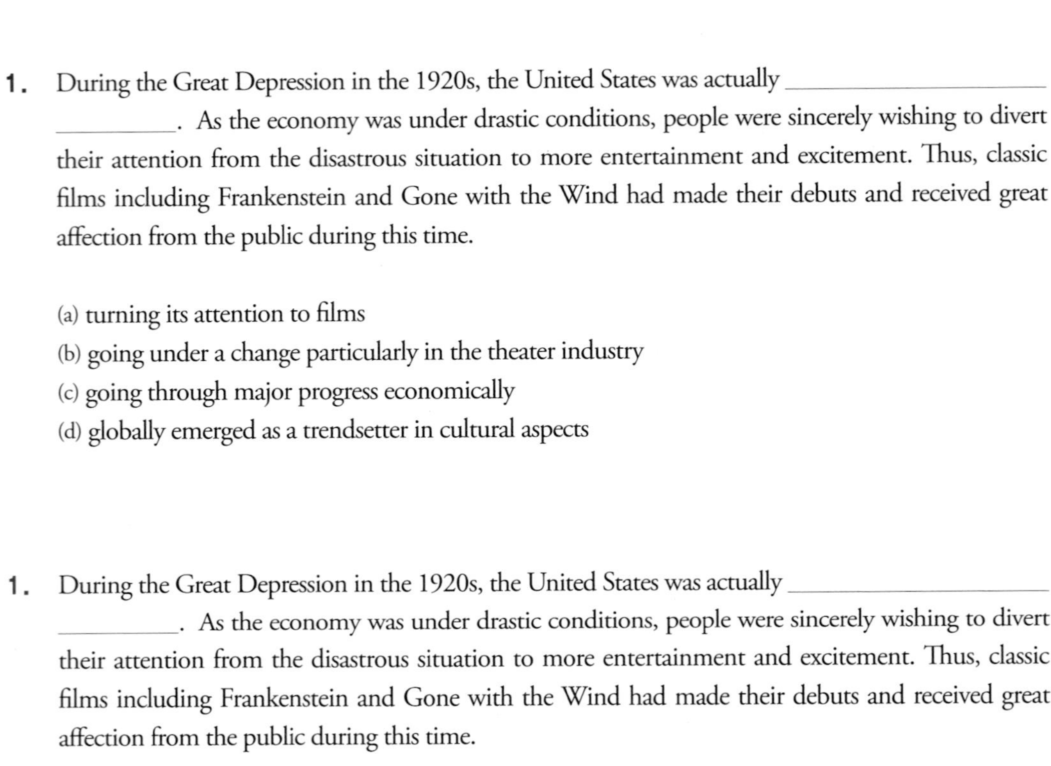

1. During the Great Depression in the 1920s, the United States was actually ____________________. As the economy was under drastic conditions, people were sincerely wishing to divert their attention from the disastrous situation to more entertainment and excitement. Thus, classic films including Frankenstein and Gone with the Wind had made their debuts and received great affection from the public during this time.

(a) turning its attention to films
(b) going under a change particularly in the theater industry
(c) going through major progress economically
(d) globally emerged as a trendsetter in cultural aspects

1. During the Great Depression in the 1920s, the United States was actually ____________________. As the economy was under drastic conditions, people were sincerely wishing to divert their attention from the disastrous situation to more entertainment and excitement. Thus, classic films including Frankenstein and Gone with the Wind had made their debuts and received great affection from the public during this time.

(a) turning its attention to films
(b) going under a change particularly in the theater industry
(c) going through major progress economically
(d) globally emerged as a trendsetter in cultural aspects

2. In the book the Last Lecture, Randy Pausch ______________________. Randy is a professor at Carnegie Mellon and is diagnosed with pancreatic cancer, which only gives him 3 to 6 months to live. He gradually starts the process of letting go of the little and irrelevant things in life such as fighting with his wife over who does the laundry or worrying about the stains on his car. He, thus, realizes how important spending time with family and friends is and how meaningless and time-consuming some of his previous jobs have been.

(a) explains how cancer influenced his family
(b) realizes the value of time in one's life
(c) bemoans being cursed with pancreatic cancer
(d) rediscovers his love for life

제1부
제2부
제3부
제4부

2. In the book the Last Lecture, Randy Pausch ______________________. Randy is a professor at Carnegie Mellon and is diagnosed with pancreatic cancer, which only gives him 3 to 6 months to live. He gradually starts the process of letting go of the little and irrelevant things in life such as fighting with his wife over who does the laundry or worrying about the stains on his car. He, thus, realizes how important spending time with family and friends is and how meaningless and time-consuming some of his previous jobs have been.

(a) explains how cancer influenced his family
(b) realizes the value of time in one's life
(c) bemoans being cursed with pancreatic cancer
(d) rediscovers his love for life

3. Recently an energy drink called the "Energy Bottle" has been on sale in local malls. Containing the ingredient Glyzerintine, the drink is known to keep a person awake for 26 hours. For students and businessmen who have limited amount of time and an intensive amount of workload, it may seem efficient to boost up work productivity by consuming the drink. Nevertheless, the World Health Organization recently published a research report claiming that Glyzerintine is toxic, and may increase the risk of heart disease. Therefore taking this into account, people ________________________.

(a) should be more cautious of having the energy drink
(b) should not stay up for 26 hours
(c) are advised to drink coffee instead
(d) should study the benefits of "Energy Bottle"

3. Recently an energy drink called the "Energy Bottle" has been on sale in local malls. Containing the ingredient Glyzerintine, the drink is known to keep a person awake for 26 hours. For students and businessmen who have limited amount of time and an intensive amount of workload, it may seem efficient to boost up work productivity by consuming the drink. Nevertheless, the World Health Organization recently published a research report claiming that Glyzerintine is toxic, and may increase the risk of heart disease. Therefore taking this into account, people ________________________.

(a) should be more cautious of having the energy drink
(b) should not stay up for 26 hours
(c) are advised to drink coffee instead
(d) should study the benefits of "Energy Bottle"

4. Korean high schools have only themselves to blame if they find that their students are not attentive during the morning. Most competitive high schools in Korea require students to come to school by 7:40 in the morning. To come to school by this time, students usually need to wake up at six or even earlier. Most studies conducted by psychologists and sleep experts claim that our brain is not fully awake and active by this time. Therefore a better strategy would be to ________________________________.

(a) change the schools into night schools
(b) provide more take home assignments
(c) wake up earlier than six o' clock
(d) start school at a later time

4. Korean high schools have only themselves to blame if they find that their students are not attentive during the morning. Most competitive high schools in Korea require students to come to school by 7:40 in the morning. To come to school by this time, students usually need to wake up at six or even earlier. Most studies conducted by psychologists and sleep experts claim that our brain is not fully awake and active by this time. Therefore a better strategy would be to ________________________________.

(a) change the schools into night schools
(b) provide more take home assignments
(c) wake up earlier than six o' clock
(d) start school at a later time

5. Many teenagers who are into building muscle want to take supplements. These include protein shakes, BCAAs, multi-vitamins, fish oil and etc. All these are dedicated to help building muscle faster and to provide more energy for workouts. Or so they say. There are plenty of evidence and studies that show these supplements to be useless. So it is no wonder that parents are ______________________________________.

(a) working out at a less efficient rate than their children.
(b) joining their kids in purchasing these products.
(c) hesitant when it comes to buying these products for their children
(d) concerned about health issues from consuming supplements

5. Many teenagers who are into building muscle want to take supplements. These include protein shakes, BCAAs, multi-vitamins, fish oil and etc. All these are dedicated to help building muscle faster and to provide more energy for workouts. Or so they say. There are plenty of evidence and studies that show these supplements to be useless. So it is no wonder that parents aree ______________________________________.

(a) working out at a less efficient rate than their children.
(b) joining their kids in purchasing these products.
(c) hesitant when it comes to buying these products for their children
(d) concerned about health issues from consuming supplements

지문 패턴#10
연결어 뉘앙스

제1부
지문의 19가지 유형

INTERMEDIATE 지문 구조 ▷

PATTERN 10 연결어 뉘앙스

영작 전문가들은 개별 연결어들의 뉘앙스를 따로 정리해서 문단 전개의 특성에 맞춰 사용하도록 교육을 받는다. 자신이 표현하고자 하는 내용을 독자에게 제대로 전달하기 위하여 사용하는 도구가 바로 "연결어"라는 것이다. 우리는 이런 연결어들의 뉘앙스를 미리 파악하면 뒤따를 내용의 예측이 가능한 것이다. 또한, 연결어들이 나온다는 것은 특정 부분이 강조 되고 있다는 뜻이므로 주제가 될 확률이 높아진다는 것도 참고해야 한다.

쏘아보기 단서

따로 없음.
지문을 읽는 과정에서 발견되는 모든 연결어.

원리 설명

특정 연결어들은 문장 내에서 A라는 부분을 부정하면서 B를 긍정하곤 한다.
시험에서 이러한 연결어들이 나온다면 A를 피해 B를 읽어야 하기도 하지만, B에 강조된다는 것을 알아야 한다. 또한, 지문 내에서 같은 부분이 이중으로 강조된다면 그 부분이 주제가 되는 것이다. "이중 강조는 주제."를 기억하자.
만약 연결어 뉘앙스[10단원]에 해당하는 연결어가 첫 문장에 나온다면 그것이 주제문이 되는 것이다.

문제 풀이

쏘아보기가 아닌 문제 풀이 단계에서 지문을 읽을 때 연결어가 등장한다면 B를 표시하고 읽는다. 정답에 B 부분이 연결 될 가능성이 크기 때문이다.

While A, B.

Although A, B.

Despite A, B.

Even though A, B.

✓ 이중 강조는 주제.

제1부
제2부
제3부
제4부

연습문제

우선 30~40초동안 문제를 먼저 풀어보세요

1. While the so-called "dumb" phones are disappearing quickly, some other electronic gadgets are disappearing even faster. Digital cameras, portable gaming console, PDAs and mp3 players have almost disappeared off the market since 2010, and they may become completely obsolete by the next few years. The leading factor contributing to their demise is the sheer multi-functionality of smart phones. With their phones becoming more versatile and compact than ever, people are no longer feeling the need for bulky separate devices.

Q: What is the passage mainly about?
(a) The inconvenience of using separate devices
(b) The demise of numerous electronic devices
(c) The disappearance of dumb phones from the market
(d) The versatility and compactness of smartphones

1. While the so-called "dumb" phones are disappearing quickly, some other electronic gadgets are disappearing even faster. Digital cameras, portable gaming console, PDAs and mp3 players have almost disappeared off the market since 2010, and they may become completely obsolete by the next few years. The leading factor contributing to their demise is the sheer multi-functionality of smart phones. With their phones becoming more versatile and compact than ever, people are no longer feeling the need for bulky separate devices.

Q: What is the passage mainly about?
(a) The inconvenience of using separate devices
(b) The demise of numerous electronic devices
(c) The disappearance of dumb phones from the market
(d) The versatility and compactness of smartphones

2. Tobacco Gum was prevalent in Major League Baseball in the United States during the mid to late 20th century, even though it ______________________________. As people were finding out that these tobacco products could lead to cancer, and when the children, after seeing their favorite players use chewing tobacco, were trying them out, Major League officials started banning the use of these products. The players, in the end, chose bubble gum, which was both healthier and more visually appealing.

(a) was mainly consumed in Europe
(b) caused no health hazards for the players
(c) contained many carcinogenic substances
(d) was against the will of the fans

2. Tobacco Gum was prevalent in Major League Baseball in the United States during the mid to late 20th century, even though it ______________________________. As people were finding out that these tobacco products could lead to cancer, and when the children, after seeing their favorite players use chewing tobacco, were trying them out, Major League officials started banning the use of these products. The players, in the end, chose bubble gum, which was both healthier and more visually appealing.

(a) was mainly consumed in Europe
(b) caused no health hazards for the players
(c) contained many carcinogenic substances
(d) was against the will of the fans

3. The head coach of the 2010 Korean speed skating national team, Leonardo Kim, has long been praised for his ______________________________. Even though he spent most of his skating career on the Korean national team where he earned three gold medals, it was his agility and creative skating skills that considerably influenced the world of speed skating. For instance, in the 1998 Olympic Games, Leonardo first disclosed his cross-legging skating style which is still the fastest known way to skate in a corner and is used by all skaters in speed skating.

(a) outstanding contributions to the development of speed skating
(b) medals for victories during the 1998 Olympic Games
(c) construction of the Korean Olympics ice rink stadium
(d) coaching skills he showed after his retirement as a professional

3. The head coach of the 2010 Korean speed skating national team, Leonardo Kim, has long been praised for his ______________________________. Even though he spent most of his skating career on the Korean national team where he earned three gold medals, it was his agility and creative skating skills that considerably influenced the world of speed skating. For instance, in the 1998 Olympic Games, Leonardo first disclosed his cross-legging skating style which is still the fastest known way to skate in a corner and is used by all skaters in speed skating.

(a) outstanding contributions to the development of speed skating
(b) medals for victories during the 1998 Olympic Games
(c) construction of the Korean Olympics ice rink stadium
(d) coaching skills he showed after his retirement as a professional

4. The phenomenon of group conformity is surprisingly prevalent in various occasions. Despite the fact that an individual knew the answer to a simple test question with certainty, the subject ended up providing the wrong answer to go along with the crowd. Psychologically, people actually convince themselves that they are thinking what the group is thinking. The tendency is highly probable when in great uncertainty. Also, the feeling of assimilation plays a crucial role in such behavioral inclination. People's primary motivation is to be liked and accepted by others and their greatest fear is to be different and alienated.

Q: What is the passage mainly about?
(a) The feeling of fear that affects one's decision-making process
(b) Experimenting with the subject excluded from the majority group
(c) Reasons why an individual had the wrong answer
(d) The attitude and action of the majority having profound influence on individuals

4. The phenomenon of group conformity is surprisingly prevalent in various occasions. Despite the fact that an individual knew the answer to a simple test question with certainty, the subject ended up providing the wrong answer to go along with the crowd. Psychologically, people actually convince themselves that they are thinking what the group is thinking. The tendency is highly probable when in great uncertainty. Also, the feeling of assimilation plays a crucial role in such behavioral inclination. People's primary motivation is to be liked and accepted by others and their greatest fear is to be different and alienated.

Q: What is the passage mainly about?
(a) The feeling of fear that affects one's decision-making process
(b) Experimenting with the subject excluded from the majority group
(c) Reasons why an individual had the wrong answer
(d) The attitude and action of the majority having profound influence on individuals

5. Although it may seem difficult to sleep when you suffer from insomnia, ________________________ ______________. Various simple measures will help you. For instance, try counting sheep, or drink a cup of warm milk before you lie down. Think about complex mathematical equations that would make your brain fried. If it still doesn't work, take a thick academic book and read it for about 5 minutes. You would find your eyelids slowly getting heavier.

(a) you should find a comfortable bed to help you sleep
(b) there are ways to make falling asleep easier
(c) you should always be more active during the day
(d) sufficient rest is important for a healthy body

5. Although it may seem difficult to sleep when you suffer from insomnia, ________________________ ______________. Various simple measures will help you. For instance, try counting sheep, or drink a cup of warm milk before you lie down. Think about complex mathematical equations that would make your brain fried. If it still doesn't work, take a thick academic book and read it for about 5 minutes. You would find your eyelids slowly getting heavier.

(a) you should find a comfortable bed to help you sleep
(b) there are ways to make falling asleep easier
(c) you should always be more active during the day
(d) sufficient rest is important for a healthy body

지문 패턴#11
부정 후엔 긍정

제1부
지문의 19가지 유형

INTERMEDIATE 지문 구조 ▷

PATTERN 11 부정 후엔 긍정

이번 단원 "부정 후엔 긍정"은 A is not B but C라는 간단한 구문에서 출발하는 것이다. 이 간단한 구문이 텝스 지문 한 문장 한 문장에 쓰이기도 하지만 텝스 지문의 전체 구조에 여러 문장에 거쳐서 나타나기도 한다. 각각의 경우에 어떻게 문제풀이를 해 나가야 하는지 감만 잡는다면 시간 절약이 확실히 될 것이다.

쏘아보기 단서

쏘아보기 단서는 따로 없음.
문장 내에서 not only, but also

원리 설명

1. 문장 내에 A is not B but C. 라는 구조는 A=C 라는 메시지를 전달하고 싶은 것이다. 그 속에 B를 부정함으로써 C를 강조하는 것이다.
   A is not B but C.
   A는 B가 아니라 C이다.
   A는 B보다 C이다.
   A is not only B, but also C.

2. 지문을 통틀어서 이런 구조가 나타날 수 있다. A is not B but C라는 것은 결국 A is not B. __________ 이렇게 두 개로 나뉠 수 있다. 그렇다면 첫 문장에 A is not B.라는 글이 나온다면, 지문 중반부 혹은 후반부에 __________가 나올 것으로 예측할 수 있다. 또한, 결국 A is not B라는 것은 중요하지 않은 것이니 오로지 __________만 파악하면 주제는 파악 되는 것이다. "A는 B가 아니다."라는 것을 주제로 하는 글은 없을 것이다.

문제 풀이

원리 설명에서 다뤘다시피 B를 발견하는 순간 C가 있을 것을 인지하고 바로 C를 찾아 나서야 한다.

연습문제

우선 30~40초동안 문제를 먼저 풀어보세요

1. Most grievances about parents from their children don't concern perceptible inequalities, like quitting a job so they can help their children with their homework or studies or giving them much freedom, such as a big allowance, a lot of spare time, and easy access to the internet. What they complain about most is communication, saying that their parents do not try to understand what they say. Most children, as a matter of fact, feel affection not when they receive much freedom, but rather when they feel understood.

Q: What is the main idea of the passage?
(a) Parents are much better communicators than children
(b) Children want more freedom from their parents
(c) Children understand that parents want to communicate
(d) Children want to be better understood by their parents

1. Most grievances about parents from their children don't concern perceptible inequalities, like quitting a job so they can help their children with their homework or studies or giving them much freedom, such as a big allowance, a lot of spare time, and easy access to the internet. What they complain about most is communication, saying that their parents do not try to understand what they say. Most children, as a matter of fact, feel affection not when they receive much freedom, but rather when they feel understood.

Q: What is the main idea of the passage?
(a) Parents are much better communicators than children
(b) Children want more freedom from their parents
(c) Children understand that parents want to communicate
(d) Children want to be better understood by their parents

2. Military boot camp is, in a way, a cycle. Newly incoming soldiers enter boot camp every month. Then, they are put into a series of training that will push them to their limits not only physically but also mentally and emotionally. But that doesn't mean they don't have a good time because they form bonds with all the people around them. These bonds are very powerful and so a lot of soldiers are motivated to come back to base camp and work as drill officers. Because of this, ____.

(a) forming a sense of camaraderie in the boot camp is the most important.
(b) many trainees become a different person once they leave the camp
(c) there is always an adequate supply of people willing to be a drill officer in boot camp
(d) the number of incoming soldiers increase annually

2. Military boot camp is, in a way, a cycle. Newly incoming soldiers enter boot camp every month. Then, they are put into a series of training that will push them to their limits not only physically but also mentally and emotionally. But that doesn't mean they don't have a good time because they form bonds with all the people around them. These bonds are very powerful and so a lot of soldiers are motivated to come back to base camp and work as drill officers. Because of this, ____.

(a) forming a sense of camaraderie in the boot camp is the most important.
(b) many trainees become a different person once they leave the camp
(c) there is always an adequate supply of people in boot camp
(d) the number of incoming soldiers increase annually

3. The Korean ______________________________. Samsung Electronics is playing a big role in this area, with its innovative ideas shaping the lifestyles of the ordinary people. Its recent release of the Galaxy Series has been receiving positive appeal not only in the local market, but also in the international market. People now get to enjoy new technologies which make their daily lives more efficient and convenient.

(a) economy is led by a few major IT companies
(b) IT companies are affecting the lives of the global population
(c) government is striving for new ways to develop technology
(d) market is declining due to the recent economic crisis

3. The Korean ______________________________. Samsung Electronics is playing a big role in this area, with its innovative ideas shaping the lifestyles of the ordinary people. Its recent release of the Galaxy Series has been receiving positive appeal not only in the local market, but also in the international market. People now get to enjoy new technologies which make their daily lives more efficient and convenient.

(a) economy is led by a few major IT companies
(b) IT companies are affecting the lives of the global population
(c) government is striving for new ways to develop technology
(d) market is declining due to the recent economic crisis

지문 패턴#12 연구내용 / 결과

제1부
지문의 19가지 유형

INTERMEDIATE 지문 구조 ▷

PATTERN 12 연구내용 / 결과

텝스 지문에서 어떤 시험이나 연구 내용이 나온다면, 그 내용의 역할은 정해져 있다.
텝스 문제에서 실제 연구/실험의 내용을 묻진 않는다.
_______은 읽을 필요 없이 오로지 _______에만 집중하면 되는 것이다. 정말 많이 등장하는 유형이므로 꼭 숙지하도록 한다.

쏘아보기 단서

study, evidence, survey, research
~shows that~
experimental results
observed, found

원리 설명

연구 내용과 연구 결과라는 것은 비슷한 듯 보이지만 텝스 지문에선 아예 다른 역할을 한다.
________은 구체적으로 어떤 연구가 진행됐는지 설명하는 부분이다.
반면에 ___________는 어떤 결론이 도출되었는지 보여준다. 정답인 주제는 결론에서 나오고, 결국 정답도 에서 나오는 것이다.

문제 풀이

결국, 우리는 결과만 필요한 것이니 앞으로 study/experiment가 등장한다면 ________를 찾는 것이 중요하다. ________은 전혀 중요하지 않다.

제1부 제2부 제3부 제4부

연습문제

우선 30~40초동안 문제를 먼저 풀어보세요

1. French gourmet and connoisseur Jean Grandetgras proposed the term "amuse-bouche" in 1963 to name the small, bite-sized dishes which became fashionable recently for master chefs to serve before the meal. He observed that the dish was not ordered from the menu by patrons, but often served freely by the chef's choice alone. The custom soon provided an arena of competition for chefs to show their mastery of cooking. Shortly after, the competition resulted in the chefs using the finest ingredients and the most avant-garde of recipes, that the gourmet named it "amuse-bouche", meaning "mouth amuser".

   Q: What is the main idea about Amuse-bouche according to the passage?
   (a) The Gourmet Jean Grandetgras first coined the term in 1913
   (b) An amuse-bouche is cooked and designed according to the diner's wishes
   (c) It was observed by the gourmet that amuse-bouche was often neglected by patrons
   (d) Amuse-bouche became very high-quality soon after its introduction, due to competition

1. French gourmet and connoisseur Jean Grandetgras proposed the term "amuse-bouche" in 1963 to name the small, bite-sized dishes which became fashionable recently for master chefs to serve before the meal. He observed that the dish was not ordered from the menu by patrons, but often served freely by the chef's choice alone. The custom soon provided an arena of competition for chefs to show their mastery of cooking. Shortly after, the competition resulted in the chefs using the finest ingredients and the most avant-garde of recipes, that the gourmet named it "amuse-bouche", meaning "mouth amuser".

   Q: What is the main idea about Amuse-bouche according to the passage?
   (a) The Gourmet Jean Grandetgras first coined the term in 1913
   (b) An amuse-bouche is cooked and designed according to the diner's wishes
   (c) It was observed by the gourmet that amuse-bouche was often neglected by patrons
   (d) Amuse-bouche became very high-quality soon after its introduction, due to competition

2. British scientists from the University of Oxford and Cambridge have come to the conclusion that Branch Chain Amino Acids, a supplement often used by bodybuilders for faster muscle growth and recovery, ______________________________. 100 athletes all around England were given BCAAs in the form of pills and their muscle growth was measured over a period of one year. However, the results showed no difference from the muscle growth of the control group which received no such supplements.

(a) can cause liver disease
(b) decrease muscle mass
(c) do not live up to its description
(d) are only effective on women

2. British scientists from the University of Oxford and Cambridge have come to the conclusion that Branch Chain Amino Acids, a supplement often used by bodybuilders for faster muscle growth and recovery, ______________________________. 100 athletes all around England were given BCAAs in the form of pills and their muscle growth was measured over a period of one year. However, the results showed no difference from the muscle growth of the control group which received no such supplements.

(a) can cause liver disease
(b) decrease muscle mass
(c) do not live up to its description
(d) are only effective on women

3. With the city of Seoul trying to reduce toxic water, oysters just might be the answer. Studies conducted by the University of Oxford show that oysters breathe in toxic water and let out relatively cleaner water in whatever environment they are in. Inserting 500 oysters into a body of water the size of Lake Eerie will decrease the toxic level by 4.7% in a time span of three weeks. Experts claim that this is the best way to ____________________.

(a) deal with Seoul's water pollution
(b) drive up the toxic level in Seoul
(c) make Lake Eerie clean once and for all
(d) create a safe ecosystem for oysters

3. With the city of Seoul trying to reduce toxic water, oysters just might be the answer. Studies conducted by the University of Oxford show that oysters breathe in toxic water and let out relatively cleaner water in whatever environment they are in. Inserting 500 oysters into a body of water the size of Lake Eerie will decrease the toxic level by 4.7% in a time span of three weeks. Experts claim that this is the best way to ____________________.

(a) deal with Seoul's water pollution
(b) drive up the toxic level in Seoul
(c) make Lake Eerie clean once and for all
(d) create a safe ecosystem for oysters

4. A new study suggests that if mothers were to avoid using the microwave, they may have a better chance of preventing cancer in their future children. Researchers, through careful examination of 4000 pregnant women, have concluded that microwaves cause prenatal cancer genes to form in the fetus. They found that every ten minutes of exposure to an operating microwave increases the chance of cancer by one percent. The discovery indicates an evident correlation between microwave exposure and the risk of the future offspring contracting cancer.

Q: What is the passage mainly about?

(a) Microwave exposure can cause infertility in mothers
(b) Microwave ovens increase the risk of cancer in mothers
(c) The need for future children to avoid using the microwave
(d) Exposure to microwaves can increase the chance of cancer in unborn children

4. A new study suggests that if mothers were to avoid using the microwave, they may have a better chance of preventing cancer in their future children. Researchers, through careful examination of 4000 pregnant women, have concluded that microwaves cause prenatal cancer genes to form in the fetus. They found that every ten minutes of exposure to an operating microwave increases the chance of cancer by one percent. The discovery indicates an evident correlation between microwave exposure and the risk of the future offspring contracting cancer.

Q: What is the passage mainly about?

(a) Microwave exposure can cause infertility in mothers
(b) Microwave ovens increase the risk of cancer in mothers
(c) The need for future children to avoid using the microwave
(d) Exposure to microwaves can increase the chance of cancer in unborn children

5. Structural stress in aluminum fuselages cause some of the molecular alignment to become condensed. In other words, the originally linear alignment becomes jagged and irregular when structural force is applied. While this change may harmlessly increase the overall durability of the structure, it eventually causes the tensile strength to deteriorate drastically and become dangerously brittle. A research conducted on crashed aircrafts discovered that aluminum fuselages that suffered from prolonged structural stress absorbed less shock from the impact, resulting in higher casualty counts.

Q: What is the main idea of the passage?

(a) Structural stress sometimes strengthens an aluminum structure in the short term

(b) Structural stress is the main cause of many aircraft crashes

(c) Structural stress is detrimental to the structural safety of a fuselage

(d) Prolonged structural stress can have devastating results unless special caution is taken during use

5. Structural stress in aluminum fuselages cause some of the molecular alignment to become condensed. In other words, the originally linear alignment becomes jagged and irregular when structural force is applied. While this change may harmlessly increase the overall durability of the structure, it eventually causes the tensile strength to deteriorate drastically and become dangerously brittle. A research conducted on crashed aircrafts discovered that aluminum fuselages that suffered from prolonged structural stress absorbed less shock from the impact, resulting in higher casualty counts.

Q: What is the main idea of the passage?

(a) Structural stress sometimes strengthens an aluminum structure in the short term

(b) Structural stress is the main cause of many aircraft crashes

(c) Structural stress is detrimental to the structural safety of a fuselage

(d) Prolonged structural stress can have devastating results unless special caution is taken during use

지문 패턴#13
동급 나열식

제1부
지문의 19가지 유형

ADVANCED 지문 구조 ▷

PATTERN

13 동급 나열식

첫 문장 ____.
첫째, ~~~~~~~
둘째, ~~~~~~~
셋째, ~~~~~~~

첫 문장에 빈칸이 들어가 있고, 지문 나머지엔 첫째, 둘째, 셋째라는 동급 구조로 진행이 되는 지문 구조를 "동급 나열식 구조"라고 한다.

쏘아보기 단서

First, Second, Third, Lastly,
Also,
Another,
These
In addition, Furthermore

원리 설명

쏘아보기 시 First, Second, Third, Lastly, Also, Another, These, In addition, Furthermore이 나온다면 동급 나열식 구조라는 것을 파악할 수 있다. 동급 나열식이라는 것이 파악 된다면 결국 A/B/C 구조를 나눠서 표시한다.

문제 풀이

A/B/C 중의 하나(가장 짧은 것)를 먼저 읽고, 선택지로 가서 정답이 불가능한 선택지들은 제거한다. 그다음 나머지 두 개 중의 하나를 고르고 선택지로 다시 가면 된다.

제1부
제2부
제3부
제4부

연습문제

우선 30~40초동안 문제를 먼저 풀어보세요

1. Linking protection of natural environment to manufacturing firms will assure that the firms ________________. In accordance with this, official documents describing the mechanics of the new policy have been sent by the federal government to all the manufacturing companies in the country. There are two main goals in plan. First, the government wishes to make the companies feel the responsibility of the surrounding environment. Second, through an appropriate reward system, the government encourages the companies to see the environment as one of their assets and to increase economic profits while protecting the environment.

(a) maximize their profits by developing on the protected land
(b) endeavor to successfully keep the natural environment healthy
(c) work with each other to evade the environmental laws
(d) make double profits by protecting the environment

1. Linking protection of natural environment to manufacturing firms will assure that the firms ________________. In accordance with this, official documents describing the mechanics of the new policy have been sent by the federal government to all the manufacturing companies in the country. There are two main goals in plan. First, the government wishes to make the companies feel the responsibility of the surrounding environment. Second, through an appropriate reward system, the government encourages the companies to see the environment as one of their assets and to increase economic profits while protecting the environment.

(a) maximize their profits by developing on the protected land
(b) endeavor to successfully keep the natural environment healthy
(c) work with each other to evade the environmental laws
(d) make double profits by protecting the environment

2. Results from the Statistics Department of the Bank of Korea suggest that____. First of all, the Gross National Product of Korea has increased greatly over the past ten years. Furthermore, unemployment rates are down to almost half of what they used to be. These results reflect the government's constant efforts to bring back what used to be before the Great Recession of 2008.

(a) the Korean economy is starting to boom
(b) the economy in Korea is always be fluctuating
(c) korea will face an economic recession
(d) the country should take use of open trade

2. Results from the Statistics Department of the Bank of Korea suggest that____. First of all, the Gross National Product of Korea has increased greatly over the past ten years. Furthermore, unemployment rates are down to almost half of what they used to be. These results reflect the government's constant efforts to bring back what used to be before the Great Recession of 2008.

(a) the Korean economy is starting to boom
(b) the economy in Korea is always be fluctuating
(c) korea will face an economic recession
(d) the country should take use of open trade

3. Making a piñata is not as difficult as people might think. First, make paper mache paste by mixing a bowl of flour with water. Second, tear some newspapers into strips. They should be about 2 inches wide and 6 to 8 inches long, making the newspaper to lie nice and flat on the balloon. Next, apply paper mache in a crisscross pattern until the entire balloon is covered. Let the piñata sit until it is completely dried and hardened. After that, pop the balloon and remove it, leaving the mold empty in a balloon-shaped.

Q: What is the passage mainly about?
(a) How to make a sphere-shaped mold
(b) Being careful with handling a balloon
(c) Solution to difficulties of making a piñata with paper mache
(d) Steps necessary for constructing a piñata

3. Making a piñata is not as difficult as people might think. First, make paper mache paste by mixing a bowl of flour with water. Second, tear some newspapers into strips. They should be about 2 inches wide and 6 to 8 inches long, making the newspaper to lie nice and flat on the balloon. Next, apply paper mache in a crisscross pattern until the entire balloon is covered. Let the piñata sit until it is completely dried and hardened. After that, pop the balloon and remove it, leaving the mold empty in a balloon-shaped.

Q: What is the passage mainly about?
(a) How to make a sphere-shaped mold
(b) Being careful with handling a balloon
(c) Solution to difficulties of making a piñata with paper mache
(d) Steps necessary for constructing a piñata

4. The terminology, "Quantum physics" is a branch of science dealing with physical phenomena on a diminutive level. It provides a mathematical description of 'particle-like' and 'wave-like' behavior and interactions of energy and matter. In epitome, one of the main ideas of Quantum Theory states that it is physically impossible to know both the position and the particle's momentum at the same time. Another idea of the theory claims that the atomic world is nothing like the world we live in. While these may sound unfamiliar and strange at a glance, Quantum physics provides clues to the field of science and the fundamental nature of the universe.

Q: What is the main topic of the passage?
(a) The ways in which particles and matters interact with one another
(b) Energy decides the momentum of a particle
(c) An overall explanation on Quantum physics
(d) A description on the scientific theories provided by Quantum

4. The terminology, "Quantum physics" is a branch of science dealing with physical phenomena on a diminutive level. It provides a mathematical description of 'particle-like' and 'wave-like' behavior and interactions of energy and matter. In epitome, one of the main ideas of Quantum Theory states that it is physically impossible to know both the position and the particle's momentum at the same time. Another idea of the theory claims that the atomic world is nothing like the world we live in. While these may sound unfamiliar and strange at a glance, Quantum physics provides clues to the field of science and the fundamental nature of the universe.

Q: What is the main topic of the passage?
(a) The ways in which particles and matters interact with one another
(b) Energy decides the momentum of a particle
(c) An overall explanation on Quantum physics
(d) A description on the scientific theories provided by Quantum

5. ______________________________ is definitely not an ambition that most elementary school teachers would try to accomplish, yet Donna Caterano was a woman of overflowing passion. She voluntarily invested her free time to help blind and deaf children start from a blank slate and gradually develop their academic skills one step at a time. With her teeming desire to support the children, she has succeeded in helping more than 100 blind and deaf elementary students to reach the level of other students in subjects which include but are not limited to writing, math, and science. Furthermore, Donna continued her progress even outside of the elementary school; by helping the disabled elderly who wish to go back to studying academics fulfill their dreams through weekly night classes.

(a) Granting free education for students lacking money
(b) Providing academics for disabled children rather than recreational activities
(c) Implementing math and science night classes for elderly
(d) Helping people with disabilities catch up on academics

5. ______________________________ is definitely not an ambition that most elementary school teachers would try to accomplish, yet Donna Caterano was a woman of overflowing passion. She voluntarily invested her free time to help blind and deaf children start from a blank slate and gradually develop their academic skills one step at a time. With her teeming desire to support the children, she has succeeded in helping more than 100 blind and deaf elementary students to reach the level of other students in subjects which include but are not limited to writing, math, and science. Furthermore, Donna continued her progress even outside of the elementary school; by helping the disabled elderly who wish to go back to studying academics fulfill their dreams through weekly night classes.

(a) Granting free education for students lacking money
(b) Providing academics for disabled children rather than recreational activities
(c) Implementing math and science night classes for elderly
(d) Helping people with disabilities catch up on academics

지문 패턴#14
꼬리의 꼬리 물기

제1부
지문의 19가지 유형

ADVANCED 지문 구조 ▷

PATTERN

14 꼬리의 꼬리 물기

이번 단원의 부제는 "역추론"이라고 할 수 있겠다. 일반적인 문제풀이 방법은 "정추론"에 해당이 된다. 앞에서부터 중요도 상관없이 읽기 때문에 "정"추론인 것이다. 하지만 우리는 중요한 부분부터 차례대로 읽는다. 중요한 문장을 읽게 되면 결국 빈칸에서 묻는 것과 일치하는 경우가 90% 이상이다. 나머지 경우에 꼬리의 꼬리물기 기술이 적용되는 것이다.

쏘아보기 단서

This, These

원리 설명

This를 번역하면 '이것'이다. 즉, This 라는 단어가 나온다는 것은, 바로 앞 문장에 대한 부연 설명을 한다는 것이다. 앞 문장의 '이것'과 관련된 부연설명이 나열 되는 것이기 때문이다. 즉, THIS가 나온다면 앞 문장과 뒷 문장은 한 문장이라고 간주하면 될 것이고, 앞 문장에 강조점이 간다는 것도 확인해야 한다.

문제 풀이

쏘아보기 단서들을 기준으로 중요한 문장 두 문장을 찾았다고 하고, 그 문장 중 한 문장이 THIS로 시작한다고 하면, THIS가 등장한 문장 앞 문장에 집중 해야 한다.
예를 들어, For example 앞의 문장이 This로 시작한다면 For example 앞의 앞 문장을 읽어야 한다.

연습문제

우선 30~40초동안 문제를 먼저 풀어보세요

1. According to the teachings of Bei Tsu, there is one most important factor that decides the harvest of a certain year. It is the frequency and the amount of annual rainfall. He says that the amount of rainfall throughout a year controls the success of the year's harvest. This is shown by the fact that some areas harvest more crops at the end of the year, even though the fertility of the soil was judged to be similar. For example, ancient records show that two fields with similar fertility and different rainfall had significantly different harvests, whereas two fields with similar rainfall and different fertility did not show much difference in the end. The obvious conclusion Bei Tsu made was that rainfall is ______________________.

(a) the deciding factor in a year's harvest is in the amount of rainfall
(b) irrelevant to deciding how much crops will be harvested that year
(c) detrimental to the growing of rice crops in some very fertile lands
(d) one of the most important factors which decide the fertility of the soil

1. According to the teachings of Bei Tsu, there is one most important factor that decides the harvest of a certain year. It is the frequency and the amount of annual rainfall. He says that the amount of rainfall throughout a year controls the success of the year's harvest. This is shown by the fact that some areas harvest more crops at the end of the year, even though the fertility of the soil was judged to be similar. For example, ancient records show that two fields with similar fertility and different rainfall had significantly different harvests, whereas two fields with similar rainfall and different fertility did not show much difference in the end. The obvious conclusion Bei Tsu made was that rainfall is ______________________.

(a) the deciding factor in a year's harvest is in the amount of rainfall
(b) irrelevant to deciding how much crops will be harvested that year
(c) detrimental to the growing of rice crops in some very fertile lands
(d) one of the most important factors which decide the fertility of the soil

2. Liquid-State Drive (LSD) is a newly invented memory storage system adopted in the most cutting-edge computer systems of today. A strange thing about this new technology is that high performance computers with high capacity LSDs tend to malfunction when used in space stations. This is because the liquid state of the drive, which normally allows the drive to change flexibly depending on what sector the necessary data is stored in, makes it float around haphazardly around the computer, causing short circuits and memory corruption. The weightless state in space stations were not put into consideration when LSD was first invented. Thus, the weightlessness makes the LSDs original advantages ______________________.

(a) not as effective as it is back down on Earth
(b) possible to be used for different purposes
(c) offset its disadvantages of its liquid state
(d) become a problem that needs to be solved

2. Liquid-State Drive (LSD) is a newly invented memory storage system adopted in the most cutting-edge computer systems of today. A strange thing about this new technology is that high performance computers with high capacity LSDs tend to malfunction when used in space stations. This is because the liquid state of the drive, which normally allows the drive to change flexibly depending on what sector the necessary data is stored in, makes it float around haphazardly around the computer, causing short circuits and memory corruption. The weightless state in space stations were not put into consideration when LSD was first invented. Thus, the weightlessness makes the LSDs original advantages ______________________.

(a) not as effective as it is back down on Earth
(b) possible to be used for different purposes
(c) offset its disadvantages of its liquid state
(d) become a problem that needs to be solved

3. On December 18, 1992, the thermometers in Svericoldjorn read a record low temperature of -73 degrees Celsius, leaving the power plant and several important electronic equipment out of function, and a large number of people dead due to hypothermia. While the people were stuck in the city, with their cars not starting and heaters not working, the citizens decided to pull down the UNESCO-protected Nordic ruin of Djontsburn, and burn it for fuel. Despite the outrageousness of the idea, this last resort was later accepted and understood worldwide, considering it was the only way to save their lives. From these events, a new provision has been added to the UNESCO cultural heritage regulations, adding that ________________________________.

(a) a protected cultural heritage site should never be jeopardized
(b) cold regions are henceforth exempt from some of the rules thereof
(c) protection of human life is always a priority over protecting heritage sites
(d) the heritage sites in areas with extreme conditions should be relocated

3. On December 18, 1992, the thermometers in Svericoldjorn read a record low temperature of -73 degrees Celsius, leaving the power plant and several important electronic equipment out of function, and a large number of people dead due to hypothermia. While the people were stuck in the city, with their cars not starting and heaters not working, the citizens decided to pull down the UNESCO-protected Nordic ruin of Djontsburn, and burn it for fuel. Despite the outrageousness of the idea, this last resort was later accepted and understood worldwide, considering it was the only way to save their lives. From these events, a new provision has been added to the UNESCO cultural heritage regulations, adding that ________________________________.

(a) a protected cultural heritage site should never be jeopardized
(b) cold regions are henceforth exempt from some of the rules thereof
(c) protection of human life is always a priority over protecting heritage sites
(d) the heritage sites in areas with extreme conditions should be relocated

4. Military boot camp is, in a way, a cycle. Newly incoming soldiers enter boot camp every month. Then, they are put into a series of training that will push them to their limits not only physically but mentally and emotionally. But that doesn't mean they don't have a good time because they form bonds with all the people around them. These bonds are very powerful and so a lot of soldiers are motivated to come back to base camp and work as drill officers. Because of this, ______________ ______________.

(a) forming a sense of camaraderie in the boot camp is the most important.
(b) many trainees become a different person once they leave the camp
(c) there is always an adequate supply of people willing to be a drill officer in boot camp
(d) the number of incoming soldiers increase annually

4. Military boot camp is, in a way, a cycle. Newly incoming soldiers enter boot camp every month. Then, they are put into a series of training that will push them to their limits not only physically but mentally and emotionally. But that doesn't mean they don't have a good time because they form bonds with all the people around them. These bonds are very powerful and so a lot of soldiers are motivated to come back to base camp and work as drill officers. Because of this, ______________ ______________.

(a) forming a sense of camaraderie in the boot camp is the most important.
(b) many trainees become a different person once they leave the camp
(c) there is always an adequate supply of people willing to be a drill officer in boot camp
(d) the number of incoming soldiers increase annually

5. Immigrant workers are forced to confront critical difficulties regarding insurance problems. As they lack authorized documents, they have no method of being issued insurances in a legal manner. This is especially a major problem in one specific area: health insurance. Visiting the doctor for even simple medical check-ups cost a fortune without the possession of a health insurance, and consequently the illegal immigrants seldom go to the hospital, resulting in frequent illness and constant fatigue. So, an answer to this problem is ____.

(a) to aid workers in the process of receiving medical check-ups
(b) to make the process of obtaining authorized documents easier for immigrant workers
(c) to improve the working conditions of immigrant workers
(d) not to show negative opinions about people lacking health insurances

5. Immigrant workers are forced to confront critical difficulties regarding insurance problems. As they lack authorized documents, they have no method of being issued insurances in a legal manner. This is especially a major problem in one specific area: health insurance. Visiting the doctor for even simple md consequently the illegal immigrants seldom go to the hospital, resulting in frequent illness and constant fatigue. So, an answer to this problem is ____.

(a) to aid workers in the process of receiving medical check-ups
(b) to make the process of obtaining authorized documents easier for immigrant workers
(c) to improve the working conditions of immigrant workers
(d) not to show negative opinions about people lacking health insurances

지문 패턴#15
인과 관계

제1부
지문의 19가지 유형

ADVANCED 지문 구조 ▷

PATTERN 15 인과 관계

X 때문에 Y가 되었다. 라고 하는 인과 구조에서 X가 원인 Y가 결과라는 것을 알 수 있을 것이다. 텝스 시험에서 인과관계가 등장한다면 결과에 초점을 둬야 하는 것이 맞다. 이번 단원에선 인과관계를 나타내는 단서들과 이 단서들이 모여서 이뤄지는 인과관계 유형이 어떤 것인지 살펴본다.

쏘아보기 단서

원리 설명

지문의 유형 중 시험 당 한 문제 정도 등장하는 것이 바로 인과 관계 구조의 유형이다. 이 유형의 지문들에는 인과 관계가 여러 번 반복해서 등장한다. 위 그림에서 보다시피 인과가 계속 맞물리게 되면, 마지막 문장이 가장 중요하게 되는 것이다. 일반적인 글 읽기 시 첫 문장부터 차례대로 읽으며 마지막 문장을 이해하게 되겠지만, 쏘아보기를 통해 발견을 한다면 수월하게 문제를 풀 수 있다.

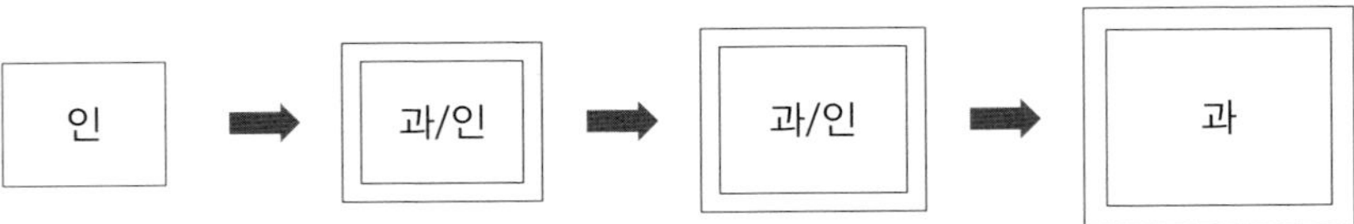

문제 풀이

- 빈칸이 마지막에 있고
- 마지막 문장이 So, Then, Consequently, As a result 로 시작하고
- ______________________________

지문은 인과관계로 생각하면 된다.
인과관계 유형을 발견 한다면 첫 문장과 뒤에서 두 번째 문장, 그리고 빈칸을 읽으면 문제는 풀린다.

제 1 부
제 2 부
제 3 부
제 4 부

연습문제

우선 30~40초동안 문제를 먼저 풀어보세요

1. Modern drug traffickers are constantly inventing many imaginative ways of producing, smuggling and trading drugs, and it seems the current control and surveillance is usually insufficient to counteract them. Since the police department's input of resources into the matter is so small, the police are often too slow to react to new tricks of the trade, which means the drug traffickers are always a step ahead. Consequently, by the time the police find out about a new trick the drug traffickers use, ______________________________.

(a) they are likely to have already moved onto a new one
(b) it is only a matter of time before they are tracked down
(c) they do not have enough men to crack down on them
(d) they shift their efforts to other available lucrative goods

1. Modern drug traffickers are constantly inventing many imaginative ways of producing, smuggling and trading drugs, and it seems the current control and surveillance is usually insufficient to counteract them. Since the police department's input of resources into the matter is so small, the police are often too slow to react to new tricks of the trade, which means the drug traffickers are always a step ahead. Consequently, by the time the police find out about a new trick the drug traffickers use, ______________________________.

(a) they are likely to have already moved onto a new one
(b) it is only a matter of time before they are tracked down
(c) they do not have enough men to crack down on them
(d) they shift their efforts to other available lucrative goods

2. It is very common for people to use poison to eliminate rats and mice in their homes. Just by leaving a few poisoned tablets around the corners of the house, rats, mice and various nuisances are easily gotten rid of without fuss. However, a great many species of rats have already become immune of the chemicals used in typical rat poison. As a result, most mice just fall sick for a week or two then recover, scurrying around behind walls and under the floor once again. Therefore, ______________________________.

(a) the rats and mice do not find the poison a threat
(b) it is not recommended to try to get rid of such vermin
(c) the method is no longer as effective as it used to be
(d) using poison only strengthens the rats and mice

2. It is very common for people to use poison to eliminate rats and mice in their homes. Just by leaving a few poisoned tablets around the corners of the house, rats, mice and various nuisances are easily gotten rid of without fuss. However, a great many species of rats have already become immune of the chemicals used in typical rat poison. As a result, most mice just fall sick for a week or two then recover, scurrying around behind walls and under the floor once again. Therefore, ______________________________.

(a) the rats and mice do not find the poison a threat
(b) it is not recommended to try to get rid of such vermin
(c) the method is no longer as effective as it used to be
(d) using poison only strengthens the rats and mice

3. The city of New York has recently come up with strategies to reduce noise pollution in the streets. There have been various complaints by citizens due to the excessive noise of music, cars and entertainment outside streets. A study revealed that 62% of the citizens have disrupted sleeping patterns due to the loud noise in the city. The city plans to reduce noise pollution by putting a quiet zone from 11:00pm to 2:00am on weekdays. Although many are quite skeptical of this new policy, experts claim that ______________________________.

(a) it is expected to reduce noise pollution
(b) the policy would not have any effect whatsoever
(c) the city noise level should be reduced
(d) citizens should use public transportation instead of cars

3. The city of New York has recently come up with strategies to reduce noise pollution in the streets. There have been various complaints by citizens due to the excessive noise of music, cars and entertainment outside streets. A study revealed that 62% of the citizens have disrupted sleeping patterns due to the loud noise in the city. The city plans to reduce noise pollution by putting a quiet zone from 11:00pm to 2:00am on weekdays. Although many are quite skeptical of this new policy, experts claim that ______________________________.

(a) it is expected to reduce noise pollution
(b) the policy would not have any effect whatsoever
(c) the city noise level should be reduced
(d) citizens should use public transportation instead of cars

4. Immigrant workers are forced to confront critical difficulties regarding insurance problems. As they lack authorized documents, they have no method of being issued insurances in a legal manner. This is especially a major problem in one specific area: health insurance. Visiting the doctor for even simple medical check-ups cost a fortune without the possession of a health insurance, and consequently the illegal immigrants seldom go to the hospital, resulting in frequent illness and constant fatigue. So, an answer to this problem is ____________________.

(a) to aid workers in the process of receiving medical check-ups
(b) to make the process of obtaining authorized documents easier for immigrant workers
(c) to improve the working conditions of immigrant workers
(d) not to show negative opinions about people lacking health insurances

4. Immigrant workers are forced to confront critical difficulties regarding insurance problems. As they lack authorized documents, they have no method of being issued insurances in a legal manner. This is especially a major problem in one specific area: health insurance. Visiting the doctor for even simple medical check-ups cost a fortune without the possession of a health insurance, and consequently the illegal immigrants seldom go to the hospital, resulting in frequent illness and constant fatigue. So, an answer to this problem is ____________________.

(a) to aid workers in the process of receiving medical check-ups
(b) to make the process of obtaining authorized documents easier for immigrant workers
(c) to improve the working conditions of immigrant workers
(d) not to show negative opinions about people lacking health insurances

5. Since the 1975 labor riots, the Dian'an Region's local textile industry has been in crisis. Initially, the casualties and collateral damage from such a violent uprising caused the production capacity to decrease sharply. Once the region recovered from the shock, a new problem arose for the local industry: monopolistic textile labor unions, which have made the industry much less lucrative and less competitive. Consequently, in order to try to reinvigorate the region's signature textile industry, the regional government Premier Yu Xianmei has suggested ______________________________.

(a) that the labor unions collaborate with the government to further their rights
(b) that the labor laws must be reexamined to prevent unjust labor exploitation
(c) providing government subsidies to textile companies until the issue subsides
(d) that the law be revised to limit the power of the textile labor union

5. Since the 1975 labor riots, the Dian'an Region's local textile industry has been in crisis. Initially, the casualties and collateral damage from such a violent uprising caused the production capacity to decrease sharply. Once the region recovered from the shock, a new problem arose for the local industry: monopolistic textile labor unions, which have made the industry much less lucrative and less competitive. Consequently, in order to try to reinvigorate the region's signature textile industry, the regional government Premier Yu Xianmei has suggested ______________________________.

(a) that the labor unions collaborate with the government to further their rights
(b) that the labor laws must be reexamined to prevent unjust labor exploitation
(c) providing government subsidies to textile companies until the issue subsides
(d) that the law be revised to limit the power of the textile labor union

지문 패턴#16
시간 흐름

제1부
지문의 19가지 유형

ADVANCED 지문 구조 ▷

PATTERN

16 시간 흐름

어떤 대상이 시간이 지남에 따라 변화하는 과정이 나타나는 것을 다루는 단원이다. 특정인물의 성장과정 혹은 사물/현상의 변화 과정을 나타내는 지문들은 모두 동일한 원칙이 있고, 문제풀이에 이 원칙들을 적용해 보면, 정확도가 올라 쉽고 편리하게 문제를 풀 수 있다.

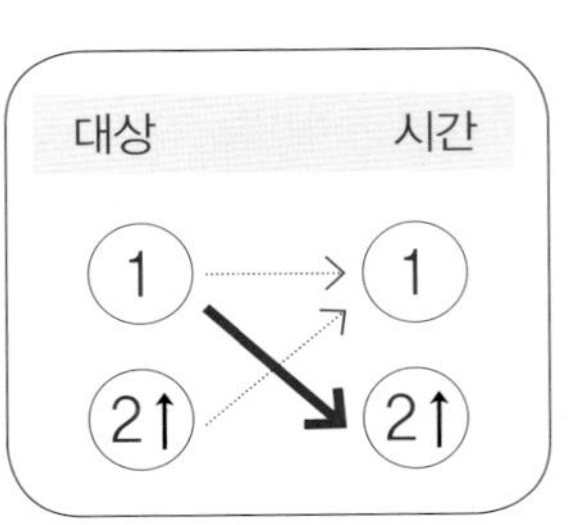

쏘아보기 단서

1. ______________________

2. 쏘아보기 단락 (문장 시작 후 2~3 단어 후 쉼표가 나오는 경우)
   EX) as time progressed, later, afterwards, 등 시간 흐름을 나타내는 단어들

3. ______________________ rise, growth, 등

원리 설명

시간 흐름은 결국 X라는 대상이 A → B → C → D 라는 시간을 지나서 변화하는 것이다. 주제는 "X의 변화과정" 이 되는 것이다. 결국, 주제 파악만 하게 된다면 모든 문제를 풀 수 있다. A단계와 D단계 중에 X의 변화 과정에서 가장 중요한 것은 D일 것이다. 주제를 파악하기 위해서는 D를 파악한다면 문제는 쉽게 풀린다.

문제 풀이

시간 흐름이 충족되려면 시간 흐름 쏘아보기 단서 중에서 ________ 이상이 등장해야, 시간 흐름이 되는 것이다. 시간 흐름 유형에 속하게 되면, 쏘아보기 단서들 중 지문 가장 뒤쪽에 위치한 단서가 들어간 문장을 읽는다. "시간 흐름"이라는 틀 속에 그 문장을 추가한다면 정답은 무조건 나온다.

연습문제

우선 30~40초동안 문제를 먼저 풀어보세요

1. In 1985, the National Land Swimming Championships Committee was established as the nation's first land swimming competition host. The first land swimming race, which was held on the Paddington Olympics Stadium, took place soon after the Committee was founded. Five years after this event in 1990, an even bigger land swimming competition was held in Los Angeles, and the sport's popularity reached its pinnacle, far exceeding that of baseball and football. The popular sport took a sharp downturn, however, when it was found in 1992 that the committee was manipulating the game results for monetary gains. As time progressed, the people slowly forgot about the sport, and now very few people remember that such a sport even existed.

Q: What is the passage mainly about?
(a) The dangers of swimming on land without proper equipment
(b) The beginning of a new popular sport which prospered in the 90s
(c) The decline of a popular sport due to accusations of game rigging
(d) The astounding speed in which people can forget about past issues

1. In 1985, the National Land Swimming Championships Committee was established as the nation's first land swimming competition host. The first land swimming race, which was held on the Paddington Olympics Stadium, took place soon after the Committee was founded. Five years after this event in 1990, an even bigger land swimming competition was held in Los Angeles, and the sport's popularity reached its pinnacle, far exceeding that of baseball and football. The popular sport took a sharp downturn, however, when it was found in 1992 that the committee was manipulating the game results for monetary gains. As time progressed, the people slowly forgot about the sport, and now very few people remember that such a sport even existed.

Q: What is the passage mainly about?
(a) The dangers of swimming on land without proper equipment
(b) The beginning of a new popular sport which prospered in the 90s
(c) The decline of a popular sport due to accusations of game rigging
(d) The astounding speed in which people can forget about past issues

2. After several tragic accidents, the public antipathy toward guns has much grown. One of the primary causes of this change was due to a catastrophic gun rampage in a college event last year, which killed 45 and injured hundreds. The increase in the number of minor gun accidents in general has been one of the reasons of the escalating stigma towards guns. Such movements have also been stimulated by the Self-Defense Act that passed congress last month, loosening qualification standards required to carry concealed-carry weapons and made it no longer illegal to hold guns in some public premises like colleges. Also the increased popularity of peace oriented cults also has stimulated this rising tension.

Q: What is the passage mainly about?
(a) Tragic incidents involving shootings which took place last year
(b) The relationships between public consensus and media coverage
(c) Weapon related regulations and its effect on the public's sentiments
(d) Reasons for the growing public autipathy towards guns

2. After several tragic accidents, the public antipathy toward guns has much grown. One of the primary causes of this change was due to a catastrophic gun rampage in a college event last year, which killed 45 and injured hundreds. The increase in the number of minor gun accidents in general has been one of the reasons of the escalating stigma towards guns. Such movements have also been stimulated by the Self-Defense Act that passed congress last month, loosening qualification standards required to carry concealed-carry weapons and made it no longer illegal to hold guns in some public premises like colleges. Also the increased popularity of peace oriented cults also has stimulated this rising tension.

Q: What is the passage mainly about?
(a) Tragic incidents involving shootings which took place last year
(b) The relationships between public consensus and media coverage
(c) Weapon related regulations and its effect on the public's sentiments
(d) Reasons for the growing public autipathy towards guns

3. The National "Cats as Pets" movement has followed along the general trend of popularizing pet animals that became mainstream from 2010 up until now. The videos produced by the partakers of this movement intended to awaken people to the cuteness of cats and to encourage cats as pets. The leaders of this movement used various methods such as Facebook and Twitter to create imaginary anthropomorphic cat personalities which would continually post pictures of its "friends". Although the beginning of this movement is unclear, it is thought to be the popularization of SNS media which allowed it to become easily known to the greater public.

Q: What is the main topic of the passage?
(a) The popularity of cats as pets from around 2010
(b) The growth of the National Cats as Pets Movement
(c) The importance of cats in the general tendency of the time
(d) The prosperity of cats as imaginary pets through the SNS media

3. The National "Cats as Pets" movement has followed along the general trend of popularizing pet animals that became mainstream from 2010 up until now. The videos produced by the partakers of this movement intended to awaken people to the cuteness of cats and to encourage cats as pets. The leaders of this movement used various methods such as Facebook and Twitter to create imaginary anthropomorphic cat personalities which would continually post pictures of its "friends". Although the beginning of this movement is unclear, it is thought to be the popularization of SNS media which allowed it to become easily known to the greater public.

Q: What is the main topic of the passage?
(a) The popularity of cats as pets from around 2010
(b) The growth of the National Cats as Pets Movement
(c) The importance of cats in the general tendency of the time
(d) The prosperity of cats as imaginary pets through the SNS media

4. In his 1433 play The Venetian Flea Chaser, Venetian playwright Lorenzo de Vecco, critically portrayed recent history, something that had never been seen in western literature. He addressed many historical controversies, especially those regarding Italian politics, including the notorious corruption in his home city Venice that once undermined the very foundation of Italian commerce. For Lorenzo, the rising prosperity of the western world during the 15th century could not hide the horrible and wasteful incidents that took place in the previous century.

Q: What is the main topic of the passage?
(a) What socio-historical conflicts Lorenzo predicted.
(b) How historical controversies were portrayed in western literature.
(c) How greater prosperity of the western world affected renaissance literature.
(d) How Lorenzo de Vecco depicted history negatively

4. In his 1433 play The Venetian Flea Chaser, Venetian playwright Lorenzo de Vecco, critically portrayed recent history, something that had never been seen in western literature. He addressed many historical controversies, especially those regarding Italian politics, including the notorious corruption in his home city Venice that once undermined the very foundation of Italian commerce. For Lorenzo, the rising prosperity of the western world during the 15th century could not hide the horrible and wasteful incidents that took place in the previous century.

Q: What is the main topic of the passage?
(a) What socio-historical conflicts Lorenzo predicted.
(b) How historical controversies were portrayed in western literature.
(c) How greater prosperity of the western world affected renaissance literature.
(d) How Lorenzo de Vecco depicted history negatively

5. During the 17th century, farmers and peasants normally ate multigrain rice. Since white rice was extremely valuable, the poor used various grains that could be easily obtained in their front yards and mixed them with pure white rice. This helped increase the volume of rice and was crucial in fighting hunger. By the end of the 20th century, however, ________________.

(a) multigrain rice had become the modern luxury good
(b) people only ate multigrain rice
(c) wheat replaced rice as the staple food
(d) white rice was no longer available

5. During the 17th century, farmers and peasants normally ate multigrain rice. Since white rice was extremely valuable, the poor used various grains that could be easily obtained in their front yards and mixed them with pure white rice. This helped increase the volume of rice and was crucial in fighting hunger. By the end of the 20th century, however, ________________.

(a) multigrain rice had become the modern luxury good
(b) people only ate multigrain rice
(c) wheat replaced rice as the staple food
(d) white rice was no longer available

지문 패턴#17
트윈타워

제1부
지문의 19가지 유형

ADVANCED 지문 구조 ▷

PATTERN 17 트윈타워

지문 내에서 두 개의 개념을 비교 대조하는 식의 글들도 자주 등장한다. 또한, 어떤 사안에 대한 찬성 반대 의견을 나타내는 글들도 많다. 이런 글들을 어떻게 발견하며 발견하게 되면 어떻게 신속히 풀 수 있는지, 그리고 이런 트윈타워 유형의 지문들의 정답들은 어떤 특징을 가졌는지 살펴보아야 한다.

쏘아보기 단서

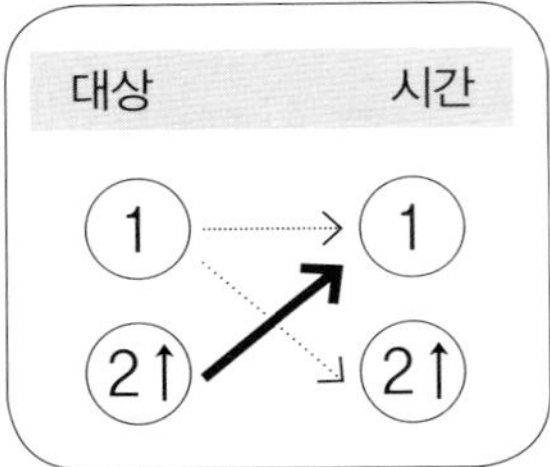

skepticism, controversy, debate, opponents/advocates
both, neither, either, whether, two (첫 문장)

원리 설명

트윈 타워라는 것을 파악한다면 결국 두 가지의 내용에 대해서 집중하기보단, ________에 대해서 생각해 봐야 한다. 정확히 A측과 B측이 어떤 이야기를 하고 있는지, 혹은 A와 B는 각각 어떤 의미가 있는지 확인하기 보단, A와 B가 어떤 ________인지만 파악하려고 노력하면 된다. 트윈타워 유형의 문제들의 모든 정답은 둘의 에 대한 것이다.

연습문제

우선 30~40초동안 문제를 먼저 풀어보세요

1. The Vesuvian Martial Arts routine has been widely assumed to suppress the appetite of an individual performing the art form. After ongoing experiments on the hunger rates of the individuals, researchers at the Ministry of Health in Battanuihi have finally confirmed the norm to be valid. However, what they have not been able to identify is whether the cause for this phenomenon is the uptempo style of movement or the repetitive bobbing motion of the head in the routine. But there also remains a possibility that both factors ____________________.

(a) will lead the Ministry of Health to find a feasible solution
(b) cause the uptempo movements
(c) are being overlooked in the research
(d) are equally responsible for the decrease in the craving for food

1. The Vesuvian Martial Arts routine has been widely assumed to suppress the appetite of an individual performing the art form. After ongoing experiments on the hunger rates of the individuals, researchers at the Ministry of Health in Battanuihi have finally confirmed the norm to be valid. However, what they have not been able to identify is whether the cause for this phenomenon is the uptempo style of movement or the repetitive bobbing motion of the head in the routine. But there also remains a possibility that both factors ____________________.

(a) will lead the Ministry of Health to find a feasible solution
(b) cause the uptempo movements
(c) are being overlooked in the research
(d) are equally responsible for the decrease in the craving for food

2. A major debate in understanding language acquisition can be divided into nativist and non-nativist schools. While nativists such as Noam Chomsky focused on hugely complex inborn cognitive abilities, non-nativists accentuated the importance of the environment in which the language is learned. Nativists argue that it is otherwise extremely difficult to explain how children within the first 5 years of life routinely master the complex grammatical rules of their native language. Non-nativists insist that environmental factors influence the way in one thinks, and so cannot be ignored. The division between these two schools is based on whether ______________________________.

(a) abilities are developed through nature or nurture
(b) children learn their mother tongue before they become five
(c) Noam Chomsky is right or wrong
(d) language acquisition is due to internal or external factors

2. A major debate in understanding language acquisition can be divided into nativist and non-nativist schools. While nativists such as Noam Chomsky focused on hugely complex inborn cognitive abilities, non-nativists accentuated the importance of the environment in which the language is learned. Nativists argue that it is otherwise extremely difficult to explain how children within the first 5 years of life routinely master the complex grammatical rules of their native language. Non-nativists insist that environmental factors influence the way in one thinks, and so cannot be ignored. The division between these two schools is based on whether ______________________________.

(a) abilities are developed through nature or nurture
(b) children learn their mother tongue before they become five
(c) Noam Chomsky is right or wrong
(d) language acquisition is due to internal or external factors

3. People who bank online are always notified beforehand that their transactions online make them liable to fraud. A research conducted on the electronic banking process in Spain has shown that many people with online bank accounts have far less protection against financial fraud than those who bank offline. At the present state, when a credit card is used fraudulently or a check is forged offline, the consumer rarely, if ever, receives the bill and thus the money is usually able to be refunded after an investigation. But this state of affairs ____________ ______________________________.

(a) does not apply for purchases conducted online
(b) is likely to be carried out in a similar matter online
(c) might not be considered important in other countries
(d) will be much more precise online

3. People who bank online are always notified beforehand that their transactions online make them liable to fraud. A research conducted on the electronic banking process in Spain has shown that many people with online bank accounts have far less protection against financial fraud than those who bank offline. At the present state, when a credit card is used fraudulently or a check is forged offline, the consumer rarely, if ever, receives the bill and thus the money is usually able to be refunded after an investigation. But this state of affairs ____________ ______________________________.

(a) does not apply for purchases conducted online
(b) is likely to be carried out in a similar matter online
(c) might not be considered important in other countries
(d) will be much more precise online

4. Linking protection of natural environment to manufacturing firms will assure that the firms. In accordance with this, official documents describing the mechanics of the new policy have been sent by the federal government to all the manufacturing companies in the country. There are two main goals in plan. First, the government wishes to make the companies feel the responsibility of the surrounding environment. Second, through an appropriate reward system, the government encourages the companies to see the environment as one of their assets and to increase economic profits while protecting the environment.

(a) maximize their profits by developing on the protected land
(b) endeavor to successfully keep the natural environment healthy
(c) work with each other to evade the environmental laws
(d) make double profits by protecting the environment

4. Linking protection of natural environment to manufacturing firms will assure that the firms. In accordance with this, official documents describing the mechanics of the new policy have been sent by the federal government to all the manufacturing companies in the country. There are two main goals in plan. First, the government wishes to make the companies feel the responsibility of the surrounding environment. Second, through an appropriate reward system, the government encourages the companies to see the environment as one of their assets and to increase economic profits while protecting the environment.

(a) maximize their profits by developing on the protected land
(b) endeavor to successfully keep the natural environment healthy
(c) work with each other to evade the environmental laws
(d) make double profits by protecting the environment

5. During the colonial period of America, Puritans, a group of Christians promoting an austere lifestyle, were predominant. Whenever its members would not follow in their footsteps, the Puritan leaders either banished or publically punished them. For example, if an individual was to involve oneself with gluttony-excessive eating and drinking-he or she would be forced to suffer public punishment in the form of a scaffold, which humiliated the offender in front of his or her peers. These types of punishments ________________________.

(a) led to the early demise of the Puritanism
(b) encouraged rebellious behaviors among citizens
(c) were against the ideals of Puritan leaders
(d) helped sustain a strict Puritan ideology

5. During the colonial period of America, Puritans, a group of Christians promoting an austere lifestyle, were predominant. Whenever its members would not follow in their footsteps, the Puritan leaders either banished or publically punished them. For example, if an individual was to involve oneself with gluttony-excessive eating and drinking-he or she would be forced to suffer public punishment in the form of a scaffold, which humiliated the offender in front of his or her peers. These types of punishments ________________________.

(a) led to the early demise of the Puritanism
(b) encouraged rebellious behaviors among citizens
(c) were against the ideals of Puritan leaders
(d) helped sustain a strict Puritan ideology

지문 패턴#18
생소개념

제1부
지문의 19가지 유형

ADVANCED 지문 구조 ▷

PATTERN 18 생소개념

이제까지 대부분의 단원에서 "강조점"을 찾는 것을 목표로 쏘아보기를 해왔을 것이다. 이번 단원에서는 가장 당연한 강조점들이 어디에 있는지 살펴본다. 지문 속의 중요한 대상에 대해 주장이나 강조를 나타내고 있다면 그것이 무조건 주제문이 된다는 원칙에서 출발한다. 문제 대부분에 해당될 수 있는 기술인만큼 쏘아보기 단서들을 꼭 숙지하도록 한다.

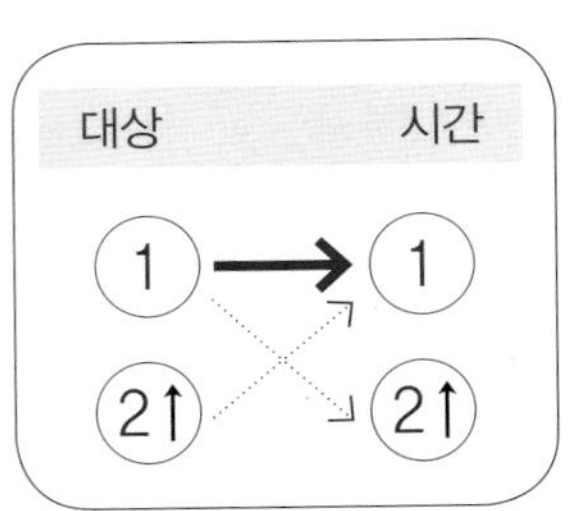

쏘아보기 단서

Allow, resemble, realize, find, which (is), believes, thinks, supports, says, is
Must, should, had better, be to, have got to, need to, insist, suggest, recommend, demand, pay attention to
It is right (natural, necessary, time) that

원리 설명

새로운 지문에서 소개하는 개념들은 모두 생소개념이라고 정의한다.
지문이 "김치"에 대한 설명을 하고 있다면, "김치"를 생소개념으로 정의하는 것이다.
김치가 우리에게 생소한 것은 아니지만, 지문이 중점적으로 설명하고 있는 대상이라면, 생소개념이 되는 것이다.
이 생소개념은 지문 내에서 여러 번 등장하게 된다. 그리고 그 중 한번이 주제문이 되는 것이다. 기존 문제 풀이 방식으로는 다 읽기 전까지 주제문을 알 수 없었지만, 이젠 생소개념 뒤에 나오는 동사들에 집중하면 수월하게 풀 수 있다.

문제 풀이

쏘아보기 혹은 첫 문장을 읽는 단계에서 생소개념을 발견하게 된다면 지문 내에 등장하는 생소개념 뒤의 동사에 집중한다.

그 중 쏘아보기 단서에 나오는 단서들이 등장한다면, 그 문장이 주제문이 되는 것이다.

웬만한 지문엔 생소개념 뒤에 단서는 단 한 번만 등장하고, 2개가 등장한다면 그 2문장을 함께 읽고 문제를 풀면 된다.

연습문제

우선 30~40초동안 문제를 먼저 풀어보세요

1. A recent investigation revealed that the material buried in the cryotic soil, also known as permafrost, is ______________________. The main object of this excavation was to subsequently revitalize the already extinct Mammuthus primigenius from approximately 12,000 years ago using the tissue frozen in the permafrost. The samples ejected from the cryotic soil were then investigated by the researchers of Sooam Biotech Research Foundation to confirm that the cells were compatible. The results of the study affirmed that an adequate nucleus was found to potentially hold DNA to create a blastocyst implantable to a surrogate mother. This recent investigation hinted at a possibility of mankind being able to bid defiance to the laws of nature.

(a) slowly melting due to global warming
(b) crucial in studying the DNA of the surrogate mother
(c) a starting point to proving human's ability to reverse time
(d) evidence of life existing 12,000 years ago

1. A recent investigation revealed that the material buried in the cryotic soil, also known as permafrost, is ______________________. The main object of this excavation was to subsequently revitalize the already extinct Mammuthus primigenius from approximately 12,000 years ago using the tissue frozen in the permafrost. The samples ejected from the cryotic soil were then investigated by the researchers of Sooam Biotech Research Foundation to confirm that the cells were compatible. The results of the study affirmed that an adequate nucleus was found to potentially hold DNA to create a blastocyst implantable to a surrogate mother. This recent investigation hinted at a possibility of mankind being able to bid defiance to the laws of nature.

(a) slowly melting due to global warming
(b) crucial in studying the DNA of the surrogate mother
(c) a starting point to proving human's ability to reverse time
(d) evidence of life existing 12,000 years ago

2. Herpes simplex virus accesses human cells, homes on the nucleus and then directs itself into the DNA using high pressure stimulated from a nanometer-scale protein shell known as the capsidpropel. This virus is known to cause infections such as influenza and HIV. However, the Herpes simplex virus is becoming resistant to medicines that aim at the viral proteins, which can instantaneously convert themselves and develop resistance to anti-viral drugs due to genetic mutation. Scientists, thus, are hoping to create a potent drug to reduce the resistance level. So far, they have experimented on mice to create an adequate drug. This could help ______________________________.

(a) detect the reason behind the genetic mutation
(b) keep the virus from seeking other viral proteins
(c) develop a new treatment to attack the influenza
(d) prevent the virus from remaining resistant to the drug

2. Herpes simplex virus accesses human cells, homes on the nucleus and then directs itself into the DNA using high pressure stimulated from a nanometer-scale protein shell known as the capsidpropel. This virus is known to cause infections such as influenza and HIV. However, the Herpes simplex virus is becoming resistant to medicines that aim at the viral proteins, which can instantaneously convert themselves and develop resistance to anti-viral drugs due to genetic mutation. Scientists, thus, are hoping to create a potent drug to reduce the resistance level. So far, they have experimented on mice to create an adequate drug. This could help ______________________________.

(a) detect the reason behind the genetic mutation
(b) keep the virus from seeking other viral proteins
(c) develop a new treatment to attack the influenza
(d) prevent the virus from remaining resistant to the drug

3. James the Vicious, who ruled Eastern India from 1540 to 1600, was the most feared king in the country's history. A man born from a poor slave family, he came to the throne through a coup-de-tat. He incessantly waged wars against adjacent nations, enjoyed brutal battles between his slaves, conscripted men as his personal body guards and robbed parents of their daughters for his pleasure. Due to such cruel deeds, he is ________________________.

(a) venerated as an audacious and strong soldier
(b) sentenced to serve maximum penalty in prison
(c) known as the most effective ruler of the century
(d) considered to be the most notorious king

3. James the Vicious, who ruled Eastern India from 1540 to 1600, was the most feared king in the country's history. A man born from a poor slave family, he came to the throne through a coup-de-tat. He incessantly waged wars against adjacent nations, enjoyed brutal battles between his slaves, conscripted men as his personal body guards and robbed parents of their daughters for his pleasure. Due to such cruel deeds, he is ________________________.

(a) venerated as an audacious and strong soldier
(b) sentenced to serve maximum penalty in prison
(c) known as the most effective ruler of the century
(d) considered to be the most notorious king

4. During the early 19th century, a style of painting called "Impressionism" emerged from the French art, which had previously been largely academic. It was associated most often with few prominent artists, among whom were Edouard Manet, Claude Monet, and Pierre-Auguste Renoir. The new impressionist art rejected classicism and the French academism. It had a liberal style which would be painted "as it is seen", employing a technique called "en plein air" or "in the open air" hinting the Impressionist tradition of painting casual subjects out in the open. The Impressionist movement significantly influenced the later flow of art, and is noted by some art historians to be the beginning of modern art.

Q: What is the main topic of the passage?
(a) The beginnings of modernism in art
(b) A brief account of the French Impressionist movement
(c) The artists who are most often mentioned in Impressionist art
(b) The influence of French Academism on the French Impressionists

제1부
제2부
제3부
제4부

4. During the early 19th century, a style of painting called "Impressionism" emerged from the French art, which had previously been largely academic. It was associated most often with few prominent artists, among whom were Edouard Manet, Claude Monet, and Pierre-Auguste Renoir. The new impressionist art rejected classicism and the French academism. It had a liberal style which would be painted "as it is seen", employing a technique called "en plein air" or "in the open air" hinting the Impressionist tradition of painting casual subjects out in the open. The Impressionist movement significantly influenced the later flow of art, and is noted by some art historians to be the beginning of modern art.

Q: What is the main topic of the passage?
(a) The beginnings of modernism in art
(b) A brief account of the French Impressionist movement
(c) The artists who are most often mentioned in Impressionist art
(b) The influence of French Academism on the French Impressionists

5. Psychodrama is commonly used as a method of therapy in which clients gain insight into their lives. The most basic form of psychodrama originates from the belief that the best way for individuals to give creative responses is by undergoing spontaneous action, which is also known as the theory of "spontaneity-creativity". Researchers have found that when an individual bases one's behaviors on impulse, they are able to acquire new solutions to complicated problems in their lives. Furthermore, the more diverse these spontaneous actions are, the more people are able to deeply understand various circumstances throughout their lives. In short, spontaneity-creativity ______________________________.

(a) connects mundane everyday actions to physical therapy
(b) plays a crucial role in making diversity within clients
(c) describes a theory relating instinctive behavior to problem solving
(d) gives therapist a chance to control innovative ideas given by the clients

5. Psychodrama is commonly used as a method of therapy in which clients gain insight into their lives. The most basic form of psychodrama originates from the belief that the best way for individuals to give creative responses is by undergoing spontaneous action, which is also known as the theory of "spontaneity-creativity". Researchers have found that when an individual bases one's behaviors on impulse, they are able to acquire new solutions to complicated problems in their lives. Furthermore, the more diverse these spontaneous actions are, the more people are able to deeply understand various circumstances throughout their lives. In short, spontaneity-creativity ______________________________.

(a) connects mundane everyday actions to physical therapy
(b) plays a crucial role in making diversity within clients
(c) describes a theory relating instinctive behavior to problem solving
(d) gives therapist a chance to control innovative ideas given by the clients

지문 패턴#19
추상 구체화

제1부
지문의 19가지 유형

PATTERN 19 추상 구체화

추상 구체화 지문은 텝스가 매우 좋아하는 유형이다. 언뜻 보기엔 주제가 없는듯 보이나, 광의의 주제와 협의의 주제가 동시에 존재한다는 점에서 매우 고급 지문이라고 할 수 있다. 1단원부터 18단원까지 모든 지문에는 1개의 주제가 있다는 것을 배웠지만, 19단원은 예외로 지문에 주제가 두개 존재한다. 출제자들은 주제에 대한 명백한 근거를 숨기기 위해 추상구체화 지문 전개 구조의 출제 빈도를 높인 것으로 보인다. 따라서, 특별히 이러한 추상구체화 유형들을 공략 가능한 방법론을 제시한다.

쏘아보기 단서

particular (particularly), specific (specifically), most, best, important, this, example, in fact, especially

원리 설명

- 추상 구체화의 핵심은, 광의의 주제와 협의의 주제를 파악하는 것이다. 쏘아보기 단서가 존재하고, 그 뒤로 동급 나열식이 아닌 경우 추상 구체화라고 할 수 있다. (Example 뒤에 다른 예시 없이 그 example 에 대한 얘기만 쭉 늘어지는 경우만 추상 구체화로 인정.)
- 특히 두번째 문장에 쏘아보기 단서가 있을 경우, 확률은 더욱 높아진다.
- “운동은 건강에 좋다. 특히, 줄넘기는 남녀노소에게 유익하다.” 류의 지문이 있다면, 두 문장 모두 주제가 될 수 있다. 단, 줄넘기와 관련된 내용이 협의에 속하며 정답으로 출제될 확률은 더 높다.

연습문제

우선 30~40초동안 문제를 먼저 풀어보세요

1. In his 1433 play The Venetian Flea Chaser, Venetian playwright Lorenzo de Vecco, critically portrayed recent history, something that had never been seen in western literature. He addressed many historical controversies, especially those regarding Italian politics, including the notorious corruption in his home city Venice that once undermined the very foundation of Italian commerce. For Lorenzo, the rising prosperity of the western world during the 15th century could not hide the horrible and wasteful incidents that took place in the previous century.

Q: What is the main topic of the passage?
(a) What socio-historical conflicts Lorenzo predicted.
(b) How historical controversies were portrayed in western literature.
(c) How greater prosperity of the western world affected renaissance literature.
(d) How Lorenzo de Vecco depicted history negatively

1. In his 1433 play The Venetian Flea Chaser, Venetian playwright Lorenzo de Vecco, critically portrayed recent history, something that had never been seen in western literature. He addressed many historical controversies, especially those regarding Italian politics, including the notorious corruption in his home city Venice that once undermined the very foundation of Italian commerce. For Lorenzo, the rising prosperity of the western world during the 15th century could not hide the horrible and wasteful incidents that took place in the previous century.

Q: What is the main topic of the passage?
(a) What socio-historical conflicts Lorenzo predicted.
(b) How historical controversies were portrayed in western literature.
(c) How greater prosperity of the western world affected renaissance literature.
(d) How Lorenzo de Vecco depicted history negatively

제1부
제2부
제3부
제4부

2. The Swiss psychiatrist and psychoanalyst Carl Gustav Jung published his paper Zentralblatt fur Psychotherapie in 1931. At the time, a popular view among the psychotherapists in Europe was that the Nazi regime was justifiable. In defiance of this anti-semitism, Jung argued that there should be no hostility to, prejudice against, nor discrimination against Jews. Specifically, he believed that Hitler was not to be sympathized and his actions were beyond exemption.

Q: What is the main topic of the passage?
(a) Jung's research of the psychotherapists in Europe
(b) Jung's analysis of the psychological aspects of Hitler
(c) Jung's advice to have sympathy for the Nazi regime
(d) Jung's criticism to the anti-semitic view

2. The Swiss psychiatrist and psychoanalyst Carl Gustav Jung published his paper Zentralblatt fur Psychotherapie in 1931. At the time, a popular view among the psychotherapists in Europe was that the Nazi regime was justifiable. In defiance of this anti-semitism, Jung argued that there should be no hostility to, prejudice against, nor discrimination against Jews. Specifically, he believed that Hitler was not to be sympathized and his actions were beyond exemption.

Q: What is the main topic of the passage?
(a) Jung's research of the psychotherapists in Europe
(b) Jung's analysis of the psychological aspects of Hitler
(c) Jung's advice to have sympathy for the Nazi regime
(d) Jung's criticism to the anti-semitic view

3. Teachers and students in a foreign language classroom are well aware that doing exactly the same thing twice is boring. It is therefore of particular in importance that teachers recognize that the "repeats" within any cyclical learning are not exact repeats; each repeat must be a development. If it does appear so to the students, then the teacher should be prepared to explain why something is being done again, and how the repeat will be different from the previous performance.

Q: What is the main idea of the passage?

(a) Teachers should never repeat what has been done already.

(b) Teachers should communicate well with their students.

(c) Language learning materials should be fun and fresh.

(d) Repeating in language learning should be developmental.

3. Teachers and students in a foreign language classroom are well aware that doing exactly the same thing twice is boring. It is therefore of particular in importance that teachers recognize that the "repeats" within any cyclical learning are not exact repeats; each repeat must be a development. If it does appear so to the students, then the teacher should be prepared to explain why something is being done again, and how the repeat will be different from the previous performance.

Q: What is the main idea of the passage?

(a) Teachers should never repeat what has been done already.

(b) Teachers should communicate well with their students.

(c) Language learning materials should be fun and fresh.

(d) Repeating in language learning should be developmental.

4. Conventional histories of Scottish literature have for over a century resembled their British and Irish counterparts in ______________________. Particularly when the subject is the later eighteenth and the earlier nineteenth centuries, the period usually dubbed the Romantic, the relative exclusion of women is singular in light of their considerable literary activity. There are of course many reasons for the modern marginalization of Scottish women poets of the Romantic period, not the least of which is the extraordinary prominence of Robert Burns and Walter Scott in Scotland's literary landscape during the era.

(a) the absence of any cultural diversity
(b) showing strong nationalist tendencies
(c) their strongly gender biased orientation
(d) finding a balance between culture and art

4. Conventional histories of Scottish literature have for over a century resembled their British and Irish counterparts in ______________________. Particularly when the subject is the later eighteenth and the earlier nineteenth centuries, the period usually dubbed the Romantic, the relative exclusion of women is singular in light of their considerable literary activity. There are of course many reasons for the modern marginalization of Scottish women poets of the Romantic period, not the least of which is the extraordinary prominence of Robert Burns and Walter Scott in Scotland's literary landscape during the era.

(a) the absence of any cultural diversity
(b) showing strong nationalist tendencies
(c) their strongly gender biased orientation
(d) finding a balance between culture and art

5. At Vets Plus, we have embarked on a mission to team up with the best to enhance our vision of providing the best possible medical care for animals. To this end, we have partnered with several companies and our valued partners now include the National Animal Hospital Association, Network of Professional Veterinarians, and Animal Friends Market Researchers. Vets Plus is proud of the fact that such fine organizations have joined us in sharing a passion for providing high-quality animal care. If you are interested in ________________, please contact our Marketing Department at 814-466-0542.

(a) offering the best veterinary service to customers
(b) a partnership with our organization
(c) new products that customers will appreciate
(d) introducing us to veterinarians who meet our standard

5. At Vets Plus, we have embarked on a mission to team up with the best to enhance our vision of providing the best possible medical care for animals. To this end, we have partnered with several companies and our valued partners now include the National Animal Hospital Association, Network of Professional Veterinarians, and Animal Friends Market Researchers. Vets Plus is proud of the fact that such fine organizations have joined us in sharing a passion for providing high-quality animal care. If you are interested in ________________, please contact our Marketing Department at 814-466-0542.

(a) offering the best veterinary service to customers
(b) a partnership with our organization
(c) new products that customers will appreciate
(d) introducing us to veterinarians who meet our standard

제2부

문제의 7가지 유형

텝스가 원하는 정답의 기준이란?

"내가 예뻐? 김태희가 예뻐?"

여자친구가 어느 날 물어본다. 여기서 어느 선택지를 고를지 고민한다면, 여자친구(출제자)의 정답의 기준을 정확히 파악하지 못한 것이다.
출제자는 매력적 오답을 제시했지만, 정답의 기준만 명확하다면 오답 함정에 걸리지 않고 곧바로 정답을 택할 수 있다. 반면에 출제자의 의도를 명확히 파악을 하지 못한다면 고민은 고민대로 하고 매력적 오답을 택하고 결과적으로 문제를 틀릴(!!) 가능성도 높다.

TEPS 독해 시험도 마찬가지다.
7가지 문제 유형은 각각 개별적인 정답의 기준이 있다. 각 문제 유형 별 정답이 어떻게 출제가 되고 어떤 요소가 가장 중요한지 "텝스가 원하는 정답의 기준"을 명확히 파악해야 한다.

텝스 시험에는 정확한 정답의 기준이 존재한다. 어디에서도 이러한 기준을 설명해주지 않지만, 텝스가 원하는 정답의 기준은 분명히 존재한다.

수험생들은 이러한 기준이 정립되지 않았기 때문에 시험을 치를 때 선택지 두 개 사이에서 계속 고민하게 되고, 정답을 바라보면서도 자기 나름대로 다른 오답도 말이 될 수 있지 않을까 하고 합리화 하게 된다.

실제 시험에서도 선택지 두 개 사이에서 고민하다가 한 문제에서 3~4분을 날린 경험이 있을 것이다. 막심한 후회 속에 퇴실하며, "다음부턴 그러지 말아야지" 정도의 다짐만으로 반성을 마친다. 하지만 이런 습관은 마음가짐의 변화 로 개선할 수 있는 부분이 아니다. 분명한 기준이 정립 되어야 하며 그 기준이 정립되지 못한다면 다음 시험에서 또다시 선택지 두 개 사이에서 계속 고민하게 될 것이다.

그래서 이 책의 모든 단원을 학습하면서도 항상 "텝스가 원하는 정답의 기준"의 내용을 생각하며 문제 풀이에 임해야 한다. 정답의 기준이 없는 사람이 쉽게 빠져 들 수 있는 함정들은 너무 많다. 이것은 영어 실력과 무관하며 쉬운 문제들에도 나타난다. 다음 문제들을 풀어보도록 하자.

Do you hate having to choose what to wear every day? Would you rather prefer 5 more minutes of sleep than having to decide in the morning what to wear? Then just call ClothesFit today for a 7-day free trial of preselected clothes every morning. We offer competitive monthly expenses, discounts for high school students, and trustworthy courteous service. Sign a monthly contract with us before January 6th and get 19% off. Don't ____________________, just call ClothesFit at 4660542

(a) lose 5 minutes of your sleep
(b) give your clothes selection another thought
(c) hesitate any longer
(d) worry about the trendiness of the style selection

While the so-called "dumb" phones are disappearing quickly, some other electronic gadgets are disappearing even faster. Digital cameras, portable gaming console, PDAs and mp3 players have almost disappeared off the market since 2010, and they may become completely obsolete by the next few years. The leading factor contributing to their demise is the sheer multi-functionality of smart phones. With their phones becoming more versatile and compact than ever, people are no longer feeling the need for bulky separate devices.

Q. What is the passage mainly about?
(a) The inconvenience of using separate devices
(b) The demise of numerous electronic devices.
(c) The disappearance of dumb phones from the market
(d) The versatility and compactness of smartphones

다 풀 때까지 페이지를 넘기지 말자. 정답은 다음 페이지에.

1번 문제는 아마 A, B, C 중에 고민을 했을 것이다.
그렇다면 정답은 무엇일까? 그리고 정답은 하나뿐일까?
정답은 B다.
A와 C는 정답이 될 수 없는 이유가 명확히 존재한다. 이 문제를 만약 시험장에서 접했다면 여러분의 대다수는 이 문제에 2분 이상의 시간을 투자하였을 것이다.
왜냐? 지문 자체가 쉬우므로 '이렇게 쉬운 문제를 틀리면 아깝다'는 생각이 들기 때문인데, 정답의 기준이 확립되지 않았기 때문에 결국 고민 끝에 A, B, C 중에 하나를 찍게 되는 것이다.
정답의 기준만 확실하다면 30초 안에도 풀 수 있었던 문제인데 말이다.

2번 문제는 정답이 B일까 D일까?
정답은 B다. 이것도 마찬가지로 정답의 기준만 명확히 알고 있다면 쉽게 풀 수 있는 문제였다.

이처럼 텝스가 원하는 정답의 기준은 명확히 존재하는데, 이는 각 part 별 유형과 출제 이유에 따라 상이하다.

독해 시험

1 ~ 8 빈칸 채우기
9 ~10 연결어 채우기
11~12 흐름상 어색한 문장
13~16 주제 찾기
17~22 코렉트
23~25 추론
26~35 세트 문제

독해 시험은 위와 같이 7가지 문제 유형으로 구분하고, 각 유형 별 문제 풀이 전략을 달리해야 한다. 제 2부에서는 각 문제 유형 및 정답의 기준을 파악하는 풀이법을 익히도록 하자.

문제 패턴#1
빈칸 채우기

제2부
문제의 7가지 유형

PATTERN 1

빈칸 채우기 (#1~8)

빈칸 채우기 유형은 가장 텝스스러운 문제들이 출제되는 유형 중 하나다. 제1부에서 학습한 지문의 논리 전개 패턴 19개 중 하나로 출제되기 때문에, 쏘아보기를 활용해 문제풀이에 임할 시 가장 효율적으로 풀어낼 수 있다.

연습문제

우선 30~40초동안 문제를 먼저 풀어보세요

1. The Vesuvian Martial Arts routine has been widely assumed to suppress the appetite of an individual performing the art form. After ongoing experiments on the hunger rates of the individuals, researchers at the Ministry of Health in Battanuihi have finally confirmed the norm to be valid. However, what they have not been able to identify is whether the cause for this phenomenon is the uptempo style of movement or the repetitive bobbing motion of the head in the routine. But there also remains a possibility that both factors ________________.

(a) will lead the Ministry of Health to find a feasible solution
(b) cause the uptempo movements
(c) are being overlooked in the research
(d) are equally responsible for the decrease in the craving for food

1. The Vesuvian Martial Arts routine has been widely assumed to suppress the appetite of an individual performing the art form. After ongoing experiments on the hunger rates of the individuals, researchers at the Ministry of Health in Battanuihi have finally confirmed the norm to be valid. However, what they have not been able to identify is whether the cause for this phenomenon is the uptempo style of movement or the repetitive bobbing motion of the head in the routine. But there also remains a possibility that both factors ________________.

(a) will lead the Ministry of Health to find a feasible solution
(b) cause the uptempo movements
(c) are being overlooked in the research
(d) are equally responsible for the decrease in the craving for food

제1부 제2부 제3부 제4부

2. I, James White, on behalf of the townspeople, ______________________________. A recent research conducted by a team of urban engineers revealed that the new construction by I&C Company will greatly affect the local ecosystem. The parking space planned to be built would be placed over an area of Atwood Woods, meaning that the construction will require lumbering of the precious Sequoia trees. These trees are indispensable as they play the most important role in keeping the nearby ecosystem healthy. Anyone who wants to support the petition is asked to please sign it at the city hall before July 25th.

(a) ask for a transfer of the Sequoia Trees
(b) demand that the new trees be planted in town
(c) am joining the I&C Company to help with the construction
(d) appeal an official petition over the new parking lot

2. I, James White, on behalf of the townspeople, ______________________________. A recent research conducted by a team of urban engineers revealed that the new construction by I&C Company will greatly affect the local ecosystem. The parking space planned to be built would be placed over an area of Atwood Woods, meaning that the construction will require lumbering of the precious Sequoia trees. These trees are indispensable as they play the most important role in keeping the nearby ecosystem healthy. Anyone who wants to support the petition is asked to please sign it at the city hall before July 25th.

(a) ask for a transfer of the Sequoia Trees
(b) demand that the new trees be planted in town
(c) am joining the I&C Company to help with the construction
(d) appeal an official petition over the new parking lot

3. Although former presidents of the United States have always been guaranteed a place in history, many of them have ________________. America's founders believed pensions smacked of royal privilege, so retired presidents lived on their own. Their post-presidential lives were often heart-rending and dramatic until the latter part of the twentieth century, when former presidents began earning millions of dollars in book royalties and speaking fees. Being a former president these days means being part of a very exclusive and lucrative club.

(a) owned private businesses
(b) ended their lives in poverty and debt
(c) led graceful and quiet lives
(d) received financial support from the country

3. Although former presidents of the United States have always been guaranteed a place in history, many of them have ________________. America's founders believed pensions smacked of royal privilege, so retired presidents lived on their own. Their post-presidential lives were often heart-rending and dramatic until the latter part of the twentieth century, when former presidents began earning millions of dollars in book royalties and speaking fees. Being a former president these days means being part of a very exclusive and lucrative club.

(a) owned private businesses
(b) ended their lives in poverty and debt
(c) led graceful and quiet lives
(d) received financial support from the country

4. Planned by the Quaker William Penn, Philadelphia grew rapidly into ____________________. By the 1750s, many groups besides the Quakers had added their numbers to this community, and the city reflected their cultures and the success of their business ventures. Additionally, Philadelphia had become the main market for produce. As one settler said, "Our lands have been grateful to us and have begun to reward our labors with abounding crops of corn." Philadelphia merchants made fortunes shipping this corn, as well as wheat, barley, biscuits, fruits, and meat, to Massachusetts, Rhode Island, and New York.

(a) a major center of trade
(b) a community of farmers
(c) a poorly populated city
(d) a rich agricultural land

4. Planned by the Quaker William Penn, Philadelphia grew rapidly into ____________________. By the 1750s, many groups besides the Quakers had added their numbers to this community, and the city reflected their cultures and the success of their business ventures. Additionally, Philadelphia had become the main market for produce. As one settler said, "Our lands have been grateful to us and have begun to reward our labors with abounding crops of corn." Philadelphia merchants made fortunes shipping this corn, as well as wheat, barley, biscuits, fruits, and meat, to Massachusetts, Rhode Island, and New York.

(a) a major center of trade
(b) a community of farmers
(c) a poorly populated city
(d) a rich agricultural land

5. The key to writing successful children's books is to look at the world ____________. They don't want to read stories about big strong people doing heroic things, because they are not big and strong. They don't want to read stories in which children meekly obey the rules, because they already have to do that themselves. What they want is to read stories in which people who start off small and weak manage to overcome great hardships, usually by ignoring whatever rules they are supposed to be following.

(a) with a view to educating children
(b) by taking a religious perspective
(c) through a profoundly moral lens
(d) from a child's point of view

5. The key to writing successful children's books is to look at the world ____________. They don't want to read stories about big strong people doing heroic things, because they are not big and strong. They don't want to read stories in which children meekly obey the rules, because they already have to do that themselves. What they want is to read stories in which people who start off small and weak manage to overcome great hardships, usually by ignoring whatever rules they are supposed to be following.

(a) with a view to educating children
(b) by taking a religious perspective
(c) through a profoundly moral lens
(d) from a child's point of view

문제 패턴#2

연결어

제2부
문제의 7가지 유형

PATTERN 2 연결어 (#9~10)

지문 속 빈칸에 들어가야할 연결어는 2문제가 출제된다. 글의 흐름을 정확히 파악가능한지 평가하고자 하는 문제이기 때문에 (1) 전반적인 지문의 흐름과 (2) 빈칸 전후에서의 논리 전개를 파악하여 풀어야 한다.

연습문제

 우선 30~40초동안 문제를 먼저 풀어보세요

1. The movement of dancers in the 19th century of Barbuda was interpreted as gruesome and grotesque. The society in general was obstinate about being relatively conservative; misinterpreting the performance art they did to symbolize social wrongdoings. The locomotion of exposing their thighs and staring at the audience irritated the viewers. ______________, these artists tried to enlighten the uncritical citizens, and as such, they enhanced the social awareness of exploitations that were surging at that time.

(a) Nonetheless
(b) Hence
(c) Similarly
(d) In addition

1. The movement of dancers in the 19th century of Barbuda was interpreted as gruesome and grotesque. The society in general was obstinate about being relatively conservative; misinterpreting the performance art they did to symbolize social wrongdoings. The locomotion of exposing their thighs and staring at the audience irritated the viewers. ______________, these artists tried to enlighten the uncritical citizens, and as such, they enhanced the social awareness of exploitations that were surging at that time.

(a) Nonetheless
(b) Hence
(c) Similarly
(d) In addition

2. Long lines, irritable waiters, cramped quarters, and questionable food have accounted for customers refusing to dine at Haggle's Scullery. Moreover, contemplate that in one four-month period in 2013, 80% of entrees arrived at least 40 minutes after the order was made, causing irritation to approximately 6000 consumers. This year August, thousands of reservations were cancelled-60% more, in fact, than the year before. ____________, the industry suffered a huge loss because of the economic crisis.

(a) Thus
(b) For instance
(c) Furthermore
(d) Nevertheless

2. Long lines, irritable waiters, cramped quarters, and questionable food have accounted for customers refusing to dine at Haggle's Scullery. Moreover, contemplate that in one four-month period in 2013, 80% of entrees arrived at least 40 minutes after the order was made, causing irritation to approximately 6000 consumers. This year August, thousands of reservations were cancelled-60% more, in fact, than the year before. ____________, the industry suffered a huge loss because of the economic crisis.

(a) Thus
(b) For instance
(c) Furthermore
(d) Nevertheless

3. In some East Asian countries, company executives face the difficult task of enjoying their wealth and living in modesty at the same time. They are torn because they want to live as luxuriously as they can, but they are also worried that people will stigmatize them as exploitative tycoons. ______________, in the US, rich people don't find it embarrassing to spend as much as they please. They show off their wealth by purchasing yachts, private jets, or large mansions.

(a) Otherwise
(b) Likewise
(c) In contrast
(d) By the same toke

3. In some East Asian countries, company executives face the difficult task of enjoying their wealth and living in modesty at the same time. They are torn because they want to live as luxuriously as they can, but they are also worried that people will stigmatize them as exploitative tycoons. ______________, in the US, rich people don't find it embarrassing to spend as much as they please. They show off their wealth by purchasing yachts, private jets, or large mansions.

(a) Otherwise
(b) Likewise
(c) In contrast
(d) By the same toke

4. Studies show that we experience a sensation of temperature with color. On the color wheel, red-orange is the warmest and blue-green is the coolest. These are referred to as the warm and cold poles of the wheel. The hues in between these poles can be experienced as warm or cold, depending on what colors they are contrasted with. ______________, violet paired with cool colors will appear warm but will appear cool if paired with warm colors. In cold climates, rooms painted with deep, warm colors will seem warmer, while in the tropics light, pastel colors create the impression of coolness.

(a) Hence
(b) For all that
(c) For instance
(d) At the same time

4. Studies show that we experience a sensation of temperature with color. On the color wheel, red-orange is the warmest and blue-green is the coolest. These are referred to as the warm and cold poles of the wheel. The hues in between these poles can be experienced as warm or cold, depending on what colors they are contrasted with. ______________, violet paired with cool colors will appear warm but will appear cool if paired with warm colors. In cold climates, rooms painted with deep, warm colors will seem warmer, while in the tropics light, pastel colors create the impression of coolness.

(a) Hence
(b) For all that
(c) For instance
(d) At the same time

문제 패턴# 3

흐름상 어색한 문장

제2부
문제의 7가지 유형

PATTERN 3

흐름상 어색한 문장 (#11~12)

11,12번 문제는 지문 속 흐름상 어색한 문장을 찾아내는 문제다. 앞뒤 문장들은 유기적으로 연결되어 있어야 하며, 첫 문장과 개별 문장들의 논리적 방향성도 일치하는 경우가 많다.

연습문제

우선 30~40초동안 문제를 먼저 풀어보세요

1. Some of the fashion that we see in old movies or photos, somehow seem very awkward to people in these days. (a) Some of the reason may be attributed to the change of taste in the general public. (b) Back in the days, people may have thought that the wide trunk jeans were polishing through influences of the media. (c) Additionally, it was not until the early 21 century that fashion magazines became popular, playing the role of a trend leader. (d) Today standards of fashion have changed dramatically, giving cold looks to those wearing 'out of fashion' clothes

1. Some of the fashion that we see in old movies or photos, somehow seem very awkward to people in these days. (a) Some of the reason may be attributed to the change of taste in the general public. (b) Back in the days, people may have thought that the wide trunk jeans were polishing through influences of the media. (c) Additionally, it was not until the early 21 century that fashion magazines became popular, playing the role of a trend leader. (d) Today standards of fashion have changed dramatically, giving cold looks to those wearing 'out of fashion' clothes

2. Welcome to the most outstanding dining place around New York City. (a) Our menus are varied that even the regulars try out something different once every month or so. (b) No wonder why the 32 year old Chile wine was so popular among the regulars. (c) For people who are not fond of any kind of meat is our traditional menu which is only composed of fish grills. (d) On the other hand, for others who are maniacs of all kinds of meat, they may choose from the other set of menu only to be consisted of beef and pork.

제1부

제2부

제3부

제4부

2. Welcome to the most outstanding dining place around New York City. (a) Our menus are varied that even the regulars try out something different once every month or so. (b) No wonder why the 32 year old Chile wine was so popular among the regulars. (c) For people who are not fond of any kind of meat is our traditional menu which is only composed of fish grills. (d) On the other hand, for others who are maniacs of all kinds of meat, they may choose from the other set of menu only to be consisted of beef and pork.

3. If you love drinking soda, you may be putting yourself at risk of pancreatic cancer, a new study has revealed. (a) The study involved over 60,000 men and women volunteers in Singapore and was conducted over 14 years. (b) The recent hot weather in Singapore has made people thirsty, and many quenched their thirst with soda. (c) Volunteers who drank over two sodas a week showed a much higher chance of getting pancreatic cancer. (d) Researchers cited sugar as the reason, since heavy doses of sugar force the pancreas to produce more insulin

3. If you love drinking soda, you may be putting yourself at risk of pancreatic cancer, a new study has revealed. (a) The study involved over 60,000 men and women volunteers in Singapore and was conducted over 14 years. (b) The recent hot weather in Singapore has made people thirsty, and many quenched their thirst with soda. (c) Volunteers who drank over two sodas a week showed a much higher chance of getting pancreatic cancer. (d) Researchers cited sugar as the reason, since heavy doses of sugar force the pancreas to produce more insulin

4. One of the greatest American novels in the 1930's is John Steinbeck's novel The Grapes of Wrath. (a) The novel tells the story of poor farmers from the Southwest who are driven off the land by the Great Depression, dust storms and the banks. (b) Packing all of their possessions in broken trucks, they travel the long Route 66 highway which will take them to California and a dream of a new life. (c) In Steinbeck's novel, however, that dream becomes a fading hope as the family suffers loss and humiliation on the journey westward. (d) The image of a turtle struggling, again and again, to cross a busy highway in the novel symbolizes nature and its struggle to survive and endure.

제1부

제2부

4. One of the greatest American novels in the 1930's is John Steinbeck's novel The Grapes of Wrath. (a) The novel tells the story of poor farmers from the Southwest who are driven off the land by the Great Depression, dust storms and the banks. (b) Packing all of their possessions in broken trucks, they travel the long Route 66 highway which will take them to California and a dream of a new life. (c) In Steinbeck's novel, however, that dream becomes a fading hope as the family suffers loss and humiliation on the journey westward. (d) The image of a turtle struggling, again and again, to cross a busy highway in the novel symbolizes nature and its struggle to survive and endure.

제3부

제4부

문제 패턴# 4
주제 찾기

제2부
문제의 7가지 유형

PATTERN 4

주제 찾기 (#13~16)

지문의 "주제"를 파악해야 풀 수 있는 문제이다. 지문 전체를 읽기보단, 지문의 전반적인 구조를 미리 파악하고, 핵심 내용 위주로 정독을 하며 기타 디테일은 가볍게 읽고 지나치는 선택과 집중 독해법이 중요하다. 주제 찾기 문제들도 제1부의 쏘아보기가 중요한 단원이다. 주제 찾기 문제는 단독으로는 4문제(#13~16)가 출제되지만, 세트 문제(#26~35)에서 추가 3문제가 출제된다

연습문제

우선 30~40초동안 문제를 먼저 풀어보세요

1. Making a piñata is not as difficult as people might think. First, make paper mache paste by mixing a bowl of flour with water. Second, tear some newspapers into strips. They should be about 2 inches wide and 6 to 8 inches long; making the newspaper to lie nice and flat on the balloon. Next, apply paper mache in a crisscross pattern until the entire balloon is covered. Let the piñata sit until it is completely dried and hardened. After that, pop the balloon and remove it, leaving the mold empty in a balloon-shaped.

Q: What is the passage mainly about?
(a) How to make a sphere-shaped mold
(b) Being careful with handling a balloon
(c) Solution to difficulties of making a piñata with paper mache
(d) Steps necessary for constructing a piñata

1. Making a piñata is not as difficult as people might think. First, make paper mache paste by mixing a bowl of flour with water. Second, tear some newspapers into strips. They should be about 2 inches wide and 6 to 8 inches long; making the newspaper to lie nice and flat on the balloon. Next, apply paper mache in a crisscross pattern until the entire balloon is covered. Let the piñata sit until it is completely dried and hardened. After that, pop the balloon and remove it, leaving the mold empty in a balloon-shaped.

Q: What is the passage mainly about?
(a) How to make a sphere-shaped mold
(b) Being careful with handling a balloon
(c) Solution to difficulties of making a piñata with paper mache
(d) Steps necessary for constructing a piñata

2. Despite safety measures, Pneumotraumatic Fibrosis is a prevalent condition amongst our factory personnel, affecting nearly 56% of all full-time workers. The employee policy at Newt & Claire Co. entitles all personnel suffering from the disorder to employee welfare benefits. Around 50% of the employees are currently beneficiaries of this policy, and this is causing quite a burden on our company welfare budget. Although the exact number is uncertain, the benefit costs the company approximately 500,000 dollars each year. This is outrageous, and must be brought to attention immediately.

Q: What is the passage mainly about?
(a) Health problems prevalent among Newt & Claire workers
(b) The symptoms of pneumotraumatic fibrosis on Newt & Claire workers
(c) The heavy burden of employee healthcare on the company welfare budget
(d) A plan to build another welfare center for the company board of directors in Newt & Claire

2. Despite safety measures, Pneumotraumatic Fibrosis is a prevalent condition amongst our factory personnel, affecting nearly 56% of all full-time workers. The employee policy at Newt & Claire Co. entitles all personnel suffering from the disorder to employee welfare benefits. Around 50% of the employees are currently beneficiaries of this policy, and this is causing quite a burden on our company welfare budget. Although the exact number is uncertain, the benefit costs the company approximately 500,000 dollars each year. This is outrageous, and must be brought to attention immediately.

Q: What is the passage mainly about?
(a) Health problems prevalent among Newt & Claire workers
(b) The symptoms of pneumotraumatic fibrosis on Newt & Claire workers
(c) The heavy burden of employee healthcare on the company welfare budget
(d) A plan to build another welfare center for the company board of directors in Newt & Claire

3. Since there is no written record of how prehistoric doctors treated medical conditions, today's scientists look to artifacts and bones to determine how patients were treated. For instance, scientists examine herbs or plants found near a body to see if they were used for treatment in any way. They also examine the bones of human remains to look for marks, such as those made from a knife or other tool, to try to understand whether they were made by a doctor trying to heal a patient.

Q: What is the main topic of the passage?
(a) Advances in prehistoric medicine
(b) Use of knives in treatments by ancient doctors
(c) Use of plants to treat diseases in ancient times
(d) Methods for examining ancient medical practices

3. Since there is no written record of how prehistoric doctors treated medical conditions, today's scientists look to artifacts and bones to determine how patients were treated. For instance, scientists examine herbs or plants found near a body to see if they were used for treatment in any way. They also examine the bones of human remains to look for marks, such as those made from a knife or other tool, to try to understand whether they were made by a doctor trying to heal a patient.

Q: What is the main topic of the passage?
(a) Advances in prehistoric medicine
(b) Use of knives in treatments by ancient doctors
(c) Use of plants to treat diseases in ancient times
(d) Methods for examining ancient medical practices

4. Instead of relying solely on the conventional internal combustion engine, a hybrid vehicle uses both a gas engine and one or more electric motors. The energy needed by the electric motors is stored in rechargeable batteries. The computer system on a hybrid determines which energy source to use at different times, based on maximizing efficiency while providing safety and comfort. Most hybrids use advanced technologies to achieve greater fuel economy, which implies reduced petroleum consumption and air pollution emissions, making them environment-friendly vehicles.

Q: What is the passage mainly about?
(a) Why a hybrid vehicle is environment-friendly
(b) Why two energy sources are required
(c) How a hybrid vehicle operates
(d) How electric motors improve fuel efficiency

4. Instead of relying solely on the conventional internal combustion engine, a hybrid vehicle uses both a gas engine and one or more electric motors. The energy needed by the electric motors is stored in rechargeable batteries. The computer system on a hybrid determines which energy source to use at different times, based on maximizing efficiency while providing safety and comfort. Most hybrids use advanced technologies to achieve greater fuel economy, which implies reduced petroleum consumption and air pollution emissions, making them environment-friendly vehicles.

Q: What is the passage mainly about?
(a) Why a hybrid vehicle is environment-friendly
(b) Why two energy sources are required
(c) How a hybrid vehicle operates
(d) How electric motors improve fuel efficiency

5. Renowned psychologists and linguists have continuously researched the correlation of the human mind and language. Widely known as "The Power of Words," scientists have been proving how a simple change of words could lead to tremendous or unexpected transitions. In epitome, people simply ignored and passed by a blind man holding a sign of "Changes Appreciated" on the subway. However, as the blind man held up a new sign that says, "It is a beautiful day, but I cannot see it", people were moved by the inspiring phrase, donating their change and even large amounts of money to help the blind man.

Q: What is the passage mainly about?

(a) How the relationship between language and human psychology has led to a mishap
(b) The experiment done to a blind man on the subway
(c) The profound influence of donation on a person
(d) The display of Power of Words and its effect

5. Renowned psychologists and linguists have continuously researched the correlation of the human mind and language. Widely known as "The Power of Words," scientists have been proving how a simple change of words could lead to tremendous or unexpected transitions. In epitome, people simply ignored and passed by a blind man holding a sign of "Changes Appreciated" on the subway. However, as the blind man held up a new sign that says, "It is a beautiful day, but I cannot see it", people were moved by the inspiring phrase, donating their change and even large amounts of money to help the blind man.

Q: What is the passage mainly about?

(a) How the relationship between language and human psychology has led to a mishap
(b) The experiment done to a blind man on the subway
(c) The profound influence of donation on a person
(d) The display of Power of Words and its effect

문제 패턴# 5
코렉트

제2부
문제의 7가지 유형

PATTERN 5

코렉트 (#17~22)

연습문제

우선 30~40초동안 문제를 먼저 풀어보세요

1. The social welfare policies established by the South Korean government since 2000 have presented more complications for the lower class than they had in the late 1990s. According to statistics, the lower class have not benefited in any way from the new policies and inefficient measures have only complicated procedures people go through to receive medical care. The statistics showed comparative analysis of data from early 1990s to late 2000. However, more analysis into the effects of these new social welfare policies will be needed in order to prove the inefficiency of the new enactments.

Q: Which of the following is correct according to the passage?
(a) The lower class may have been better off in the late 1990s
(b) The statistics involved data from the 1970s to the 1990s
(c) The recent welfare policies have made the lives of the lower class well-off
(d) The statistics have been proven by many other sources

1. The social welfare policies established by the South Korean government since 2000 have presented more complications for the lower class than they had in the late 1990s. According to statistics, the lower class have not benefited in any way from the new policies and inefficient measures have only complicated procedures people go through to receive medical care. The statistics showed comparative analysis of data from early 1990s to late 2000. However, more analysis into the effects of these new social welfare policies will be needed in order to prove the inefficiency of the new enactments.

Q: Which of the following is correct according to the passage?
(a) The lower class may have been better off in the late 1990s
(b) The statistics involved data from the 1970s to the 1990s
(c) The recent welfare policies have made the lives of the lower class well-off
(d) The statistics have been proven by many other sources

2. The invention of the steam engine brought about many changes to 18th century Europe. Firstly, it helped people travel faster, farther and with more people. For example, trains that used steam engines as power sources could carry large amounts of cargo such as wood, coal and fur. Steam engine-powered boats were also used until the 20th century. Furthermore, steam engine created industrial tools capable of producing goods at a much faster rate than humans. In this way the steam engine is deemed to be central to the industrial revolution.

Q: Which of the following is correct according to the passage?
(a) The steam engine was invented in the 20th century
(b) The steam engine enhanced the quality of transportation in numerous ways
(c) Trains powered by steam were limited in their cargo capacity
(d) The steam engine ultimately slowed down Europe's industrialization

2. The invention of the steam engine brought about many changes to 18th century Europe. Firstly, it helped people travel faster, farther and with more people. For example, trains that used steam engines as power sources could carry large amounts of cargo such as wood, coal and fur. Steam engine-powered boats were also used until the 20th century. Furthermore, steam engine created industrial tools capable of producing goods at a much faster rate than humans. In this way the steam engine is deemed to be central to the industrial revolution.

Q: Which of the following is correct according to the passage?
(a) The steam engine was invented in the 20th century
(b) The steam engine enhanced the quality of transportation in numerous ways
(c) Trains powered by steam were limited in their cargo capacity
(d) The steam engine ultimately slowed down Europe's industrialization

3. This textbook aims to help students develop skills in becoming a true law professional. Students will come across many different aspects such as game theory, logical reasoning, and law practices and theories. Students will gain a greater understanding into various law cases on both national and international level. A thorough reading of this book will broaden students' understanding of law and the practice of law. Prior reading of "The Fundamentals of Law" is needed as a prerequisite before reading this book.

Q. Which of the following is correct about the text book according to this passage?
(a) It allows students to learn the various aspects related to law
(b) It focuses on the failed attempts of law professionals
(c) It has an in-depth analysis into various law cases
(d) It requires students to take an off-line course

3. This textbook aims to help students develop skills in becoming a true law professional. Students will come across many different aspects such as game theory, logical reasoning, and law practices and theories. Students will gain a greater understanding into various law cases on both national and international level. A thorough reading of this book will broaden students' understanding of law and the practice of law. Prior reading of "The Fundamentals of Law" is needed as a prerequisite before reading this book.

Q. Which of the following is correct about the text book according to this passage?
(a) It allows students to learn the various aspects related to law
(b) It focuses on the failed attempts of law professionals
(c) It has an in-depth analysis into various law cases
(d) It requires students to take an off-line course

4. The loss of cultural diversity is happening at an unprecedented speed in recent years. As people become more influenced by the idea of assimilation, diversity is losing its value in all aspects. This is proven by cultures in many Asian countries such as China, Japan, and South Korea where media plays an important role in re-establishing the meaning and importance of diversity. It is still doubtful whether, if any, efforts can be made to put a stop to the loss of such diversity in societies alike.

Q. Which of the following is correct about the loss of cultural diversity?
(a) It is a rare and new phenomenon in the contemporary society
(b) Its occurrence is concentrated around many Asian countries
(c) In China, media is crucial regarding diversity
(d) It is a phenomenon not worth putting an end to

4. The loss of cultural diversity is happening at an unprecedented speed in recent years. As people become more influenced by the idea of assimilation, diversity is losing its value in all aspects. This is proven by cultures in many Asian countries such as China, Japan, and South Korea where media plays an important role in re-establishing the meaning and importance of diversity. It is still doubtful whether, if any, efforts can be made to put a stop to the loss of such diversity in societies alike.

Q. Which of the following is correct about the loss of cultural diversity?
(a) It is a rare and new phenomenon in the contemporary society
(b) Its occurrence is concentrated around many Asian countries
(c) In China, media is crucial regarding diversity
(d) It is a phenomenon not worth putting an end to

5. Earnest Miller Hemingway's well-known novel The Indian Camp received harsh criticism when it was first published in 1952. The novel's theme highlighted on an Indian boy who deeply loved a girl in his town. However, the book came under blatant attack by the media for lack of originality and what they termed "recycling used ideas". In addition, Hemingway had written the novel based on the inspiration he got after reading Tom Huntington's The Inuit Boy, a praised novel that shows love between an Eskimo boy and a girl. Hemingway came under fire for having simply written the modern version of Huntington's novel with just a different setting.

Q. Which of the following is correct about The Indian Camp according to the passage?

(a) Hemingway was revered by the book critics when it was first published.
(b) The main theme in the book involved a love affair between two Eskimos
(c) Hemingway was sued for using too much of the content from The Inuit Boy
(d) The novel is allegedly based too strongly on Huntington's celebrated book

5. Earnest Miller Hemingway's well-known novel The Indian Camp received harsh criticism when it was first published in 1952. The novel's theme highlighted on an Indian boy who deeply loved a girl in his town. However, the book came under blatant attack by the media for lack of originality and what they termed "recycling used ideas". In addition, Hemingway had written the novel based on the inspiration he got after reading Tom Huntington's The Inuit Boy, a praised novel that shows love between an Eskimo boy and a girl. Hemingway came under fire for having simply written the modern version of Huntington's novel with just a different setting.

Q. Which of the following is correct about The Indian Camp according to the passage?

(a) Hemingway was revered by the book critics when it was first published.
(b) The main theme in the book involved a love affair between two Eskimos
(c) Hemingway was sued for using too much of the content from The Inuit Boy
(d) The novel is allegedly based too strongly on Huntington's celebrated book

6. The European Union (EU) and other nations in Europe have agreed on the need to find cooperative solutions for the current economic recession the whole world is facing. A gathering of 23 major countries ended with a unanimous decision to improve unemployment rate as a first step of overcoming economic recession, but have yet to finalize upon specific policies regarding individual countries. In addition, countries like Germany and Sweden seem poised to be at the forefront of the attempt to save the Eurozone from crumbling and most importantly, to address concerns about the currency of Euro itself. The world's attention is concentrated on the long-term outcome of this meeting, considered to be critical in shaping the future of Europe.

Q. Which of the following is correct about the current situation according to the passage?
(a) The issue of unemployment rate is a major priority for European nations
(b) The procedures to reduce unemployment rate reached a consensus at the meeting
(c) Germany and Sweden are prepared to lead Europe out of the continuous recession
(d) The Eurozone is in danger of being replaced by a new currency order

6. The European Union (EU) and other nations in Europe have agreed on the need to find cooperative solutions for the current economic recession the whole world is facing. A gathering of 23 major countries ended with a unanimous decision to improve unemployment rate as a first step of overcoming economic recession, but have yet to finalize upon specific policies regarding individual countries. In addition, countries like Germany and Sweden seem poised to be at the forefront of the attempt to save the Eurozone from crumbling and most importantly, to address concerns about the currency of Euro itself. The world's attention is concentrated on the long-term outcome of this meeting, considered to be critical in shaping the future of Europe.

Q. Which of the following is correct about the current situation according to the passage?
(a) The issue of unemployment rate is a major priority for European nations
(b) The procedures to reduce unemployment rate reached a consensus at the meeting
(c) Germany and Sweden are prepared to lead Europe out of the continuous recession
(d) The Eurozone is in danger of being replaced by a new currency order

7. Timepiece Plus has introduced a brand new line of watches. These new, Swiss-made watches offer four different types of bands-stainless steel, rubber, titanium and ceramic to suit the customers' taste. All watches come with a lifetime warranty protection, meaning that the manufacturers will either repair or replace any watches that may have gotten damaged. The watches are water resistant at up to 300 meters and can be worn during aquatic activities such as swimming, snorkeling or scuba diving.

Q. Which of the following is correct about the new line of Timepiece Plus watches?
(a) They are available in leather bands
(b) They are custom-made for each individual customer
(c) The quality is guaranteed for an unlimited period of time
(d) It can be worn in water at 300 meters only when doing aquatic activities

7. Timepiece Plus has introduced a brand new line of watches. These new, Swiss-made watches offer four different types of bands-stainless steel, rubber, titanium and ceramic to suit the customers' taste. All watches come with a lifetime warranty protection, meaning that the manufacturers will either repair or replace any watches that may have gotten damaged. The watches are water resistant at up to 300 meters and can be worn during aquatic activities such as swimming, snorkeling or scuba diving.

Q. Which of the following is correct about the new line of Timepiece Plus watches?
(a) They are available in leather bands
(b) They are custom-made for each individual customer
(c) The quality is guaranteed for an unlimited period of time
(d) It can be worn in water at 300 meters only when doing aquatic activities

8. After many centuries of state-endorsed religion, various new factors in Europe caused a large part of the new generation to become indifferent about religion. A recent survey by the Orchard-Pumpkins Foundation found that 77% of Europeans in their twenties are secularists, putting the number of believers at 60% lower than 100 years ago. Still, however, the Church and its doctrines hold sway over the lifestyle and culture in Europe. Moreover, with new and more moderate branches of Christianity attracting new believers, it is unclear whether Europe will become more secular in the coming century.

Q. Which of the following is correct according to the passage?
(a) The number of secularists has been on the decrease over the last century
(b) A vast majority of Europeans in their twenties have been found to be strident atheists
(c) The new branches of Christianity are attracting new believers with their radical doctrines
(d) Whether Europe will become less religious in the future remains to be seen

8. After many centuries of state-endorsed religion, various new factors in Europe caused a large part of the new generation to become indifferent about religion. A recent survey by the Orchard-Pumpkins Foundation found that 77% of Europeans in their twenties are secularists, putting the number of believers at 60% lower than 100 years ago. Still, however, the Church and its doctrines hold sway over the lifestyle and culture in Europe. Moreover, with new and more moderate branches of Christianity attracting new believers, it is unclear whether Europe will become more secular in the coming century.

Q. Which of the following is correct according to the passage?
(a) The number of secularists has been on the decrease over the last century
(b) A vast majority of Europeans in their twenties have been found to be strident atheists
(c) The new branches of Christianity are attracting new believers with their radical doctrines
(d) Whether Europe will become less religious in the future remains to be seen

9. Timepiece Plus has introduced a brand new line of watches. These new, Swiss-made watches offer four different types of bands-stainless steel, rubber, titanium and ceramic to suit the customers' taste. All watches come with a lifetime warranty protection, meaning that the manufacturers will either repair or replace any watches that may have gotten damaged. The watches are water resistant at up to 300 meters and can be worn during aquatic activities such as swimming, snorkeling or scuba diving.

Q. Which of the following is correct about the new line of Timepiece Plus watches?
(a) They are available in leather bands
(b) They are custom-made for each individual customer
(c) The quality is guaranteed for an unlimited period of time
(d) It can be worn in water at 300 meters only when doing aquatic activities

9. Timepiece Plus has introduced a brand new line of watches. These new, Swiss-made watches offer four different types of bands-stainless steel, rubber, titanium and ceramic to suit the customers' taste. All watches come with a lifetime warranty protection, meaning that the manufacturers will either repair or replace any watches that may have gotten damaged. The watches are water resistant at up to 300 meters and can be worn during aquatic activities such as swimming, snorkeling or scuba diving.

Q. Which of the following is correct about the new line of Timepiece Plus watches?
(a) They are available in leather bands
(b) They are custom-made for each individual customer
(c) The quality is guaranteed for an unlimited period of time
(d) It can be worn in water at 300 meters only when doing aquatic activities

문제 패턴# 6

추론

제2부
문제의 7가지 유형

PATTERN 6

추론 (#23~25)

연습문제

우선 30~40초동안 문제를 먼저 풀어보세요

1. Benedict Anderson's book Imagined Communities is a reflection on the origins and diffusion of Nationalism. He mainly provides his readers with a thoughtful explanation of how people collectively created "imagined" nations to segment themselves from the rest of the world. Cultural roots, national consciousness, old and new languages, imperialism, and racism are all concepts Anderson uses to support his ideas. For those who are interested in the inexplicable behavior of people acting on behalf of the nation, Anderson's book will most definitely provide some answers for you.

   Q. What can be inferred about Benedict Anderson from the book review?
   (a) He led a socialist movement in his time
   (b) He supports the idea of cultural imperialism
   (c) He believes the concept of nation is mostly illusional
   (d) He thinks geographical boundaries of a nation are useless

1. Benedict Anderson's book Imagined Communities is a reflection on the origins and diffusion of Nationalism. He mainly provides his readers with a thoughtful explanation of how people collectively created "imagined" nations to segment themselves from the rest of the world. Cultural roots, national consciousness, old and new languages, imperialism, and racism are all concepts Anderson uses to support his ideas. For those who are interested in the inexplicable behavior of people acting on behalf of the nation, Anderson's book will most definitely provide some answers for you.

   Q. What can be inferred about Benedict Anderson from the book review?
   (a) He led a socialist movement in his time
   (b) He supports the idea of cultural imperialism
   (c) He believes the concept of nation is mostly illusional
   (d) He thinks geographical boundaries of a nation are useless

2. Due to sudden changes in fashion trends, Zaba Fashion will be tidying up old stock to make room for the new inventory. In addition to the already existing 50% discounted retail price, for a limited time, you can purchase the old merchandise for even a cheaper fee. We are also providing the service of allowing consumers to either return or exchange the products for another item if they are dissatisfied. Visit Zaba Fashion from the 16th of September to the 30th of September to make use of this amazing opportunity!

Q: What can be inferred about Zaba Fashion from the passage?
(a) Fashion trends always have a tendency to change abruptly
(b) The new inventory will be sold at a price cheaper than the 50% discounted one
(c) It is holding a sale for a limited time period
(d) Customers have suffered from product dissatisfaction

2. Due to sudden changes in fashion trends, Zaba Fashion will be tidying up old stock to make room for the new inventory. In addition to the already existing 50% discounted retail price, for a limited time, you can purchase the old merchandise for even a cheaper fee. We are also providing the service of allowing consumers to either return or exchange the products for another item if they are dissatisfied. Visit Zaba Fashion from the 16th of September to the 30th of September to make use of this amazing opportunity!

Q: What can be inferred about Zaba Fashion from the passage?
(a) Fashion trends always have a tendency to change abruptly
(b) The new inventory will be sold at a price cheaper than the 50% discounted one
(c) It is holding a sale for a limited time period
(d) Customers have suffered from product dissatisfaction

3. A talented Norwegian football player, Horten Pamst Pedersen, was not only an athlete but also, an actor and singer. He is primarily remembered for playing a vital role in winning the super bowl of 1978 by throwing the last touchdown pass for the Alabama Tigers. On top of his physical abilities, he made appearances in over ten movies and recorded seven albums over his lifetime. However, Pedersen died prematurely after a car accident in 1985 at the age of 37. Even though Pedersen was promptly taken into medical service, he passed away having bled copious amounts of blood in the ambulance

Q: What can be inferred about Horten Pamst Pedersen from the passage?
(a) He owes his movie career to his touchdown pass
(b) He is best known to the world for his music talents
(c) He was a renowned football player until 1985
(d) Excessive bleeding was the cause of his death

3. A talented Norwegian football player, Horten Pamst Pedersen, was not only an athlete but also, an actor and singer. He is primarily remembered for playing a vital role in winning the super bowl of 1978 by throwing the last touchdown pass for the Alabama Tigers. On top of his physical abilities, he made appearances in over ten movies and recorded seven albums over his lifetime. However, Pedersen died prematurely after a car accident in 1985 at the age of 37. Even though Pedersen was promptly taken into medical service, he passed away having bled copious amounts of blood in the ambulance

Q: What can be inferred about Horten Pamst Pedersen from the passage?
(a) He owes his movie career to his touchdown pass
(b) He is best known to the world for his music talents
(c) He was a renowned football player until 1985
(d) Excessive bleeding was the cause of his death

제1부
제2부
제3부
제4부

4. Swine influenza can cause chills, fever, muscle pain, severe headache, and general discomfort. If your child has similar symptoms, you should consult a doctor immediately due to the contagiousness of this disease. Although the source of the virus is from swines, human to human transimission takes up a majority of hospital admissions. The prevention of transmission can be quite simple: frequently wash your hands after being out in public. Moreover, carrying alcohol-based hand sanitizers to wash your hands throughout the day can significantly help your chances.

Q: What can be inferred about swine influenza from the passage?
(a) Washing hands thoroughly can cure the symptoms
(b) It is necessary for patients to be admitted to the hospital for a lengthy time
(c) It is more infectious to children than adults
(d) Measures regarding hygiene are effective for prevention

4. Swine influenza can cause chills, fever, muscle pain, severe headache, and general discomfort. If your child has similar symptoms, you should consult a doctor immediately due to the contagiousness of this disease. Although the source of the virus is from swines, human to human transimission takes up a majority of hospital admissions. The prevention of transmission can be quite simple: frequently wash your hands after being out in public. Moreover, carrying alcohol-based hand sanitizers to wash your hands throughout the day can significantly help your chances.

Q: What can be inferred about swine influenza from the passage?
(a) Washing hands thoroughly can cure the symptoms
(b) It is necessary for patients to be admitted to the hospital for a lengthy time
(c) It is more infectious to children than adults
(d) Measures regarding hygiene are effective for prevention

5. The Henry & Jerry Tugnutt Memorial was erected to commemorate the Tugnutt Brothers' contribution to the field of electrical engineering. The Memorial is currently under construction to engrave the names of previously unknown associates onto the far-west side of the main monument. If anyone happens to have more personal information (birth dates, middle names, etc.) about the previously undisclosed associates, please contact co-director Jack Gordon at 978-4999. We are dedicated to making sure the Brothers' contributions are not forgotten by the city.

Q. What will most likely follow the passage?

(a) The cause of the Tugnutt Brother's death
(b) The Tugnutt Brother's achievements to date
(c) The Tugnetts' relationship with the city
(d) Henry and Jerry's stardom

5. The Henry & Jerry Tugnutt Memorial was erected to commemorate the Tugnutt Brothers' contribution to the field of electrical engineering. The Memorial is currently under construction to engrave the names of previously unknown associates onto the far-west side of the main monument. If anyone happens to have more personal information (birth dates, middle names, etc.) about the previously undisclosed associates, please contact co-director Jack Gordon at 978-4999. We are dedicated to making sure the Brothers' contributions are not forgotten by the city.

Q. What will most likely follow the passage?

(a) The cause of the Tugnutt Brother's death
(b) The Tugnutt Brother's achievements to date
(c) The Tugnetts' relationship with the city
(d) Henry and Jerry's stardom

6. Many people associate science with facts and evidence. They believe that justification, which includes proving something with 100% certainty, is science itself which is an idea people have not been accustomed to yet. However, an important part of science is to understand uncertainty. Applying new ideas to a wide range of situations is what tests their limitations. In order to fully understand science we need to pull ourselves away from sterile and controlled experiments and plunge into the pool of indefinite occurrences. Approaching science in such a manner wouldn't be forcing two unrelated concepts together but would instead boost one's understanding of the subject.

Q.What can be inferred about the writer of the passage?

(a) He doubts the existence of hard facts

(b) He considers experiments to be ineffective in revealing truths about the world

(c) He thinks the study of liberal arts is more useful than science

(d) He believes current widespread understanding of science is one-sided

6. Many people associate science with facts and evidence. They believe that justification, which includes proving something with 100% certainty, is science itself which is an idea people have not been accustomed to yet. However, an important part of science is to understand uncertainty. Applying new ideas to a wide range of situations is what tests their limitations. In order to fully understand science we need to pull ourselves away from sterile and controlled experiments and plunge into the pool of indefinite occurrences. Approaching science in such a manner wouldn't be forcing two unrelated concepts together but would instead boost one's understanding of the subject.

Q.What can be inferred about the writer of the passage?

(a) He doubts the existence of hard facts

(b) He considers experiments to be ineffective in revealing truths about the world

(c) He thinks the study of liberal arts is more useful than science

(d) He believes current widespread understanding of science is one-sided

문제 패턴#7
세트 문제

제2부
문제의 7가지 유형

PATTERN

7 세트 문제 (#26~35)

"세트 문제"는 독해 시험 35문제 중 10문제를 차지하는 매우 중요한 유형이다. 기존 텝스가 1지문 1문항 원칙을 포기하며 추가한 문제 유형인 만큼, 논리적으로 매우 깔끔한 문제들이 출제된다. 지문이 한 문단 이상으로 출제되는 경우가 대부분이며, 각 문단 간의 논리 관계를 파악하면 지문의 흐름을 금방 파악할 수 있다. 1지문에 2문항이 출제되며, 주제 유형, 코렉트 유형, 추론 유형, 세부 유형 등이 혼합되어 출제된다.

세트 문제의 지문은 길이가 늘어났기 때문에 제1부의 '쏘아보기'가 보다 더 효율적이며, 출제되는 개별 문제들은 제2부에서 학습해온 유형의 문제들이 출제되기에 문제 유형별 훈련도 필수다. 제1부의 쏘아보기와 제2부의 유형별 접근법을 모두 활용하여 문제풀이에 임할 경우, Part4는 문제당 평균 40초(세트당 80초)에 풀어낼 수 있는 효자 영역이 된다.

연습문제

우선 30~40초동안 문제를 먼저 풀어보세요

The Citiville Times

Home / **Opinion** / Politics / Business / International / Culture / Sports

Opinion: Why Technology Will Divide Our Country

(Read full article)

Comments

Vivian Davies | 12 hours ago

We are living in the age of rapid technological advances. There is simply no denying it. We cannot be stuck in the trenches arguing for and against new innovations that have already brought about changes in our industries. Rather, we should deliberate about how all of us can move forward as a society.

We, as a society, have always found ways to adapt to significant changes and overcome insurmountable obstacles. We have welcomed innovations that have vastly transformed the ways we eat, work, and live. We can embrace change without alienating certain social groups. We are a society that can forge our own path ahead.

Q 1: What is the main purpose of Vivian Davies' comment?

(a) To encourage American society to pursue innovations

(b) To congratulate the progress humans have made

(c) To shift the perspective on the debate over technological innovations

(d) To argue that social advancement is dependent upon technology

Q 2: Which statement would the author most likely agree with?

(a) Social divide does not necessarily cause technological divide.

(b) The significance of technological changes has been immensely overrated.

(c) Technological advancement does not have an impact on economic growth.

(d) Arguing about the pros and cons of technology is futile.

Documentary Review
Sicko by Michael Moore

Michael Moore is regarded as "the JK Rowling of the documentary industry." He has filmed a plethora of critical documentaries, from Fahrenheit 9/11 to Where to Invade Next. Although America is highly advanced in technological and medical developments, Moore is acutely aware that surgeries and drugs in America are too expensive for the average citizen.

That is why he has filmed this documentary which provides potential methods of decreasing healthcare costs.

Moore starts this documentary by talking about how countries like India decrease drug prices by revoking patents for life-saving medicine, including the drug for HIV. In fact, he has devoted a significant section of the documentary to HIV drugs. He regards HIV as one of the most serious problems in all countries. Just like India, Moore suggests to the audience that America should revoke patents for life-saving medicine. Of course, Moore also suggests other solutions like government regulations on drug prices.

Anyone who wants to learn about issues regarding the American healthcare system and how to resolve these issues should watch this engaging documentary.

Q 3: According to the passage, what is Fahrenheit 9/11?
(a) A documentary criticising the healthcare system of the United States
(b) A successful documentary regarding global warming
(c) A failing book that Michael Moore wrote when he was young
(d) A documentary filmed by the director of Where to Invade Next

Q 4: What can be inferred from the review?
(a) Moore owns a medical company
(b) Michael Moore admires Indian culture
(c) Where to Invade Next contradicts the content of Sicko
(d) Moore is concerned about the high healthcare costs in America

제3부

오답의 7가지 유형

출제자는 오답을 어떻게 출제할까? (오답7유형)

지문 해석이 생각보다 잘 되어 자신만만하게 선택지로 내려갔더니, 헷갈리는 선택지들… 매 시험 마지막 순간까지 고민하다 아쉽게 틀리는 3~4 문제의 함정… 그 함정들에 빠지는 이유는 무엇일까? 그리고 그것은 단순히 내 '실수'였을까?

텝스 독해 문제를 구성하는 3요소 (지문, 질문, 선택지) 중 마지막 요소는 "선택지"다. 아무리 지문 독해를 잘했다 하더라도 선택지를 제대로 풀어내지 못한다면 결국 문제 풀이는 실패하게 되는 것이다. 지문을 정확히 이해하고 자신 있게 선택지로 내려왔는데 선택지 2개 사이에서 고민을 하다 시간을 날린 경험은 누구나 한 번 쯤 있다.

특히 새롭게 개정된 TEPS 독해 시험엔 논리력을 중점적으로 평가하는 문항들이 산재되어 있기 때문에, 지문보다 선택지가 까다롭게 출제되는 문항들도 다수 존재한다.
제 3부에서는 TEPS 독해 영역의 최빈출 함정 7가지를 정리했다. TEPS가 가장 좋아하는 "매력적 오답 7 유형"을 익혀 대비할 수 있도록 하자.

	Easy 지문	Hard 지문
Easy 선택지	10%	40%
Hard 선택지	40%	10%

기출문제들의 출제 경향을 기반으로 측정한 TEPS 출제 분포도이다. 지문과 선택지가 각각 쉽고 어렵게 출제가 될 수 있는데, 전체 문제 중 지문이 어렵게 출제가 되는 확률이 50%이며 선택지가 어렵게 출제가 되는 경우도 50%이다.

위 표 속 [Easy 선택지] 의 경우, 지문 구조 및 질문의 내용만 정확히 파악했다면 풀 수 있는 문제들이다. 즉, 지문 구조에서 명백한 정답이 존재하거나, 선택지들 중 매력적 오답이 따로 출제되지 않은 경우에 해당이 된다. 제3부는 〈Hard 선택지〉에 속하는 50%의 문제에 해당이 되는 "매력적 오답"들의 유형을 다루게 된다. 〈Hard 선택지+Easy 지문〉 문제 유형들(시험의 약 40%)의 경우 한정된 영어 실력으로도 충분히 역전이 가능한 성격의 문제들이니, 오답 유형들의 함정들을 꼼꼼히 학습하도록 하자.

선택지 비교법

선택지를 접근 할 때에 확실하게 해야 하는 부분이 있다. 시험에서 선택지가 문제가 되는 것은 선택지 4개 중에 2개가 남았을 때 일 것이다.

선택지 2개가 남았을 때 어떻게 정답을 고를지 그 기준을 모르겠고, 선택지 2개가 남았을 때 고민하는 시간이 오히려 길어진 경험을 했을 것이다.

"선택지 비교법"은 결국 선택지가 두 개 남았을 때 어떻게 최단 기간 내에 가장 정확하게 둘을 비교할지에 대한 방법론이다. 대부분 사람들은 선택지가 두 개 (a, c) 남는다면 a를 한번 읽어보고 c를 한번 읽어본다. 그다음 둘 중에서 고민을 하면서 a에 관련해서 맞는지 틀린 지 확인하기 위해 지문으로 올라가서 여기 저기 읽는다. 그래도 모르겠으면 시간 압박도 있으니 c를 한번 읽어보고 지문으로 올라가서 c가 맞는지 파악하려고 한다.

결국 이 과정 속에서 지문에 대한 이해도가 크게 높아지지 않을뿐더러, 결국 정답을 맞힐 확률도 높아지지 않는다. 더군다나 지문을 여러 번 반복적으로 읽게 되므로 결국 엄청난 시간을 낭비하게 된다. 이러한 접근은 잘못된 것이다.

결국, 선택지가 두 개 남았을 때엔 접근법이 바뀌어야 한다. (만약 선택지a와 선택지c 사이에서 고민 중이라면,)

선택지 비교법

1. a와c를 꼼꼼히 읽는다.
2. a와c의 차이점이 무엇인지 찾아낸다.
3. a와c의 차이점을 각각 키워드 하나로 표현한다.
4. 키워드를 가지고 지문에 올라가서 검증한다.

1~4 순서대로 진행을 한다면 결국 훨씬 수월하게 문제를 접근 할 수 있을 것이다. 고민하는 시간도 줄어들 것이고, 정확도는 완벽에 가까워질 것이다. 앞으로 학습할 오답의 7유형까지 체득하여, 더 이상 텝스가 자주 출제하는 함정들에 빠져들지 말자!

제1부
제2부
제3부
제4부

제3부
오답의 7가지 유형

오답 패턴#1
지엽성

PATTERN 1 지엽성

연습문제

우선 30~40초동안 문제를 먼저 풀어보세요

1. Many viewers of the renowned opera 'Notre Dame de Paris' make the mistake of assuming that ____. This mistake in perception is understandable since Claude Frollo is constantly persecuting Esmerelda and her fellow gypsies. However, towards the end of the opera, Claude Frollo confides in god that he is only persecuting Esmerelda because she has declined his offer of marriage. His confession is a small but significant detail that the majority of viewers fail to recall after watching the opera.

(a) Frollo's confession is an insignificant detail
(b) Claude Frollo is harassing Esmerelda due to his unrequited love
(c) Esmerelda is not a gypsy
(d) Frollo torments Esmerelda due to his hatred of gypsies

1. Many viewers of the renowned opera 'Notre Dame de Paris' make the mistake of assuming that ____. This mistake in perception is understandable since Claude Frollo is constantly persecuting Esmerelda and her fellow gypsies. However, towards the end of the opera, Claude Frollo confides in god that he is only persecuting Esmerelda because she has declined his offer of marriage. His confession is a small but significant detail that the majority of viewers fail to recall after watching the opera.

(a) Frollo's confession is an insignificant detail
(b) Claude Frollo is harassing Esmerelda due to his unrequited love
(c) Esmerelda is not a gypsy
(d) Frollo torments Esmerelda due to his hatred of gypsies

2. Many fans of the universally popular Harry Potter series labor to correct misconceptions shared by others, one of the most common of which being that ______________________.
Since the series consists of seven long books, it is understandable that many find it much easier to watch the movies only. Films are much more limited in scope or length compared to books, though, and there have been many alterations to fit such needs with Harry Potter as well. Hardcore fans, of course, would be quite outraged by "Muggles" thinking that it was Neville who gave Harry gillyweed in the Triwizard Tournament, or completely unaware of the existence of Peeves the Poltergeist.

(a) the books take too long to read compared to the films
(b) Peeves is not a significant character in the series
(c) the movies are exactly in accord with the original books
(d) all the characters are equally important

제1부 제2부 제3부 제4부

2. Many fans of the universally popular Harry Potter series labor to correct misconceptions shared by others, one of the most common of which being that ______________________.
Since the series consists of seven long books, it is understandable that many find it much easier to watch the movies only. Films are much more limited in scope or length compared to books, though, and there have been many alterations to fit such needs with Harry Potter as well. Hardcore fans, of course, would be quite outraged by "Muggles" thinking that it was Neville who gave Harry gillyweed in the Triwizard Tournament, or completely unaware of the existence of Peeves the Poltergeist.

(a) the books take too long to read compared to the films
(b) Peeves is not a significant character in the series
(c) the movies are exactly in accord with the original books
(d) all the characters are equally important

3. The World History Research Center (WHRC) and History Restoration Association (HRA) have recently announced the joint publication of a World History Book that is to be selected as a guideline to all teachers. As an educator, you may always choose to add on elaborations or different viewpoints in the process of teaching. However, the factual analysis and interpretation of the joint World History Book must be prioritized. The book's content must be highlighted and should be the gist of all class materials. Other interpretations or insights, if substituted, must be clearly distinguished from the book's main point to ensure that they remain secondary.

Q: What is the main purpose of the announcement?

(a) To announce a joint publication between the WHRC and the HRA

(b) To inform teachers of the necessary prioritization of the joint book in history education

(c) To tell students that different viewpoints may exist

(d) To highlight the differences between the new book and previous variations of history books

3. The World History Research Center (WHRC) and History Restoration Association (HRA) have recently announced the joint publication of a World History Book that is to be selected as a guideline to all teachers. As an educator, you may always choose to add on elaborations or different viewpoints in the process of teaching. However, the factual analysis and interpretation of the joint World History Book must be prioritized. The book's content must be highlighted and should be the gist of all class materials. Other interpretations or insights, if substituted, must be clearly distinguished from the book's main point to ensure that they remain secondary.

Q: What is the main purpose of the announcement?

(a) To announce a joint publication between the WHRC and the HRA

(b) To inform teachers of the necessary prioritization of the joint book in history education

(c) To tell students that different viewpoints may exist

(d) To highlight the differences between the new book and previous variations of history books

4. The American Bank has announced its new policy of reinforcing its restriction on mortgage products due to the emerging financial crisis. We put our client's safety as our first priority and are willing to take full actions to support our goal. In the recent months, we detected that there were declines in residential investment and that more and more banks are failing to meet the desirable risk ratings. Therefore in order to respond to the economic crisis which is becoming more visible, we will only provide mortgage contracts to our prime clients-this means that subprime and alt-a clients will not be subject to applying for a mortgage in our bank.

Q: What is the main purpose of this announcement?
(a) To announce the changes in the subjects who can apply for a mortgage in the American Bank.
(b) To inform that the financial crisis is becoming more serious.
(c) To promote a new mortgage that can be attractive for newly-weds.
(d) To compare its mortgage offers with that of other banks.

4. The American Bank has announced its new policy of reinforcing its restriction on mortgage products due to the emerging financial crisis. We put our client's safety as our first priority and are willing to take full actions to support our goal. In the recent months, we detected that there were declines in residential investment and that more and more banks are failing to meet the desirable risk ratings. Therefore in order to respond to the economic crisis which is becoming more visible, we will only provide mortgage contracts to our prime clients-this means that subprime and alt-a clients will not be subject to applying for a mortgage in our bank.

Q: What is the main purpose of this announcement?
(a) To announce the changes in the subjects who can apply for a mortgage in the American Bank.
(b) To inform that the financial crisis is becoming more serious.
(c) To promote a new mortgage that can be attractive for newly-weds.
(d) To compare its mortgage offers with that of other banks.

5. The Barnum Effect refers to a human tendency to credit statements about one's personality as highly accurate while in reality they are vaguely broad and applicable to the general public. This human phenomenon was proven to be true with a thought experiment by a group of psychologists in Northwestern University. The experiment revealed that the students tended to give high accuracy ratings to broad personality descriptions which seemingly appear to be designed for the individual. The study suggest that people must approach horoscopic predictions with caution and not take them into serious account.

Q: What is the passage mainly about?
(a) Differences in the accuracy of predictions in horoscopes
(b) The most effective way to incorporate pseudoscience to one's benefit
(c) Human tendency to approach horoscopic prophecies with a biased view
(d) The effect of 'self-serving prophecy' on peoples' decision making

5. The Barnum Effect refers to a human tendency to credit statements about one's personality as highly accurate while in reality they are vaguely broad and applicable to the general public. This human phenomenon was proven to be true with a thought experiment by a group of psychologists in Northwestern University. The experiment revealed that the students tended to give high accuracy ratings to broad personality descriptions which seemingly appear to be designed for the individual. The study suggest that people must approach horoscopic predictions with caution and not take them into serious account.

Q: What is the passage mainly about?
(a) Differences in the accuracy of predictions in horoscopes
(b) The most effective way to incorporate pseudoscience to one's benefit
(c) Human tendency to approach horoscopic prophecies with a biased view
(d) The effect of 'self-serving prophecy' on peoples' decision making

6. Throughout the past decade, the number of casual smokers increased in almost a twofold, with especially focused the middle-class population. Casual smoking refers to a behavioral pattern of smoking regularly (two or more times a day) and consuming more than one package a week. While social discourse mostly laments the spread of cigars and highly condemns its usage, more and more people are turning to smoking as a stress-relief device. However, anti-smoking laws are making it increasingly difficult for people to smoke in places. Furthermore, the increase in taxes regarding cigarette sales has led to a constant increase in prices, making smoking a much less cost-effective way to relieve stress.

Q. What is the topic of the passage?

(a) The problem with casual smoking to oneself and the surrounding people
(b) The decrease in favorability of smoking as a getaway device for people
(c) Recently established regulations regarding smoking and buying cigarettes
(d) The increasing social awareness against public smoking

6. Throughout the past decade, the number of casual smokers increased in almost a twofold, with especially focused the middle-class population. Casual smoking refers to a behavioral pattern of smoking regularly (two or more times a day) and consuming more than one package a week. While social discourse mostly laments the spread of cigars and highly condemns its usage, more and more people are turning to smoking as a stress-relief device. However, anti-smoking laws are making it increasingly difficult for people to smoke in places. Furthermore, the increase in taxes regarding cigarette sales has led to a constant increase in prices, making smoking a much less cost-effective way to relieve stress.

Q. What is the topic of the passage?

(a) The problem with casual smoking to oneself and the surrounding people
(b) The decrease in favorability of smoking as a getaway device for people
(c) Recently established regulations regarding smoking and buying cigarettes
(d) The increasing social awareness against public smoking

7. Dear Mr. and Mrs. Johnson:

Thank you for participating in the parent teacher conference last week. I could see that both of you are interested in understanding your son Tim and want to provide him with high quality education. As Tim's homeroom teacher, I am trying to help him adjust to his first year of middle school. As Tim is active and playful, I am certain he will make friends and become accustomed to the school very soon.

Unfortunately, I must mention that although Tim participates actively in all other classes, he does not seem interested in studying mathematics. Tim seems to believe mathematics is unnecessary in daily life. However, mathematics is crucial for numerous events like paying taxes or shopping. Because I only see Tim at school, I cannot help Tim realize that mathematics is crucial in such events. Therefore, I hope that you will help Tim realize the importance of mathematics in daily events.

If you would like to discuss any other aspect of Tim's school life, please contact me at laurensmith@brantelyhighschool.org.

Sincerely,
Lauren Smith
Homeroom Teacher
Brantely High School

Q: What is the main purpose of the letter?

(a) To appreciate Mr. and Mrs. Johnson's participation in the parent teacher conference
(b) To congratulate Mr. and Mrs. Johnson for having helped their son improve his math skills
(c) To thank Mr. and Mrs. Johnson for sending their son to Brantely High School
(d) To ask Mr. and Mrs. Johnson to help Tim develop an interest in mathematics

제3부
오답의 7가지 유형

오답 패턴#2
일반화

PATTERN 2

일반화

1. When I first became a teacher, one of the most difficult jobs was communicating with my students. I did not want to be seen as a strict and unapproachable instructor but earning respect from the students was also necessary. At first, I did nothing but compliment all students for even the tiniest actions. However I realized that not only was this inefficient in bonding with the students, but that they thought such praise lacked sincerity. So I decided to change my course and gave only relevant appraisals and constructive criticism when needed, which led to a more intimate relationship with my students. This experience led me to realize that ______________________.

(a) compliments help in creating a bond between the teacher and the students.
(b) teachers should try to be more sincere.
(c) criticism should be encouraged.
(d) limited usage of compliments can be useful in building a relationship with the students.

1. When I first became a teacher, one of the most difficult jobs was communicating with my students. I did not want to be seen as a strict and unapproachable instructor but earning respect from the students was also necessary. At first, I did nothing but compliment all students for even the tiniest actions. However I realized that not only was this inefficient in bonding with the students, but that they thought such praise lacked sincerity. So I decided to change my course and gave only relevant appraisals and constructive criticism when needed, which led to a more intimate relationship with my students. This experience led me to realize that ______________________.

(a) compliments help in creating a bond between the teacher and the students.
(b) teachers should try to be more sincere.
(c) criticism should be encouraged.
(d) limited usage of compliments can be useful in building a relationship with the students.

2. The day I got accepted to a foreign language high school, I promised myself that I would try my best. I wanted to be the top of my class, so I did nothing but study day and night. While this did lead to a sudden boost in my grades, they started to decline after a certain amount of time. Day after day, my grades started to drop, despite my hard work. I decided to give up everything and took a long nap for the first time in a year of my freshman life. After I woke up, I felt much better. I felt like I could concentrate and get back to reading. After weeks, my grades started to get back on track. Rather than staying up all night during exam periods, I started to make myself sleep for at least 7 hours a day. That short nap that day taught me that ________________.

(a) promises made to god should not be broken
(b) deceiving yourself to believe that you are resting while studying works best
(c) the less you study, the better it is for your grades
(d) balance between hard work and sufficient rest is crucial

2. The day I got accepted to a foreign language high school, I promised myself that I would try my best. I wanted to be the top of my class, so I did nothing but study day and night. While this did lead to a sudden boost in my grades, they started to decline after a certain amount of time. Day after day, my grades started to drop, despite my hard work. I decided to give up everything and took a long nap for the first time in a year of my freshman life. After I woke up, I felt much better. I felt like I could concentrate and get back to reading. After weeks, my grades started to get back on track. Rather than staying up all night during exam periods, I started to make myself sleep for at least 7 hours a day. That short nap that day taught me that ________________.

(a) promises made to god should not be broken
(b) deceiving yourself to believe that you are resting while studying works best
(c) the less you study, the better it is for your grades
(d) balance between hard work and sufficient rest is crucial

3. Starting my first year of university, I had a problem making new friends. I thought getting closer was all about knowing more about each other, and filled awkward silences with unnecessary information. The result was indeed longer conversations, but also more regrets on my part. I revealed everything, while gaining nothing from my partner. Eventually, I learned to be comfortable with pauses. Keeping calm was no small ordeal, but slowly I saw progress. Instead of what I dreaded, slowing down in relationships made the intercourse more relaxed and natural. This showed me that ________________________________.

(a) pauses were effective for building closer relationships
(b) asking more about the other person is always better
(c) revealing yourself loosens up the tension in relationships
(d) providing too much information backfires

3. Starting my first year of university, I had a problem making new friends. I thought getting closer was all about knowing more about each other, and filled awkward silences with unnecessary information. The result was indeed longer conversations, but also more regrets on my part. I revealed everything, while gaining nothing from my partner. Eventually, I learned to be comfortable with pauses. Keeping calm was no small ordeal, but slowly I saw progress. Instead of what I dreaded, slowing down in relationships made the intercourse more relaxed and natural. This showed me that ________________________________.

(a) pauses were effective for building closer relationships
(b) asking more about the other person is always better
(c) revealing yourself loosens up the tension in relationships
(d) providing too much information backfires

4. Dear Mr. Coleman

This is a special letter of appreciation that we decided to send to a few selected applicants. As you already know, since the results have been announced earlier today, you were not selected as one of the award recipients. That decision was based on the grounds that the "Science Fiction" division that you applied for, demands very innovative thinking and unpredictable imagination. Also, the plot and setting has to be persuasive enough to make the readers believe that such a world might exist somewhere, or in the future that lies beyond.

Your novel "Stolen Moments" did have a lot of holes in terms of delicate imagination and world persuasiveness, and hence, did not win the contest. However, we thought that it would have had higher odds of winning if it were submitted to another division. For example, the "Emotions" sector or the "Romance" division would have been better options. Your writing lacked a vivid picture of a dystopian world, however your words and sentences were powerful enough to make readers reflect on their own selves and emotions.

So we decided to send you this letter of encouragement, and offer you another chance at our next year's contest. You will not have to go through the preliminary basic writing tests, but just directly submit your work to the adequate category.

Sincerely,

Laura McKenzie,

Editor-in-chief

Sun & Moon Publishers

Q: According to the letter, why couldn't Mr. Coleman's novel win the contest?

(a) Because he lacked scientific proficiency

(b) Because there were too much love stories to be a Science-Fiction novel

(c) Because he failed to choose the most appropriate category to submit his writing

(d) Because his novel lacked certain characteristics

제1부

제2부

제3부

제4부

5. http://www.greatgatsby.com/auditionhome/tickets/audition/audience/sponsor

Casting New Daisy Buchanan!

Have you ever read the Great Gatsby? Ever wanted to reenact the lives of the characters from the novel? Ever wanted to act in front of friends and families? In that case, apply to become the new Daisy Buchanan and act for the Fitzgerald Theatre!

In contemporary films, Daisy is often portrayed as sentimental and caring. However, we plan to reenact the novel more accurately and encourage our audience to look behind the false naivety of Daisy. We portray Daisy as a character driven by her desire to gain wealth and prestige rather than love. In other words, Daisy's actions were driven by self-centered motives.

To apply for the role of Daisy, candidates should submit a video file reading the script posted on our website. The video should be no longer than 15 minutes. While reading the script, please keep in mind our interpretation of Daisy and portray her materialistic desires. If you have any further inquiries, contact Lucy Steel at lucysteel@greatgatsby.com.

Q: Which of the following is correct according to the announcement?
(a) Candidates can visit the theatre to audition in person
(b) Candidates can audition for characters in The Great Gatsby
(c) Candidates should be aware that Daisy is selfish
(d) Candidates should break away from contemporary interpretations of Daisy

제3부
오답의 7가지 유형

오답 패턴#3
극단적

PATTERN 3

극단적

연습문제

우선 30~40초동안 문제를 먼저 풀어보세요

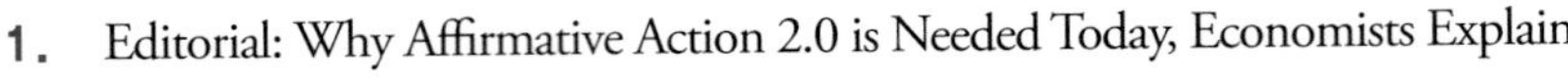

1. Editorial: Why Affirmative Action 2.0 is Needed Today, Economists Explain

Read full article

Comments

Dr. Irene Telemann | 7 hour(s) ago

Even in the diversity infused 21st century, debate regarding the economic effectiveness of establishing certain quotas in corporate recruitment processes still exists. This sole fact is enough to realize that the economic balance sheets are not the core subject in this issue. Rather, this discourse is centered in the question of what comprises a society as a whole.

We are a strictly meritocracy based society with deep roots in Anglo-Saxon dominance. We are a society which has cunningly overlooked injustices in every part of the society including discrimination against minority groups. We are a society that has constantly been criticized for the lack of diversity within the hiring field despite the endless efforts of social reform throughout the decades. We are a society that still has a long way to go in terms of realizing actual equality.

Q: What is the main purpose of Dr. Telemann's comment?

(a) To criticize the corporate society for its diminishing progress

(b) To assert that lack of diversity is the paramount of all social problems

(c) To remind of the core problem that must be addressed when discussing diversity quotas

(d) To insist that increasing diversity in the workforce will lead to economic advancement

2. http://www.barbie-dolls.org/exhibition&DIY

About us | Products | Exhibition & Experience | Contact US

An invitation back to your childhood!

All of us, especially girls, had one or two Barbie dolls next to our pillows. Personally, my sons also enjoyed playing with male doll characters! We bought clothes for them, dressed them, combed their hair, played with them and made them our friends. Even long after becoming an "adult", I couldn't help but stop by pretty doll shops and stare through the show-windows.

Founded in 1987, the Barbie Doll Company has been producing the most loved dolls for decades. As a gratitude to all our friends who have shown love and support to our dolls, we are holding an event called "Exhibition & DIY". It will take place at our company building from 10:00 a.m. through 8:00 p.m.

At our exhibition & DIY, you and your children will be able to look at series of different dolls, observe the manufacturing processes and most importantly, participate in the process yourselves and make your own doll! Since it has no precedent history of such, we will be extra careful with children and their safety.

To show our appreciation for our old friends, there will be no admission fees. However, you must bring at least one Barbie doll to be able to enter. For further information, call us at 02) 9384-4385

Q: What can be inferred from the announcement?

(a) The association only produced dolls targeting girls

(b) The event will take place in a shopping mall

(c) The event has always been hosted at the company building

(d) Participants will be able to make their own dolls

제1부
제2부
제3부
제4부

3. The Life of a French Female Musician in the 19th Century by Chantelle Delacour

Cecile Chaminade is renowned as "the queen of woodwind compositions". Her works include a number of beloved flute pieces, from Concertino in G to the Bluebird Sonata. Although she was absolutely brilliant at composing exquisite pieces, she was faced with extreme criticism as a female composer that none of her male counterparts ever encountered. In reflection of her conflictful life, one of her pupils, Chantelle Delacour has written a biography that looks into this musician's career with objectiveness.

Delacour starts this biography with Chaminade's early life as an esteemed flutist due to her early exposure to chamber music, thanks to her parents, who were both musicians. She then moves on to her life as a composer, when she officially becomes one of the first female members of the musicians' society. Delacour weaves through her various scandals and triumphs, along with her personal distresses and moments of anguish as a musician always in the spotlight.

Anyone interested in diving into the life of a female Romantic Era musician would find this biography of Cecile Chaminade both entertaining and inspiring.

Q: What can be inferred from the review?

(a) Chaminade has developed her self-contemplation skills to the paramount

(b) Chaminade's family had strong ties with the musician society

(c) The Bluebird Sonata initially gained social criticism upon its composition

(d) Chaminade went to trials of controversy throughout her career

4. Notifications Concerning Student Dormitory Regulation

The Director of the Dormitory would like to notify all students in Wellington University housing and their visitors that there has been a very important change in student dormitory regulation. From now on, drinking any kind of alcohol beverages will be strictly prohibited, inside the building as well as the back yard.

There have been many complaints concerning noise rackets and unsanitary lobbies due to alcohol consumption. The Wellington University housing put its utmost interest in promoting the security and welfare of our residents and in order to protect the dormitory from abuses caused by drinking alcohol, this action seems unavoidable.

We expect that all residents and visitors abide by the regulations of our dormitory. In case of violation of dormitory rules, corresponding penalties would be given out. Thank you for your cooperation.

Q: What can be inferred from the notice?

(a) The college dormitory puts freedom of residents as their first priority.

(b) Alcohol consumption has always been restricted in and out of the dormitory.

(c) The change in the regulation is part of the countermeasures regarding incoming complaints.

(d) Visitors are not a subject to this rule.

5. Tackling the cycle of violence towards women has always been an important issue for the global society. In the year 2000, the Security Council recognized harms to women during international conflict for the first time in its official whole session. Four pillars were mainly emphasized of women security: participation, necessity of protecting women from conflict related violence, prevention of gender based violence, and recovering of conflicts. These actions aimed in not only addressing women as victims but also as active agents. As a continuous process, the UK declared a global initiative in 2012 to prevent sexual violence in armed conflicts. This declaration addressed a wider group of victims, including men and boys. More than 120 nations signed this commitment. Today, protection of all types of victims regarding sexual violence during wartime stands as a critical agenda.

Q: What is the topic of the passage?
(a) During wartime, it is vital for the global society to protect women, the only victims of sexual crimes.
(b) Protection of victims of sexual violence during conflicts remains as a global political agenda.
(c) Men and boys are the most under rated victims in the cycle of violence.
(d) Deliberate targeting towards small boys exists during war state.

5. Tackling the cycle of violence towards women has always been an important issue for the global society. In the year 2000, the Security Council recognized harms to women during international conflict for the first time in its official whole session. Four pillars were mainly emphasized of women security: participation, necessity of protecting women from conflict related violence, prevention of gender based violence, and recovering of conflicts. These actions aimed in not only addressing women as victims but also as active agents. As a continuous process, the UK declared a global initiative in 2012 to prevent sexual violence in armed conflicts. This declaration addressed a wider group of victims, including men and boys. More than 120 nations signed this commitment. Today, protection of all types of victims regarding sexual violence during wartime stands as a critical agenda.

Q: What is the topic of the passage?
(a) During wartime, it is vital for the global society to protect women, the only victims of sexual crimes.
(b) Protection of victims of sexual violence during conflicts remains as a global political agenda.
(c) Men and boys are the most under rated victims in the cycle of violence.
(d) Deliberate targeting towards small boys exists during war state.

제3부
오답의 7가지 유형

오답 패턴# 4
정반대

PATTERN 4

정반대

연습문제

우선 30~40초동안 문제를 먼저 풀어보세요

1. Suzanne Koelle's recent art exhibition in Michigan was an unprecedented shock in terms of painting and display. The exhibition included exactly 472 pieces of paintings, which is an unbelievable number of work. However, all of the pieces were nothing more than one single paper filled with a single choice of color. The exhibition reminded the viewers of a house with 472 windows with 472 different shades of color outside. By transforming "colors" from 'tools' to create art to a 'creation' of art itself, Koelle inspired viewers to think outside of the box, allowing the notion that anything can become art to kick in their minds.

Q: What is the writer's main point about the exhibition?
(a) Suzanne Koelle's novel approach to art lead to the repugnance of fans
(b) It was very localized adhering to the Michigan population
(c) Its attempt to surprise people failed
(d) Its twist of perception regarding colors make people redefine art

1. Suzanne Koelle's recent art exhibition in Michigan was an unprecedented shock in terms of painting and display. The exhibition included exactly 472 pieces of paintings, which is an unbelievable number of work. However, all of the pieces were nothing more than one single paper filled with a single choice of color. The exhibition reminded the viewers of a house with 472 windows with 472 different shades of color outside. By transforming "colors" from 'tools' to create art to a 'creation' of art itself, Koelle inspired viewers to think outside of the box, allowing the notion that anything can become art to kick in their minds.

Q: What is the writer's main point about the exhibition?
(a) Suzanne Koelle's novel approach to art lead to the repugnance of fans
(b) It was very localized adhering to the Michigan population
(c) Its attempt to surprise people failed
(d) Its twist of perception regarding colors make people redefine art

2. The Curious Case of Benjamin Button and The Age of Adaline both deals with a character who lives a different timeline compared to normal people, yet they differ in ______________________________ __________. Benjamin Button, who was born old and became younger every moment he lived, did not fear falling in love. Benjamin sought to fight and protect his love, and make her stay. However Adaline, fearing that her loved one might leave her when her secret is disclosed, kept on running from her love. This distinction led to their different ways of treating their life and ultimately to an opposite ending.

(a) the way the protagonists react to their lovers.
(b) how their main characters cope with stressful situations.
(c) the way their characters view life.
(d) how they prepare for the last chapter of their life.

2. The Curious Case of Benjamin Button and The Age of Adaline both deals with a character who lives a different timeline compared to normal people, yet they differ in ______________________________ __________. Benjamin Button, who was born old and became younger every moment he lived, did not fear falling in love. Benjamin sought to fight and protect his love, and make her stay. However Adaline, fearing that her loved one might leave her when her secret is disclosed, kept on running from her love. This distinction led to their different ways of treating their life and ultimately to an opposite ending.

(a) the way the protagonists react to their lovers.
(b) how their main characters cope with stressful situations.
(c) the way their characters view life.
(d) how they prepare for the last chapter of their life.

3. home/tickets/audition/audience/sponsor

Casting New Daisy Buchanan!

Have you ever read the Great Gatsby? Ever wanted to reenact the lives of the characters from the novel? Ever wanted to act in front of friends and families? In that case, apply to become the new Daisy Buchanan and act for the Fitzgerald Theatre!

In contemporary films, Daisy is often portrayed as sentimental and caring. However, we plan to reenact the novel more accurately and encourage our audience to look behind the false naivety of Daisy. We portray Daisy as a character driven by her desire to gain wealth and prestige rather than love. In other words, Daisy's actions were driven by self-centered motives.

To apply for the role of Daisy, candidates should submit a video file reading the script posted on our website. The video should be no longer than 15 minutes. While reading the script, please keep in mind our interpretation of Daisy and portray her materialistic desires. If you have any further inquiries, contact Lucy Steel at lucysteel@greatgatsby.com.

Q: What can be inferred from the announcement?
(a) The theatre only shows plays related to religion.
(b) The theatre portrays Daisy as a doting character.
(c) Ms. Steel loves the new interpretation of The Great Gatsby.
(d) The casting crew has a clear expectations of Daisy's traits.

4. During the early 20th century, Scientology, a religious cult focused on spiritual fulfillment through studying and training, was highly influential. Members who deviated from the teachings of Scientology were acerbically punished. For example, if an individual consumed alcohol before sessions, he or she would be publicly humiliated and banned from attending future sessions. These harsh punishments ____________________.

(a) led to the premature demise of Scientology
(b) caused citizens to rebel
(c) were against the teachings of Scientology
(d) helped maintain strict ideologies of Scientology

4. During the early 20th century, Scientology, a religious cult focused on spiritual fulfillment through studying and training, was highly influential. Members who deviated from the teachings of Scientology were acerbically punished. For example, if an individual consumed alcohol before sessions, he or she would be publicly humiliated and banned from attending future sessions. These harsh punishments ____________________.

(a) led to the premature demise of Scientology
(b) caused citizens to rebel
(c) were against the teachings of Scientology
(d) helped maintain strict ideologies of Scientology

5. Starbucks, the global coffee chain ever attentive to consumer tastes, has newly launched the avocado smoothie this month to the ______________________________. The fruit is now trendier than ever across the globe, and is featured in numerous menus in various ways. However, it has recently come to light that the popularity of avocados is causing major deforestation in avocado-producing countries such as Mexico, with excessive demand leading to unsustainable harvest. It seems that avocados are not as green for the environment as they may be for health. Thus, organizations tied close to the matter have started demanding for efforts on resolving this issue.

(a) disappointment of avocado aficionados everywhere
(b) disbelief of Mexican farmers all over the country
(c) protest of many environmental organizations
(d) generally lukewarm reception from environmentalists

5. Starbucks, the global coffee chain ever attentive to consumer tastes, has newly launched the avocado smoothie this month to the ______________________________. The fruit is now trendier than ever across the globe, and is featured in numerous menus in various ways. However, it has recently come to light that the popularity of avocados is causing major deforestation in avocado-producing countries such as Mexico, with excessive demand leading to unsustainable harvest. It seems that avocados are not as green for the environment as they may be for health. Thus, organizations tied close to the matter have started demanding for efforts on resolving this issue.

(a) disappointment of avocado aficionados everywhere
(b) disbelief of Mexican farmers all over the country
(c) protest of many environmental organizations
(d) generally lukewarm reception from environmentalists

제3부
오답의 7가지 유형

오답 패턴# 5
논리 전개

PATTERN 5 논리 전개

제1부
제2부
제3부
제4부

연습문제

우선 30~40초동안 문제를 먼저 풀어보세요

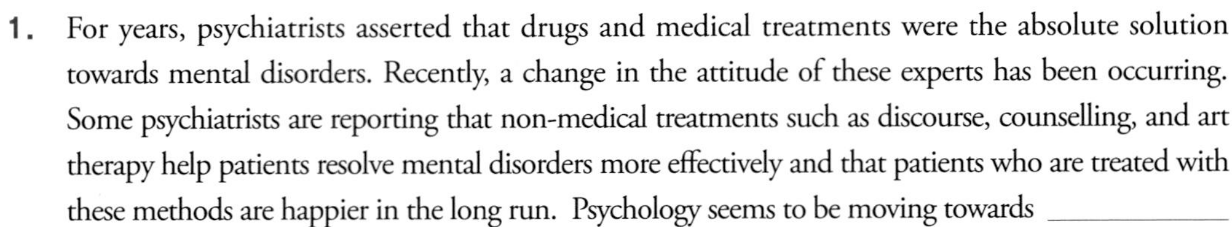

1. For years, psychiatrists asserted that drugs and medical treatments were the absolute solution towards mental disorders. Recently, a change in the attitude of these experts has been occurring. Some psychiatrists are reporting that non-medical treatments such as discourse, counselling, and art therapy help patients resolve mental disorders more effectively and that patients who are treated with these methods are happier in the long run. Psychology seems to be moving towards ______________________.

(a) increasing the number of psychiatrists
(b) utilising non-medical treatments to resolve mental disorders
(c) encouraging family members of the patient to be more supportive
(d) helping individuals use non-medical treatments

1. For years, psychiatrists asserted that drugs and medical treatments were the absolute solution towards mental disorders. Recently, a change in the attitude of these experts has been occurring. Some psychiatrists are reporting that non-medical treatments such as discourse, counselling, and art therapy help patients resolve mental disorders more effectively and that patients who are treated with these methods are happier in the long run. Psychology seems to be moving towards ______________________.

(a) increasing the number of psychiatrists
(b) utilising non-medical treatments to resolve mental disorders
(c) encouraging family members of the patient to be more supportive
(d) helping individuals use non-medical treatments

2. The "Door in the Face Effect" is psychological term coined to explain the irrational process that our mind sometimes goes through. The term explains how people tend to accept offers more easily when a more burdensome offer is suggested in advance. For example, if you ask a friend to lend you $100, the friend might feel like it is too much and refuse to lend you money. However, if you first ask her to lend you $300, get rejected, and then ask for $100, she is more likely to agree to do so. This is because the amount relatively feels less compared to the previously mentioned $300, and one rejection makes the person feel a sense of guilt that stops her from repeating it.

Q: What is the main purpose of the passage?
(a) To explain the mechanism of relativeness in the "Door in the face" effect
(b) To prove a psychological phenomenon
(c) To pass on know-hows on how to successfully borrow money from your acquaintances
(d) To stress that starting off with smaller amounts is a better approach attain your goal

2. The "Door in the Face Effect" is psychological term coined to explain the irrational process that our mind sometimes goes through. The term explains how people tend to accept offers more easily when a more burdensome offer is suggested in advance. For example, if you ask a friend to lend you $100, the friend might feel like it is too much and refuse to lend you money. However, if you first ask her to lend you $300, get rejected, and then ask for $100, she is more likely to agree to do so. This is because the amount relatively feels less compared to the previously mentioned $300, and one rejection makes the person feel a sense of guilt that stops her from repeating it.

Q: What is the main purpose of the passage?
(a) To explain the mechanism of relativeness in the "Door in the face" effect
(b) To prove a psychological phenomenon
(c) To pass on know-hows on how to successfully borrow money from your acquaintances
(d) To stress that starting off with smaller amounts is a better approach attain your goal

3. With the rising attention for skin-care, due to the increase of skin-damaging micro-dusts in the atmosphere, cucumbers just might be the answer. Seoul National University's research shows that cucumbers are very rich in vitamin C, which is widely used as ingredients for skin softeners and lotions. Also, they have chlorophylls that result in a brighter, toned-up skin. Many dermatologists agree that cucumber packs and massages are the best way to ____________________.

(a) make your skin softer and brighter
(b) damage your skin irreversibly
(c) make excellent lotion products
(d) control the quantity of cucumbers in the trade market.

3. With the rising attention for skin-care, due to the increase of skin-damaging micro-dusts in the atmosphere, cucumbers just might be the answer. Seoul National University's research shows that cucumbers are very rich in vitamin C, which is widely used as ingredients for skin softeners and lotions. Also, they have chlorophylls that result in a brighter, toned-up skin. Many dermatologists agree that cucumber packs and massages are the best way to ____________________.

(a) make your skin softer and brighter
(b) damage your skin irreversibly
(c) make excellent lotion products
(d) control the quantity of cucumbers in the trade market.

4. It is a common misconception that ingesting a lot of fat is detrimental to losing weight, leading many dieters to swear off fatty foods and instead focus on other nutrients, such as protein. However, the truth about fat and health is slowly coming to the light. According to recent research outcomes, fat is vitally needed in the human body just as much as other nutrients. It seems that new diet trends are shifting towards ______________________.

(a) minimalizing protein intake instead of fat as in the past
(b) prioritizing a balanced nutrition intake
(c) focusing on overall health instead of weight loss
(d) increasing fatty acids consumption for longevity

4. It is a common misconception that ingesting a lot of fat is detrimental to losing weight, leading many dieters to swear off fatty foods and instead focus on other nutrients, such as protein. However, the truth about fat and health is slowly coming to the light. According to recent research outcomes, fat is vitally needed in the human body just as much as other nutrients. It seems that new diet trends are shifting towards ______________________.

(a) minimalizing protein intake instead of fat as in the past
(b) prioritizing a balanced nutrition intake
(c) focusing on overall health instead of weight loss
(d) increasing fatty acids consumption for longevity

오답 패턴# 6
디테일

제3부
오답의 7가지 유형

PATTERN 6

디테일

연습문제

우선 30~40초동안 문제를 먼저 풀어보세요

1. **Casting New Daisy Buchanan!**

Have you ever read the Great Gatsby? Ever wanted to reenact the lives of the characters from the novel? Ever wanted to act in front of friends and families? In that case, apply to become the new Daisy Buchanan and act for the Fitzgerald Theatre!

In contemporary films, Daisy is often portrayed as sentimental and caring. However, we plan to reenact the novel unconventionally and encourage our audience to look behind the false naivety of Daisy. We portray Daisy as a character driven by her desire to gain wealth and prestige rather than love. In other words, Daisy's actions were driven by self-centered motives.

To apply for the role of Daisy, candidates should submit a video file reading the script posted on our website. The video should be no longer than 15 minutes. While reading the script, please keep in mind our interpretation of Daisy and portray her materialistic desires. If you have any further inquiries, contact Lucy Steel at lucysteel@greatgatsby.com.

Q: Which of the following is correct according to the announcement?
(a) Candidates can visit the theatre to audition in person
(b) Candidates can audition for characters in The Great Gatsby
(c) Candidates should be aware that Daisy is selfish
(d) Candidates should break away from contemporary interpretations of Daisy

2. A gala will be hosted celebrating the ________________ the Champs-Elysees museum. The Champs-Elysees museum was once known for exclusively featuring classic artworks such as those of Van Gough or Monet. It has recently increased the spectrum of its collection by accepting works of modern art. The museum's decision has been acclaimed by many critics worldwide and is expected to significantly increase visitor turnout. The gala will commence at 6 p.m. and is open to all members of the museum.

(a) increase in visitor turnout at
(b) diversification of the modern art selection of
(c) acceptance of contemporary works of art at
(d) debut of a new artist at

2. A gala will be hosted celebrating the ________________ the Champs-Elysees museum. The Champs-Elysees museum was once known for exclusively featuring classic artworks such as those of Van Gough or Monet. It has recently increased the spectrum of its collection by accepting works of modern art. The museum's decision has been acclaimed by many critics worldwide and is expected to significantly increase visitor turnout. The gala will commence at 6 p.m. and is open to all members of the museum.

(a) increase in visitor turnout at
(b) diversification of the modern art selection of
(c) acceptance of contemporary works of art at
(d) debut of a new artist at

3. Acclaimed writer Mary Boone is having a book signing at New York's Barnes & Noble this upcoming Friday to celebrate her ______________________________. Although Boone's previous works are mostly comprised of novels, her latest masterpiece has proved her to be equally adept at essays as well. Entitled Doing Mom, this collection of the author's own journal entries on childrearing poignantly describes the woes and joys of her recent motherhood. The New Yorker has noted this book as a must-read for new parents everywhere, and rave reviews from other major newspapers are flooding in. The signing will last for three hours, and complimentary coffee or champagne will be offered to all those present.

(a) newest novel on a young woman's passage into adulthood
(b) triumphant return to the literary scene after recent childbirth
(c) well-received dabble into poetry about her week-old child
(d) successful transition from novels to essays about her own mother

3. Acclaimed writer Mary Boone is having a book signing at New York's Barnes & Noble this upcoming Friday to celebrate her ______________________________. Although Boone's previous works are mostly comprised of novels, her latest masterpiece has proved her to be equally adept at essays as well. Entitled Doing Mom, this collection of the author's own journal entries on childrearing poignantly describes the woes and joys of her recent motherhood. The New Yorker has noted this book as a must-read for new parents everywhere, and rave reviews from other major newspapers are flooding in. The signing will last for three hours, and complimentary coffee or champagne will be offered to all those present.

(a) newest novel on a young woman's passage into adulthood
(b) triumphant return to the literary scene after recent childbirth
(c) well-received dabble into poetry about her week-old child
(d) successful transition from novels to essays about her own mother

4. When examining the statistics describing the occurrence and survival rates of diseases, a bias frequently occurs. Known as the lead-time bias, this medical jargon basically shows that people easily think one patient has survived longer than the other, but that is simply due to earlier diagnosis. Upon closer inspection of the circumstances, the actual lifespan will prove to be similar among patients after the disease comes into effect. An individual equipped with this piece of knowledge would take it into account when dealing with medical figures.

Q: What is the main purpose of the passage?
(a) To describe the meaning and reality of the lead-time bias
(b) To show a case of lead-time bias in action when using statistics
(c) To warn individuals of the consequences irrational thinking might bring
(d) To claim that logical backgrounds are needed to handle mathematical figures

4. When examining the statistics describing the occurrence and survival rates of diseases, a bias frequently occurs. Known as the lead-time bias, this medical jargon basically shows that people easily think one patient has survived longer than the other, but that is simply due to earlier diagnosis. Upon closer inspection of the circumstances, the actual lifespan will prove to be similar among patients after the disease comes into effect. An individual equipped with this piece of knowledge would take it into account when dealing with medical figures.

Q: What is the main purpose of the passage?
(a) To describe the meaning and reality of the lead-time bias
(b) To show a case of lead-time bias in action when using statistics
(c) To warn individuals of the consequences irrational thinking might bring
(d) To claim that logical backgrounds are needed to handle mathematical figures

5. The World Health Organization(WHO) has issued new measures to the Tobacco Industry Union(TIU) including the Cigarette Marketing Regulations. Companies belonging to the union must now incorporate the official text warning customers of the dangers of smoking into the packaging designs of every cigarette on the market. Whether or not to add the given photograph is free for the company to decide, but the text is mandatory. The style of the font is also a free option, but the result must follow size regulations. Finally, the position of the warning should be prominent enough, and all packaging must be inspected for acceptability.

Q: What is the main purpose of the announcement?
(a) To highlight the significance of new regulations from the WHO
(b) To explain the new enforcements on restricting cigarette packaging options
(c) To show customers how they can feel more safe consuming tobacco products
(d) To compare the new rules to the former ones governing cigarette companies

5. The World Health Organization(WHO) has issued new measures to the Tobacco Industry Union(TIU) including the Cigarette Marketing Regulations. Companies belonging to the union must now incorporate the official text warning customers of the dangers of smoking into the packaging designs of every cigarette on the market. Whether or not to add the given photograph is free for the company to decide, but the text is mandatory. The style of the font is also a free option, but the result must follow size regulations. Finally, the position of the warning should be prominent enough, and all packaging must be inspected for acceptability.

Q: What is the main purpose of the announcement?
(a) To highlight the significance of new regulations from the WHO
(b) To explain the new enforcements on restricting cigarette packaging options
(c) To show customers how they can feel more safe consuming tobacco products
(d) To compare the new rules to the former ones governing cigarette companies

오답 패턴#7
부정 내용

제3부
오답의 7가지 유형

PATTERN
7

부정 내용

연습문제

우선 30~40초동안 문제를 먼저 풀어보세요

1. This Introduction to English Linguistics edition is an updated version of 2012, originally written by the U.S. Association of Linguistics in 2008. It is not a fully informative reference for professionals in the area, but a beginner's guide meant for students majoring linguistics. As the whole association is co-authoring the book, all renowned scholars belonging to the association helped compile this edition. Any objections or opinions on the content are to be forwarded to the association's official website.

Q: Which of the following is correct according to the document?
(a) The version updated in 2012 was not written by the original author.
(b) The book is meant to aid researchers and professors in their studies.
(c) No member was exempted in the creation process of the book.
(d) Comments to the author about the book can be made in person.

1. This Introduction to English Linguistics edition is an updated version of 2012, originally written by the U.S. Association of Linguistics in 2008. It is not a fully informative reference for professionals in the area, but a beginner's guide meant for students majoring linguistics. As the whole association is co-authoring the book, all renowned scholars belonging to the association helped compile this edition. Any objections or opinions on the content are to be forwarded to the association's official website.

Q: Which of the following is correct according to the document?
(a) The version updated in 2012 was not written by the original author.
(b) The book is meant to aid researchers and professors in their studies.
(c) No member was exempted in the creation process of the book.
(d) Comments to the author about the book can be made in person.

2. Although best renowned for his masterpieces as a classical composer, Peter Ilych Tchaikovsky was also a scholar during his early-to middle ages. Normally, it was extremely difficult for a musician to work in another field, because the music industry itself was very demanding. But Tchaikovsky, unlike his contemporaries, put his passion into fields of his interest, no matter how drastic. He worked in civil service during his youth while training as a pianist, until he graduated the conservatory in 1836. Later in his life, he worked as a legal historian in Cambridge University, and eventually was awarded an honorary doctorate in 1892.

Q: Which of the following is correct about Peter Ilych Tchaikovsky according to the passage?
(a) He worked in civil service during the last years of his life.
(b) He limited his academic interest to classical music composition.
(c) He did not work in different fields.
(d) He received compensation for his academic contributions.

제1부
제2부
제3부
제4부

2. Although best renowned for his masterpieces as a classical composer, Peter Ilych Tchaikovsky was also a scholar during his early-to middle ages. Normally, it was extremely difficult for a musician to work in another field, because the music industry itself was very demanding. But Tchaikovsky, unlike his contemporaries, put his passion into fields of his interest, no matter how drastic. He worked in civil service during his youth while training as a pianist, until he graduated the conservatory in 1836. Later in his life, he worked as a legal historian in Cambridge University, and eventually was awarded an honorary doctorate in 1892.

Q: Which of the following is correct about Peter Ilych Tchaikovsky according to the passage?
(a) He worked in civil service during the last years of his life.
(b) He limited his academic interest to classical music composition.
(c) He did not work in different fields.
(d) He received compensation for his academic contributions.

3. Although Steve Jobs is famous for having dropped out of college, this was not due to lack of talent or even, pure defiance. Rather, he did not want to become a burden on his stepparents, and felt some courses were not worth following paying the fees. Further evidences suggest that Jobs had a certain attachment toward the school, seeing that he talked the superintendent to letting him stay at the dormitory and even attended several classes. One of the few lessons he took dealt with typography, and this passion that seized him led to development of the Apple true type font later on.

Q: Which of the following is correct about Steve Jobs according to the passage?
(a) He lacked academic potential for graduation.
(b) He refused any further involvement with the college after quitting.
(c) He decided the whole curriculum of the school was irrelevant with his needs.
(d) He put an end to his official education out of regard for his family.

3. Although Steve Jobs is famous for having dropped out of college, this was not due to lack of talent or even, pure defiance. Rather, he did not want to become a burden on his stepparents, and felt some courses were not worth following paying the fees. Further evidences suggest that Jobs had a certain attachment toward the school, seeing that he talked the superintendent to letting him stay at the dormitory and even attended several classes. One of the few lessons he took dealt with typography, and this passion that seized him led to development of the Apple true type font later on.

Q: Which of the following is correct about Steve Jobs according to the passage?
(a) He lacked academic potential for graduation.
(b) He refused any further involvement with the college after quitting.
(c) He decided the whole curriculum of the school was irrelevant with his needs.
(d) He put an end to his official education out of regard for his family.

4. Dear Mr. Coleman,

This is a special letter of appreciation that we decided to send to a few selected applicants. As you already know, since the results have been announced earlier today, you were not selected as one of the award recipients. That decision was based on the grounds that the "Science Fiction" division that you applied for, demands very innovative thinking and unpredictable imagination. Also, the plot and setting has to be persuasive enough to make the readers believe that such a world might exist somewhere, or in the future that lies beyond.Your novel "Stolen Moments" did have a lot of holes in terms of delicate imagination and world persuasiveness, and hence, did not win the contest. However, we thought that it would have had higher odds of winning if it were submitted to another division. For example, the "Emotions" sector or the "Romance" division would have been better options. Your writing lacked a vivid picture of a dystopian world, however your words and sentences were powerful enough to make readers reflect on their own selves and emotions. So we decided to send you this letter of encouragement, and offer you another chance at our next year's contest. You will not have to go through the preliminary basic writing tests, but just directly submit your work to the adequate category.

Sincerely,

Laura McKenzie, Editor-in-chief Sun & Moon Publishers

Q: What can be inferred from the letter?

(a) Mr. Coleman is highly likely to submit his novel to the "Science Fiction" division

(b) The Sun & Moon Publishers believe that Mr. Coleman's writing could have won an award

(c) Scientific knowledge and proficiency must be prioritized for all types of writing

(d) If Mr. Coleman wishes to re-apply, he would have to go through the same steps as everyone else

5. The Korean fishing industry is endeavoring to eliminate a foreign fish species that ____. This fish, known as the blue bass, was introduced to Korea during the early 1900s by Chinese envoys who were visiting the contemporary government. While the young blue bass is harmless, the grown bass has a devastating impact on the ecology. These adult blue bass eat up all the plankton and seaweed, depleting food resources for other fish to consume.

(a) spreads epidemic through bacteria
(b) contains toxins lethal to humans
(c) endangers the ecology in its adult stage
(d) negatively impact the environment in its youth

5. The Korean fishing industry is endeavoring to eliminate a foreign fish species that ____. This fish, known as the blue bass, was introduced to Korea during the early 1900s by Chinese envoys who were visiting the contemporary government. While the young blue bass is harmless, the grown bass has a devastating impact on the ecology. These adult blue bass eat up all the plankton and seaweed, depleting food resources for other fish to consume.

(a) spreads epidemic through bacteria
(b) contains toxins lethal to humans
(c) endangers the ecology in its adult stage
(d) negatively impact the environment in its youth

제4부

실전 모의고사

제4부
실전 모의고사

독해 실전 세트 #1

연습문제

우선 30~40초동안 문제를 먼저 풀어보세요

1. The Japanese economy _______________ during the 1960s and 70s. Skyscrapers could be seen in the midst of Tokyo for the first time. Men started to wear suits to become more respected in their businesses and because they could afford them. The general standard of living increased greatly in every aspect as well.

(a) developed at an eye-popping rate
(b) went through a recession
(c) became more globalized
(d) succeeded in overcoming a depression

2. Choi's Preowned Automobiles boasts a new hybrid line of used cars, comprising of many famous brands like Hyundai, Kia, and Toyota. Newly incorporated in the line is the famous 2012 Toyota Prius. The one year old fuel-efficient car has the following features such as a 40 km per liter fuel efficiency, a sleek and sophisticated design, and an affordable price. Moreover, drivers are better protected with the superior warranty of Toyota that non-Toyota drivers envy. So come down to Choi's _______________.

(a) for the all new 2012 Toyota Prius
(b) to purchase our new Hyundai models
(c) if you wish to gain information about a partnership with Choi's
(d) for more information about hybrid cars

3. In South Korea, ______________________________. South Koreans, mostly the younger generations, have the conception that an individual's blood type influences his or her personality. For instance, if your blood type is A, you are then more likely to be introverted. However, this false perception can sometimes have a negative impact in building relationships because a person's blood type can lead to a prejudice when establishing a first impression.

(a) many people have some sort of a blood phobia
(b) there is a unique biased culture regarding blood types
(c) the older generation tends to emphasize blood types
(d) scientists have tricked the citizens into believing the myth about blood types

4. Nevertheless, it is nowadays common to see teenage or college girls disregard such side effects and visit plastic surgeons. As lookism and discrimination according to someone's facial and bodily features are becoming rampant, procedures of plastic surgery have become the solution to this appearance-oriented society no matter what the repercussions are. Such phenomena sharply shows ______________________________.

(a) the outcome of overdoing plastic surgery
(b) the close connection of extreme "lookism" and success in society
(c) the unpleasant situation of plastic surgery in a beauty-infatuated society
(d) how plastic surgery can make you famous

5. The wildlife conservatory located in Bronx Zoo is currently operating a program for children to ____. However, many young students residing in New York City are still unaware of the current state of various endangered animals in the United States. Thus, in order to increase awareness for these children, the conservatory is conducting weekly classes that enable students to learn about different animals facing extinction. The activities require children to tour around the zoo to find endangered species, learn about their living habits, and find ways to improve their conditions.

(a) help take care of animals in the zoo
(b) give attention to animals who are close to facing extinction
(c) understand what aspects of New York City are negative for animal habitation
(d) figure out the reasons behind the animal behavior all around the states

6. Trying to ______________________________? Take a vacation at the Tamazaai Islands! You can swim all day, read books near the fireplace and get a tan near the beach. Just pay $150, and you will get 2 free tickets. Enjoy the life of luxury that you would not be able to have in your everyday life. For additional service, we give you a free meal at the Rest-in Palace Hotel, which is the best hotel in the Tamazaai Islands. Get your tickets right now!

(a) enjoy a luxurious vacation at a cheap price
(b) get 2 free tickets to the Tamazaai Islands
(c) find a place to visit on summer break
(d) find the best area for sight seein

7. The Korean ______________________. Samsung Electronics is playing a big role in this area, with its innovative ideas shaping the lifestyles of the ordinary people. Its recent release of the Galaxy 4 Series has been receiving positive appeal not only in the local market, but also in the international market. People now get to enjoy new technologies which make their daily lives more efficient and convenient.

(a) economy is led by a few major IT companies
(b) IT companies are affecting the lives of the global population
(c) government is striving for new ways to develop technology
(d) market is declining due to the recent economic crisis

8. Forensic psychologists around the world are distressed because of ______________________. A year ago, a series of murders, which are thought to have been carried out by one person, was committed in the capital city of Spain, Madrid. The pattern of these particular crimes had never been seen before. The development of criminal profiling had allowed psychologists to analyze criminals' minds in deeper and more profound manner than ever. Applied to this case however, it showed its limits. The profiling was useless in ascertaining the primary motive of the Madrid serial killer as such behavior had never been seen in serial murder cases.

(a) the limitation of the law enforcement authority in Madrid
(b) the ineffectiveness of conventional forensic psychology
(c) the pressure of the urgency to catch a criminal
(d) series of baffling cases of criminal actions

9. Testosterone, the male sex hormone, has long been thought of as inducing aggression. New research, though, shows that this is something of an oversimplification. What testosterone actually seems to induce is a deep concern for social status. In situations where violence or other aggressive behaviors are likely to win higher social status, this does indeed translate into increased aggression. __________, in social situations in which cooperation, rather than competition, is the key to winning social favor, testosterone will make individuals calmer and more reasonable.

(a) However
(b) Indeed
(c) Furthermore
(d) Therefore

10. Medical scientists are learning more and more about how specific foods can help to prevent illness and may even aid in the recovery from certain diseases. ___________, scientists at the University of California have discovered that apigenin, a compound that occurs naturally in fruits and vegetables, enhances the effectiveness of chemotherapy drugs used to treat cancer.

(a) Hence
(b) In other words
(c) For example
(d) Thus

11. Cyber-era nowadays is opening up a brand new complexion of war. (a) For instance, unlike the old days, it has become highly realistic to seize the opponent's computer base and disrupt communications. (b) Hackers are polishing up their hacking skills in order to breach the thoroughly structured security system in a blink of an eye. (c) Airplanes are now being converted into pilotless jet planes, bombing five megaton atomic bombs with just one click on the computer. (d) Submarines can also sense the near-drawing torpedoes and obliterate them while the actual controller is deep inside the fortress on land.

12. The university entrance exam was once considered the most suited method of estimating academic abilities of Taiwanese students. (a) To be utterly straightforward, however, the university entrance exam of Taiwan is at the forefront of obliterating the creativeness of its students. (b) Just simply observing the inferior outcomes of Taiwanese high school seniors in international competitions, we can see how valid this statement can be. (c) Unfortunately, at one time Taiwanese students had been well-recognized for their refined competence in the field of math and science. (d) Through outcomes like this, we surely can say that the university entrance exam isn't the optimal choice for the Korean students.

13.

Dear Mr. Rauguin

We have received your request to permanently delete your Faccialibro account. We must inform you, however, that the terms and conditions that you willingly agreed to during your registration process states that Faccialibro has no duty to remove your personal data upon the deletion of your account, and we will continue to use them for selective advertisement. Although we provide no means to remove your data, a cancellation fee of 5,000 USD will let you receive no further advertisements from our service. Please inform us of your intentions regarding this matter. Sincerely, Marco Giucoberco

Q: What is the main purpose of the letter to Mr. Rauguin?

(a) To inform him that he needs to register for an account

(b) To discuss the matter concerning the deletion of his account

(c) To ask that he pay the 5,000USD of cancellation fee as soon as possible

(d) To enquire whether or not he wishes to remove his Faccialibro account

14. Fresh Me has officially launched a new dental line, Fresh Teeth. Fresh Teeth is a non-chemical mixture of mint and eucalyptus extracts that removes stains, plaques, and even bad breathe. Apply Fresh Teeth twice a day instead of regular toothpaste, and you will definitely witness a dramatic change within a month. You will experience a plaque reduction of up to 65 percent and a dramatic whitening effect of 36 percent. This amazing offer is now available only at $20 with additional discount available with the purchase of two!

Q: What is mainly being advertised in the passage?

(a) A toothpaste that is very effective

(b) A 65% discount on toothpaste

(c) A way to reduce bad breath

(d) A plaque-free toothpaste

15. Making a piñata is not as difficult as people might think. First, make paper mache paste by mixing a bowl of flour with water. Second, tear some newspapers into strips. They should be about 2 inches wide and 6 to 8 inches long; making the newspaper to lie nice and flat on the balloon. Next, apply paper mache in a crisscross pattern until the entire balloon is covered. Let the piñata sit until it is completely dried and hardened. After that, pop the balloon and remove it, leaving the mold empty in a balloon-shaped.

Q: What is the passage mainly about?
(a) How to make a sphere-shaped mold
(b) Being careful with handling a balloon
(c) Solution to difficulties of making a piñata with paper mache
(d) Steps necessary for constructing a piñata

16. Until the late 19th century, women's garment had the silhouette of an hourglass. Blouses and dresses were full in front and a narrow waist supported by a corset was highlighted with a sash or a belt. However, the silhouette slimmed down and elongated dramatically as the new century began. Dresses became much more fluid and soft than before. In later years, women's fashion tilted towards accessibility and practicality as women entered the workforce and earned rights to vote. The constrictive corset, an imperative part of women's garments in highlighting a thin waist, became a thing of the past.

Q: What is the passage mainly about?
(a) Late 19th century fashion movement
(b) The history of women's garment in the transition of the century
(c) How dress designs changed over time
(d) Transformation in women's trend

17. Want to present your loved one with the gift of a lifetime? The new digital screen located in front of Han River will allow you to make that once-in-a-lifetime moment possible. It will guarantee not only attraction but also that special moment for your special person at the special time of your choice. This digital screen will allow any kind of video clip, letters, and pictures to be displayed on a first rate LED screen and make your special moments more presentable and long-lasting in the mind of your loved one. With this one phone call you can make all the arrangements in a heartbeat.

Q: Which of the following is correct about the digital screen located near Han River?
(a) Any music of one's choice can be played with video
(b) A video clip on the screen will not seen by the public
(c) The screen was designed initially for public attraction
(d) Reservations for use of the screen can be placed easily

18. Art Fry accidently created Post-it notes (or Sticky Notes) in the 1990s though he suffered from many problems related to patent laws during the years that followed. During his years in his career he failed to climb the corporate ladder, lacked creative ideas, and was in even debt because of issues related to family. One day, his colleague Spencer Silver accidentally created "low tack", reusable, and pressure adhesive in an attempt to create a super strong adhesive. Fry utilized this discovery by using the adhesive as a bookmark in his hymnbook. A few years later, Fry developed solidified the idea into the form of Post-its as they exist today.

Q. Which of the following is correct about Fry according to the passage?
(a)He did not have difficulties in his career before the invention of Post-its
(b) He had to deal with many legal issues
(c) He made the discovery alone
(d) He used glue that had succeeded in being created for its original purpose

19. The busy life of the city has always given me a great vibe in my life. Born in the country side, I have always pictured the city as place devoid of intimacy and life before moving to a city. In contrast, I have found out that many of my acquaintances adore country over city life. Some have even made plans to move to the country after retirement. They have found the country to be more peaceful and full of life. In fact, some of them have even went far to believe that life in the country has more excitement and often find time to travel to the countryside.

Q: Which of the following is correct about the writer?
(a) He believes that life in the country is ideal
(b) He visits the country unoccasionally
(c) He does not wish to live in the countryside.
(d) He finds city life to be devoid of friendliness

20. Ministry of Culture announced last Thursday that there will be a new campaign to eliminate copyright infringement in the music industry. The campaign seems to have been planned in reaction to an incident last week, when a major recording company was accused of having sold soundtracks without the author's consent. The ministry official said that crimes associated with copyright have so far been rampant in the industry, giving a hard time for musicians and minor recording companies. He emphasized that the time has come for us to stop. However, the public seems skeptical about the efficacy of the ministry's campaign, as several similar attempts were made before, and only in vain.

Q. Which of the following is correct about the passage?
(a) The ministry has eliminated copyright infringement regulations and laws
(b) There was an incident recently where a musician was accused of infringement
(c) There is controversial debate on the severity of punishment for copyright infringement
(d) The ministry's previous campaigns have been largely unsuccessful

21. Scientists are always looking for ways to produce more efficient renewable energy. One method that is currently under examination is a technology that utilizes banana skins to create explosive chemicals, which can be used in internal combustion engines. However, the widelyfarmed types of bananas were found unfit for this purpose. They were initially grown for its sweeter taste, which lead to the excess sugar in the banana skin interfering with the chemical distillation process. To counter the problem, scientists in the field have been breeding a new kind of banana called hydroboxylic-chlorobanana which tastes horrible, but can produce up to seven times more chemical fuel.

Q. What of the following is true according to the passage?

(a) Scientists are improving ways to make bananas taste horrible

(b) Banana skins are providing efficient renewable energy around the world

(c) A special species of bananas is being developed in order to facilitate fuel production

(d) The excess sugar in the banana skin lead to easier extraction of chemicals from it

22. In the northern lands of Skyrealm, archaeologists have discovered a gigantic Nordic ruin called Anjarvunde with an unprecedented amount of Nordic jewelry in it. The archaeologists claim that the ruin was a temple used by the Jarvundarr People, an ancient Nordic tribe that thrived around 110 CE. The ruin was found to contain mummies, which were booby trapped with explosives upon the opening of the ruin, attacking the excavation team, and several other defense mechanisms which caused a number of fatalities. Despite the loss of a few archaeology graduate students, it is a common opinion that the Nordic marvel is a discovery of the century.

Q. Which of the following is correct according to the passage.

(a) Jewelry was the only thing that the Anjarvunde ruin had inside it

(b) The Jarvundarr People flourished around late second century CE

(c) Graduate students were among the fatalities of the excavation

(d) Archaeologists are not yet sure what the purpose of the ruin was

23. Making room in your home for a new feline family member is not that difficult. Three simple tips are all you need. First, prepare a cozy surface made of sand that coagulates upon urination. Second, prepare some toys that catch the attention of your pet. Interestingly, balls of yarn are a form of attraction for all animals whose ancestry can be traced to the tiger. Third, always try to get a variety of snacks prepared. Eventually you will get to know which one your new pal enjoys the most.

Q. What can be inferred about cats from the passage?
(a) They are typically not used to sleeping on sand
(b) They are attracted to all forms of thread
(c) They possess a picky appetite regarding snacks
(d) They are categorized into the same group as tigers

24. Point of Explosion 2 is a sequel to the blockbuster Point of Explosion. When first released in China, it was banned from all but three movie theaters in the capital. Even this was a major step forward for Chinese cinemas from times of blocking anything foreign. Protective of its proud culture, so much wariness existed when came to deciding whether an alien cultural form could enter the country. Let's just say that even Chinese officials who hate Hollywood could not resist the temptation of seeing two of the greatest action stars of this generation on screen.

Q. What can be inferred about the movie from the passage?
(a) Chinese parochialism is not a big concern for Hollywood
(b) The majority of movie theaters in China are concentrated in the capital city
(c) Chinese officials are starting to change their attitude on foreign influence
(d) China is respectful of action blockbusters regardless of its cultural barrier

25. The term 'absolute poverty' refers to people living on less than $1 a day. It is not an exaggeration to say that almost an eighth of the human population fall into this category. Anthropologists have pinpointed Sub-Saharan Africa as having a high concentration of such people. The people of this region are known to starve on a regular basis and are deprived of the most basic medical care. Numerous NGOs and acclaimed figures are imploring the world to step up and take action.

Q. What can be inferred from the passage?

(a) The African continent is well-known for its impoverished population

(b) $1 is not a paltry sum of money to live on

(c) Anthropologists are interested in demographics involved in this phenomenon

(d) The Sub-Saharan Africa is in desperate need for aids and subsidies

26~27 Your article seems to exaggerate the failures of the United Nations to adequately resolve global issues. But is this really true? Occasional mishaps and delays in carrying out operations hardly represent "structural failure", as you put it. Don't forget that the United Nations succeeded in helping numerous nations develop as we can see from the example of South Korea. South Korean democracy was able to flourish thanks to the assistance of the United Nations in the Korean War. It also contributed to the rapid economic development of South Korea.
The United Nations conducts operations more successfully than individual nations. It also plays a humanitarian function, criticizing and sanctioning governments that violate the human rights of their citizens. The least we can do is to appreciate the vital roles that the United Nations is playing.

26. Q: What is the writer mainly trying to do?
(a) Acclaim the role the United Nations is playing
(b) Draw attention to the development of South Korea
(c) Contest the humanitarian function of the United Nations
(d) Criticize governments violating human rights

27. Q: Which statement would the writer most likely agree with?
(a) South Korea assisted the United Nations to develop
(b) The democracy of South Korea requires more improvement
(c) The failure of the United Nations stems from criticisms from governments
(d) The United Nations enacts missions more effectively than individual nations

28~29 Will:

Hi Emily,

I was just curious because I couldn't get back from you and consequently was worried. Last Monday I sent some flowers to your address, with a letter asking you if you'd be my date to the graduation prom. But not only did you not give a reply, you even missed school for a whole week, so I couldn't ask you in person. But above all of that, I heard about your sudden illness. Are you okay? I was so shocked from hearing this that I couldn't concentrate on anything. Please let me know if you're okay.

Emily

Hi Will,

I really don't know what to say, because I thought the letter and those flowers were for Anna, my sister, and didn't open them. You know, since she's pretty and popular. Sorry for the late answer, I am very honored to be your date to the prom ^^. About missing school, I got pneumonia and I had to stay at home. It's nothing serious. I'm fully recovered now! I'll be at school from next week. Thanks for worrying, Will. See you at school!

28. Q: Why did Emily not answer Will's date-to-prom request?

(a) Because she didn't like Will

(b) Emily couldn't attend the prom due to pneumonia

(c) She already had a date to the prom

(d) She thought the presents weren't hers

29. Q: What can be inferred from the conversation?

(a) Will is a very attractive person

(b) Delivered flowers were usually for Anna.

(c) Will will be going to prom alone

(d) Emily has been sick for months

30~31 I knew that books and language arts would be my thing ever since I was in middle school. My parents and academic advisors have always applauded my distinguished competence in composing prose, but now during the university admissions seasons in which I have clearly stated my affection in the liberal arts, their attitude has changed, saying that I should study more practical fields like engineering or economics. According to them, a penman will have a hard time establishing a stable income.

I wholeheartedly understand their concerns since the literary world is not a field that guarantees high returns or huge merit. But many people around me have managed to find value in exercising their flair for literature, and that's what I am keen on as well. The publishing sector and analytic vocations are in the scope of careers that I can incorporate my writing skills in. So, while I know that I will always take into account what my parents have to say about my career, I solely have to think for myself and value my priorities hoping that they support me nonetheless.

30. Q: What is the writer mainly writing about in the passage?

(a) Her views on career choice that diverge from her parents

(b) Her parents' ambition for her career as a successful writer

(c) The difficulty of choosing a major when applying for university

(d) The possibilities of finding a job with a degree in liberal arts

31. Q: Which of the following is correct about the writer?

(a) She is having a hard time deciding between majors

(b) Her parents believe studying literature will not pay much

(c) She has connections with few writers who work in their chosen field

(d) Her highest priority is living up to her parents' wishes

32~33

Psychology Today

The vast field of psychoanalysis led by Sigmund Freud in the early 20th century deals with observation and analysis of the human mind. Its main concern is what is known as unconsciousness, and through analyzing various involuntary actions, it aims to thoroughly understand psychological diseases and consequences. Psychoanalysis has triggered further researches on human behavior in relation to the deeper mind, and is considered to have contributed greatly across diverse fields of study. But a new theory came into the spotlight by strongly rebuking the preexisting one, saying that psychoanalysis puts psychology into a shockingly nonscientific sphere, and that psychologists as scientists should only focus on objectively observable behaviors. The term 'behaviorism' was coined for this new paradigm by John B. Watson in 1913.

Behaviorists mainly claim that any human behavior can be attained through appropriate adjustments to circumstances, and therefore delving into one's innermost mind is unnecessary. In behaviorism, the extrinsic factors are more responsible for one's actions rather than intrinsic ones, such as dreams or unconsciousness. There are two types of behavioristic models: classical and operant conditioning. Classical conditioning is more widely known by the Pavlov experiment. By repeatedly exposing a dog to a stimulus(a bell), Pavlov succeeds in associating the formerly neutral stimulus with a reward. While there still are criticisms about its lack of reference to the mental process, behaviorism is also acknowledged and studied as an influential branch of psychology.

32. Q: How does behaviorism differ from psychoanalysis?

(a) It denies the existence of unconsciousness.
(b) It focuses on more external features of human actions.
(c) It does not aim to cure mental diseases.
(d) It claims that involuntary actions are of no importance.

33. Q: Which of the following is correct about behaviorism?

(a) It associates various human actions with the mental state.
(b) A stimulus as in the Pavlov experiment is the only way to observe human behavior.
(c) It suggests human behavior is always due to circumstantial conditions.
(d) It completely overcame the attacks of its opponents.

34~35

Predicting the future

Underlying all business decisions is the process of predicting a future event. This process is called forecasting. Forecasting methods assume that the past will influence the present due to the stability in the system. There are several types of forecasting such as the Delphi method, moving average method, and linear regression.

While forecasts are seldom perfect, they play an important role in preparing future business strategies. Yes, it is true that forecasts could be costly and time consuming. Nevertheless, it provides an opportunity for the company to prepare the adequate number of products and services to cover the potential numbers of customers. Successful forecasting also leads to cutting down on unnecessary expenses such as inventory costs.

34. Q: What is the passage mainly about?

(a) The different types of forecasting methods

(b) The positive effects of forecasting on the company

(c) How forecasting methods have evolved throughout time

(d) The debate on whether forecasting is effective

35. Q: Which of the following is correct according to the passage?

(a) Business decisions are based on 100% precise planning.

(b) Some forecasting methods are better than others.

(c) Forecasting, if successfully done, can result in more products being stored.

(d) Although forecasting doesn't provide the exact numbers, it is a helpful way to prepare for the future.

제4부
실전 모의고사

독해 실전 세트 #2

연습문제

 우선 30~40초동안 문제를 먼저 풀어보세요

1. HawkVision, the most advanced technology on the market, is here to increase the impartiality in a tennis match. Using 8 ultra-high speed cameras which are installed around the tennis court, the cameras are always prepared to keep the game fair for the players and fans and to relieve the umpires of pressures of making difficult decisions. Combining the visions from all 8 cameras, the movement of the tennis ball is recorded and a 3D video image is downloaded in a database which can be shown immediately on the electronic scoreboard. The HawkVision allows ______________________________.

(a) the umpire to prevent a player from cheating
(b) the umpire to keep the players from injuries.
(c) the game to be carried out fair and square.
(d) people to see tennis games in max 8 courts.

2. A lot of inventions and technology that people use on a daily basis ____________________.
For example, the post-it note paper was not something that the developers first had in mind. Originally, they were trying to create a powerful heavy-duty glue, but a newly hired assistant mistakenly mixed in the wrong chemicals which produced glue that would barely stick paper together. Ironically, however, that failed invention became insanely popular when it was applied to a note paper which made it possible to easily attach and detach from all surfaces without residue.

(a) weren't expected to be profitable
(b) are from developers of the post-it notes
(c) were expected to rake in money
(d) are from serendipitous discoveries.

3. A new advancement in technology has major paper companies struggling to make ends meet. We live in the digital era, where everything from books to formal contracts are produced and stored electronically. Whereas people had to carry heavy paperback books or documents in paper form in the past, everything now fits perfectly inside electronic handheld devices in the form of digital files. As more and more people are starting to buy E-books or electronic books, experts claim with some certainty that paper books ______________________.

(a) are becoming more popular than ever before
(b) are no different from e-books
(c) may become obsolete very soon
(d) are products of human ingenuity

4. During this year's budget review meeting, the student council president noticed a critical flaw that ex posed ______________________. While going through last year's financial records related to allocation of club funds, she recognized that sports clubs received over 70 percent of the total budget, despite the fact that they only account for about 15 percent of total clubs. This forced cultural and religious clubs to operate solely based on the private funds collected from the members.

(a) an unfair distribution of club funds
(b) a need to augment the overall budget for club activities
(c) an abrupt change in the school's budgetary policy
(d) incidents where certain clubs were unilateral shutdowns

5. Culinary touristy is an innovative technique of travel in which tourists focus solely on the traditional food and cuisine of another region. Essentially, travelers mainly target the eatery rather than any other aspect of a foreign country. For example, a person visiting a South African province will visit local towns where they can experience ethnic food tastings or partake in cooking classes conducted by an original inhabitant. This traveling technique is not just a technique used by people who have professional training in the culinary field. It is ______________________.

(a) used as a way of experts gaining more knowledge in this area
(b) regarded as a traveling method that anyone interested in this field can enjoy
(c) best known for decreasing the difficulties that travelers experience
(d) used in enhancing the cooking abilities of chefs

6. Dear Senator Kim,
I have read your proposal you submitted to Congress last fall. With all due respect, however I disagree with your decision to allocate a number of parking spaces designated for solely female drivers. As a fellow driver, I believe that it is absolutely unfair and irrational. What I am most discordant about is that the number of female parking spots considerably exceeds the number of handicap parking spots. Policies like this will encourage radical feminism in the country. I sincerely ask you to ______________________.
Sincerely, Gil Dong, Hong

(a) reconsider your policy before this country becomes sexually biased
(b) enforce your policy to help female drivers
(c) make new parking spots designated for males
(d) suspend your policy until we hear the opinions of female drivers

7. The debut of the avant-garde filmmaker Stevie Collins and his film, Runaway Boys, resulted in the audience discovering a new realm in the topic of AIDS. Collins's ultimate goal of this controversial film was for people to alter their perceptions of AIDS patients. Instead of identifying this group of people as filthy and shallow-minded in their sexual relationships, they should be seen as no different from any other kinds of long-term disease patients. With no astonishment, his film has swiftly led to the argument in ______________________.

(a) the justification of prejudice against people suffering with AIDS
(b) whether this film appropriately deals with sexual relations
(c) which approach is better in treating AIDs patients
(d) the need for a complete change in the films dealing with AIDS

제1부
제2부
제3부
제4부

8. Our privacy on the internet is increasingly being invaded as technology is progressing. The emergence of various Social Networking Services has made it practicable for exposure of personal information to the public. Accessing a specific person's address or phone number in an incomparably short period of time is now possible for anyone using services like Facebook. This invasion to other people's privacy has become taken for granted by so many people that many people no longer find it rude or disrespectful to pry into other people's personal information. Unlike the past, ______________________.

(a) social networking services are available for all kinds of people
(b) people are vulnerable to fraud from social networking services
(c) privacy penetration has been perceived to be something natural
(d) there are more people joining into internet communities

9. There are several interesting facts about elephants. First of all, just like some people are left-handed and right-handed, elephants are also "left-tusked" and "right-tusked." Tusks are long, curved, pointed teeth that are next to their long trunk. The way to find out whether an elephant is left-tusked or right-tusked is to compare their lengths. If they are right-tusked, the right tusk is shorter since they use it more often. ____________, scientists discovered that elephants can communicate with other elephants that are very far away. They make sounds that travel over the ground, and other elephants feel this sound with their skin on their feet and trunks.

(a) Therefore
(b) In contrast
(c) For example
(d) In addition

10. Christiane Bird's account of the Al Busaidi sultans in Oman and Zanzibar during the nineteenth century is, she says, "a tale rich with modern-day themes: Islam vs. Christianity, religion vs. secularism, women's rights, human rights, multiculturalism, and a nation's right to construct its own destiny." In truth those themes are not quite so visible in The Sultan's Shadow as its author would have us believe, for despite her lucid prose and dogged research, the book never comes together into a coherent whole. ____________, it is an oddly arranged miscellany, some parts of which are exceptionally interesting, but she never manages to connect them to each other in a convincing fashion.

(a) However
(b) Therefore
(c) Instead
(d) Accordingly

11. There are several amazing signs that indicate it is soon going to be rainy. (a) For some people, right before raining, they may complain of agony in their backs and knees. (b) Also, birds fly at low altitude while frogs croak continuously over the night. (c) This is no scientific phenomenon but rather it's an empirical aspect that was observed from a long time ago. (d) On a rainy day, going outside would not be the best idea since the possibility to getting involved in an accident is much higher than what these aforementioned superstitions claim.

12. John Stuart Mill was exceptional philosopher who is treated as the person who completed the theory of Utilitarianism. (a) He was surely a prodigy, learning Greek at the age of 3, able to read Plato's 'The Dialogue' at 7, also reading convoluted Latin literatures at 8. (b) He started to study logic and economics at 12 and accumulated his own personal opinions about the abstruse subjects. (c) Usually prodigies have problems in their social life and Mill wasn't an exception. (d) The zenith of his studies was the time when he completed 'The Utilitarianism', which made people exalt Mill for a long time.

13. Police authorities have developed a new method that is effective in distinguishing fake identifications. Minors illegally forge a bogus ID mainly in order to get into bars and to purchase alcohol or cigarettes. These IDs seem legitimate to a naked eye, making it even harder for bar owners to spot. The government has come up with an authorized system, which recognizes the barcode on the back of an ID card, showing not only the general information and records but also a fingerprint for comparison. With the new technology, authorities are hoping to prevent the usage of fake IDs.

Q: What is the passage mainly about?
(a) How effectively the new system catches phony IDs
(b) The police authorities' efforts to arrest minors using forged IDs
(c) A fingerprint system that works well
(d) The introduction of a new system for catching fake identifications

14. Born in New York in 1915, the mathematician Jeremy Macbeth originally studied English literature at Harvard. Afterwards, he served in the US Army during the Second World War. As a lieutenant in the army signal corps, he gained experience in encrypting and decrypting transmissions. That was when he realized his talent in math. When the war ended, he went on to study math and cryptology. Professor Macbeth's prolific research in the field is very widely known today.

Q: What is the best title for the passage?
(a) Jeremy Macbeth's Military Service during World War II
(b) Jeremy Macbeth: How a Shakespearean turned into a mathematician
(c) Jeremy Macbeth's Unexpected Talent in Cryptology and Mathematics
(d) Jeremy Macbeth's Treason against Literature for Mathematics and Cryptology

15. When Guiltius II became the pope, he used art as an educational tool to propagate the divine wisdom even to the ignorant. He instructed the best craftsmen of the time to create sculptures and murals from the Bible. Thus were created the magnificent paintings in the Notre Dame de Montie-Python, and the masterful sculptures in the Baptistery of Saint Claus, both depicting the life and death of Christ. Such religious artworks acted as a method of teaching stories in the Bible even to the illiterate.

Q: What is the passage mainly about?
(a) Pope Guiltius II's use of artworks for religious purposes
(b) Pope Guiltius II's strong belief in educating the ignorant
(c) Pope Guiltius II's relations with religious medieval craftsmen
(d) Popo Guiltius II's achievements in the field of paintings and sculpture

16. The asteroid B-613 has a surface made up of highly rare elements, since it is constantly being bombarded with extreme cosmic radiation. An anomalous supernova nearby is spraying the asteroid with a powerful ray of energy, continuously converting rocks to uncommon matter. These elements usually have an extremely short half-life, and disappear immediately after they are created. On B-613, however, the rare elements are constantly fed energy, making it possible to sustain its unstable form. As a result, B-613 is the only known place in the universe where Doloresumbridsium and Albusdumbledorium can be found.

Q: What is the main topic of the passage?
(a) Elements on the surface of B-613
(b) The creation of rare elements in B-613
(c) The powerful radiation of an anomalous supernova
(d) The forces behind the unusual stabilization of rare elements

17. Confucianism is a philosophical system from 6th century China that has shaped the societal structures of many Asian countries since its inception. Although official Confucianism movements ended in 1905, its values and ethical philosophy are still deeply ingrained in most Asian societies. Focused on humanism, Confucianism preached values and virtues regarding how to respectfully treat other human beings. Among such values were loyalty, justice, honesty and respect. Filial piety was especially emphasized - it shaped not only family structures but also the Chinese legal system.

Q: Which of the following is correct about Confucianism according to the passage?
(a) It has only spread to other Asian countries in the recent past
(b) It reached the zenith of its influential power in early 20th century
(c) It valued respect and courteousness in an individual's conduct
(d) Filial piety is a concept developed to shape the ideal family structure in China

18. Khula trees, which are found in many parts of southern Africa, are disappearing at an alarming rate. The population has decreased from some 3 million trees to only about 800,000 in just 7 years. Experts say that the abrupt drop in population size was brought on by a rare type of fungus known as Anadara Chlymia. Once it settles in the roots of the Khula trees, this virulent fungus releases deadly toxins that disable the roots from absorbing water and other essential minerals from the soil. This causes Khula trees to dry out within a week.

Q: Which of the following is correct about Khula trees according to the passage?
(a) Their number has abruptly decreased by 800,000 in 7 years
(b) The overall demise of Khula trees is caused by human activities
(c) Toxins produced by fungus disrupt the influx of water
(d) It takes at least a couple of weeks for Khula trees to completely wither

19. The advent and popularization of the Internet have given birth to a phenomenon where more and more people are working from home. My sister, Jennifer Higgins, is a legal consultant at Goldberg Law Firm who only goes to work in her office twice a week; she works from home for the remaining three days. This allows her to take better care of her children and to manage house chores effectively. One interesting aspect of this phenomenon is that employees that frequently work at home recorded a much higher level of happiness at work. To me, there is clearly a link between the two.

Q: Which of the following is correct about the writer of the passage?
(a) She claims that an economic boom allowed more people to work from home
(b) Her sister spends a majority of her working days at home
(c) Single mothers would benefit the most from this phenomenon
(d) She suggests that people working from home are mostly unskilled workers

20. Tomorrow will be the last day for our 3-day bus tour of Washington, D.C. We will depart at exactly 9:00 am, so please check out from your hotel rooms at least 15 minutes before departure. We will arrive at the Smithsonian Museum of Natural History at approximately 10:00 am. You will be given 4 hours to view the museum. Please have lunch during this time as well, since we do not provide lunch. We ask that you return to the bus prior to 2:15 pm. At 2:20 pm we will head back to Philadelphia. We estimate that the bus ride home will take no more than 4 hours.

Q: Which of the following is correct according to the passage?
(a) The bus tour will start tomorrow
(b) It will take 15 minutes to get to the museum from the hotel
(c) At 2:15 pm., 4 hours are allotted for the museum tour
(d) The tour bus will return to Philadelphia by 6:20 pm

21.

Dear Ms. Baker, On behalf of the admissions committee, it is my honor and privilege to share with you that you have been admitted to the Johnson School of Business at University of Southern Georgia. Congratulations! I could not be more excited to welcome you to USG. Please know that we take your Early Decision Agreement very seriously and we expect you to enroll at USG, providing you are financially able to do so. You must both confirm your enrollment and withdraw all other applications by March 15. Failing to follow all the required steps will result in cancellation of your acceptance to Southern Georgia.
Sincerely, Jane Porter Assistant Vice President of Admissions

Q: Which of the following is correct according to the letter?
(a) Ms. Baker sent a letter to the University of Southern Georgia
(b) Ms. Baker has already sent the confirmation letter on March 15th
(c) University of Southern Georgia expects confirmation of enrollment before March
(d) Ms. Baker's acceptance will not be admitted if she fails to meet the deadline

22. As a response to growing fear against leak of radioactive matter in Japan, the Japanese government introduced a new measure to install radiation detectors in some major cities like Tokyo and Fukushima. The policy was announced in order to relieve anxiety of Japanese citizens, who believe the radiation level is at life-threatening stage. Some experts mentioned that radiation levels in major cities are not as high as people believe them to be, and that the fact is greatly exaggerated. Nevertheless, installation of these detectors is hoped to eliminate any potential danger that might occur and resolve doubts Japanese people have on the government.

Q: Which of the following is correct according to the passage?
(a) The Japanese government is planning to install radiation detectors in every major city.
(b) New safety precaution measures have been implemented to soothe citizens' fear
(c) Experts revealed that the radiation level is especially threatening in major cities.
(d) The new policy has resolved trust problems between the citizens and the government

23. The Environmental Protection Agency (EPA) released a large number of horned toads into the Ingoen Forest. It is the intention of the Agency to use the toads to preserve the Ingoen ecosystem, as a large number of giant mosquitos have been spawning without any formidable predator. Hundreds of toads will be feasting on the vampiric insects to return the habitat back to its original state. Many environmentalists predict that the forest will not only be healed of its bug problem but that the toads will also facilitate plant growth, as their dung has been found to have fertilizing properties.

Q. What can be inferred from the passage?

(a) All toads are eco-friendly through their lifestyle

(b) Giant mosquitos have been ravaging the natural landscape

(c) The Ingoen Forest is irreparably damaged right now from predator attacks

(d) The toads are an invaluable influence for revive the forest in numerous ways

24. A raging debate was on for 2 hours in front of 400 spectators for the KKI Debate Championship. Both the opposing teams went over the most salient aspects of the issue, weighing the important arguments of the two sides and the meaning of happiness to humans, which was thought to be a difficult subject for teens. However, the audience was gripped with tension as the two sides kept rallying back and forth with remarkable logic, tenacity and elegance. Even after two weeks, viewers claim the contest gave them something to think about happiness.

Q. What can be inferred from the article?

(a) The crowd was given the chance to vote for the winner

(b) Happiness is of utmost importance to one's quality of life

(c) The tournament was unexpectedly dazzling compared to their age group

(d) The viewers were engaged to participate in the debate and even after

25. During the 20th century the world was torn apart by war. The Second World War, with the greatest number of casualties the world had ever seen, was more than just a military battle between two sides. It was a conflict of political ideals, from conservative to radical. In the end, repressive government structures saw their downfall and gave way to the spread of democracy and capitalism. In a way, the World War II set the stage for the contemporary world that we see today.

Q. What would the writer most likely elaborate on next?

(a) The development of ideologies up to the present times

(b) Major political wars after World War II

(c) The influence of capitalism on the global political system

(d) The most influential politicians of this era

26~27

Open call: Auditions for "Wicked"

Broadway Korea is seeking actors and actresses for this year's special spring musical, "Wicked". Currently the following roles are open:
Elphaba: Conditions- Female, Age between 20-34, any ethnicity
is expected to play a character in her 20s. The "Wicked" witch. Born with emerald-green skin. She is intelligent, passionate, sincere, sensitive, sympathetic, and has great talent for magic and sorcery. Looking for an actress with a powerful, high-belt singing voice. Will have to prepare 3 songs.
Fiyero: Conditions- Male, Age between 20-34, any ethnicity, height of 5'11" or taller
is expected to play a character in his 20s. The handsome, sexy "Prince Charming". Initially, being a self-absorbed snob, he is attracted to the kind, Glinda. However, his relationship with Elphaba later on changes him. Needs a strong physique and a powerful tenor pop/rock singing voice. Will have to prepare 2 songs.
2 people will be selected for each role, with one person being the main actor and the other being the understudy (a back-up actor that takes the main's place in case the main actor cannot perform on stage due to an unexpected situation). All main actors will be paid 3 million won per show, and all understudies will be paid half a million won per show. If the understudy happens to substitute the main actor, he or she will be paid equally as the main actor.
Send your applications to apply@broadwaykorea.com

26. Q: How many songs does an actress applying for Elphaba have to prepare?
(a) Two
(b) Three
(c) Four
(d) Five

27. Q: Which of the following is correct about understudy position actors/actresses?
(a) There will be four of them selected in total
(b) They do not have to audition
(c) They are there for situations where main actors cannot perform
(d) Even if they do not perform, they are paid half as much as main actors.

28~29 In 1903, Wilber and Oliver Wright performed a stunning feat at Kitty Hawk, a coastal town located in North Carolina. Utilizing giant spruce wood and fabric to create the first airplane, the Wright Brothers named their craft 'the Flyer' and successfully initiated four short flights. Many spectators described the sight as breathtaking.

Initially, many people disregarded the claim of the Wright brothers that they had created a functioning aircraft as a blatant lie. It was not until credible sources such as the media started reporting about the successful flight of the Wright brothers that people began to believe the Wright brothers. So how did they manage to build the first aircraft? When the Wright brothers finally revealed the design of their aircraft several years later, the secret was revealed. The aircraft was comprised of several sections: an engine, numerous propellers, and a movable rudder. To support the weight of the aforementioned components, the Wright brothers designed immense wings larger than 500 square feet.

28. Q: What is the passage mainly about?

(a) The first aircraft built by the Wright brothers
(b) The lies spread by the media regarding 'the Flyer'
(c) How to build an aircraft
(d) A method of building planes pioneered by the Wright brothers

29. Q: What can be inferred from the passage?

(a) The aircraft designed by the Wright brothers was very dangerous
(b) The design of 'the Flyer' was initially kept secret
(c) The engine had to be modified because it was too heavy
(d) The media did not want to report news about 'the Flyer'

30~31

Editorial: Wage disparity between men and women in the workplace

Comments

I agree with your claim that the wage disparity between men and women in the workplace should be solved through new legislations forbidding the discrimination of women. Oftentimes women are paid less for equal amounts of labour. Congress agrees that this is a grave issue as all members of congress approved a law banning companies from committing wage discrimination. Now, all companies will be obligated to pay women and men equal wages for the same amount of labor.

Although this is a positive change, the law has drawbacks that you have not mentioned in your editorial. To begin with, it only focuses on discrimination against women inside of corporations. Discrimination occurs in diverse environments like the household and school, but these environments are all neglected by the new law. On top of that, simply obligating companies to pay equal wages does not focus on changing the negative social perception of women. Forcing companies to pay equal wages does not mean that society will start to perceive women as equally capable workers. If we truly want to solve discrimination in society, all these issues should be addressed.

30. Q: Which of the following is correct according to the letter?

(a) Corporations have been paying women less money for the same labor

(b) Some members of congress dissented to the law

(c) Companies are the most discriminatory environments for women

(d) The new law solves discrimination in all environments

31. Q: What is the main purpose of the letter?

(a) To understand why women are being discriminated in the workplace

(b) To criticize the editorial's stance on the implementation of the new law

(c) To point out insufficiencies of the new law on wage discrimination

(d) To encourage the government to help mitigate discrimination

32~33 CONNECTICUT- Starting this April, be ready to pay more at New England Museum. Executive members have agreed upon a rise in fees ranging from $2 to $5, with the biggest blow to tourists who need translation. The increase in exhibition fees will go to funding a new maintenance program in order to take better care of and preserve museum property.

Even though there is a visible surge in fees, New England Museum will still remain as the third lowest priced museum of its size in the States. As of now, exhibitions fees cost a maximum of $10 for special exhibitions, $ 8 for regular exhibitions, and $2 for renting translation modules; and guided tours cost $ 15. After May 31, those will increase to $13, $10, $7, and $18, respectively. But gift shop prices will not change, and visitors can still take advantage of the free brochures that are available to everyone.

Response to such forecasted price changes are ambivalent. Helen Lee, who regularly goes to the museum's monthly special exhibitions has admitted that the three-dollar increase has come to be a new burden in her hands. On the other hand, some museum goers like Tom Chang welcome this change. According to him, the increase in fees will lead to higher quality exhibitions in the long run since the museum will focus more on preserving property.

32. Q: Which of the following will NOT be changed?

(a) The rate for renting translating devices

(b) The price of brochures in the gift shop.

(c) The special exhibition fee

(d) The regular exhibition fee

33. Q: What can be inferred from the news article?

(a) New England Museum lacks demand for guided tours.

(b) The decision could lead to a decrease in translator rentals.

(c) The decision to increase fees was decided in a majority vote by board members.

(d) There are not as many visitors in special exhibitions as in regular ones.

34~35 In 1913, the Russian composer Stravinsky made pandemonium in the Theatre de Champs Elysees with his new *Rite of Spring*. The ballet piece, was not like any of its predecessors. It was loud, and disturbing. Stravinsky was a renowned and distinguished artist of his time, and he was aware that his composition had potential to completely trigger public protest. And that is what happened-*Rite of Spring*, when first played in Paris, created a huge fuss and was publicly denounced in the media.

While the majority of people hated Stravinsky's new work, some found it fascinating. These people started arguing for *Rite of Spring* under the grounds that it enkindles an intrinsic sensation that can't be seen in the Nutcracker or Swan Lake. This dispute between scandal and revolution led to popularization of the work into the limelight. *Rite of Spring* was exalted as the initiator of a new movement in the musical industry, which led to a new dimension of diversity of expression. Today, this piece is Stravinsky's most influential and frequently performed piece.

34. Q: What is the main topic of the passage?

(a) How *Rite of Spring* led to the ban of Stravinsky's music
(b) Why Stravinsky hesitated the production of *Rite of Spring*
(c) Why some initially received *Rite of Spring* negatively
(d) How *Rite of Spring* eventually started a new age of music

35. Q: What can be inferred about *Rite of Spring*?

(a) *Rite of Spring* was not premiered in Stravinsky's motherland.
(b) Most of the public enjoyed the initial performance.
(c) Public protest ultimately led to the ban of Stravinsky's music.
(d) Stravinsky had ambition to start a new age of music with *Rite of Spring*.

제4부
실전 모의고사

독해 실전 세트 #3

연습문제

우선 30~40초동안 문제를 먼저 풀어보세요

1. One of the first color movies was shown on the big screen in France in 1934. The title of the movie was House and one of the most famous actors of all time, Jack Sparrow, starred in it. Due to lack of technology and financial support, House did not display spectacular lights and actions that movies nowadays do. However, colors on the big screen were a sensational shock to movie goers then, to whom black and white movies were the norm. As a result, the movie topped the film charts for more than a year. House definitely is ______________________.

(a) one of the worst movies in cinema history.
(b) comparable in its qualities to the blockbusters of these days.
(c) a masterpiece for the great actor Jack Sparrow.
(d) a milestone in the business of Cinema.

2. It is a common misunderstanding that establishing many relationships with people can help one in overcoming an illness. In fact, it has been found in a research that what is more important is ______________________. The research was conducted by Amie Song, a distinguished professor at Harvard Medical School in Massachusetts. According to Song, although having numerous relationships might seem to help the patient at first, shallow relationships and meetings eventually leave the patient with a sense of futility, thereby worsening the illness. Having a deep and intimate relationship with even just one person can greatly increase the chance of overcoming an ailment.

(a) the level of medical support one is receiving.
(b) the will to overcome the sickness.
(c) having friends to cover for one's medical expenses.
(d) the depth and intimacy of the relationships.

3. As a leading company in space travels, Easy Space now provides civilians with opportunities to travel into space. With our ion-propelled rocket engine and launch platforms in 30 countries around the world, you may start your travel to the moon in less than a day. All the technology and equipment have been certified by NASA and the highest level of safety is guaranteed. Contact our travel agent now ______________________.

(a) to find out how many civilians traveled to the moon
(b) why ion-propelled rocket engines are better than fossil fueled ones
(c) for advice to creating your own rocket engines
(d) for a quick and safe trip to space

4. Cadets chosen as members of the Bluerock Project are ______________________. Moving in secrecy to effectuate higher orders is the ultimate target of the Bluerock Project, and all constituents are asked to please render themselves to fulfill this motion. The individual policies and agendas on proper comportment will be stated in the confidential files accessible to only the cadets involved. We command all cadets to heed by the orders. Without exceptions, violations of the policies will result in expulsion.

(a) provided with financial aid nationally
(b) obliged to abide by the edict
(c) free to trespass the headquarters with an authorized identification
(d) required to follow highly confidential governmental orders

5. Mehlenbacher's Human is a book that ______________________________.
The objective of this publication is criticism on the stereotypical assumption that humans are all self-centered. With reference to Hsun-tzu and Hobbes, Mehlenbacher refutes the points claimed both in the oriental and western society. Mehlenbacher also descriptively explains the social background that led to concluding human's nature in a misconstrued way.

(a) is acknowledged for its political views on moral characteristics
(b) sarcastically ridicules human's fundamentally good nature
(c) uses metaphors to portray about egocentrism
(d) contradicts the misconception of human's innate personality

6. Last year, the Supreme Court finally ruled "bullying" as a criminal offense, prompting more draconian rules against bullying in high schools. Not only physical violence but also verbal abuse and cyber bullying can be prosecuted under the new law. This means that school administrators and teachers must now report to police authorities when confronted with a case of bullying. This has, however, resulted in a phenomenon where schools ignore cases of bullying, fearing that they may damage the school's reputation. For such reasons, the Ministry of Education is considering ______________________________.

(a) a policy allowing schools to handle bullying cases by themselves
(b) a surprise police visit to all high schools across the country
(c) to lower the rate of cyber bullying in schools by conducting a scan of school computers
(d) the expulsion of students who are bullied

7. There are many ways to ______________________. Any small helping hand is actually a huge contribution. You can erase the blackboard before the start of each session. You can also make sure that all the technological equipment is in order. Even simple acts such as these will be a great help to your classmates and your teacher and will thus be highly appreciated.

(a) give help to your teacher
(b) get involved in your classroom setting
(c) get along with your classmates
(d) earn the respect of your teacher.

8. Up until the First World War, also known as the Great War, people still considered war to be a glorious thing. Many texts and books from that time, 1914, suggest that people were actually excited with the beginning of a war. People saw this as a chance to show that they were washed away from their selfishness and wanted to show patriotism and dedication for their country. However the brutality of this war changed this conception and so ______________________.

(a) war became something to be feared rather than looked forward to
(b) war was the symbol of energy and glory
(c) World War 2 broke out soon after
(d) more and more people enlisted in the forces

9. Many educators are finding that touch-screen computer tablets are opening up new ways of interacting with their students who have special needs. In particular, educators are finding that they can more easily use images to communicate with their students. ___________, they can now easily store a large library of images that they can quickly browse through and display to the students.

(a) In sum
(b) For instance
(c) Moreover
(d) Meanwhile

10. Archaeological excavations in southern Turkey recently brought to the surface a magnificent marble statue depicting Emperor Marcus Aurelius. Renowned as a popular leader of the empire during the second century, the discovery has prompted many to ask: what was Marcus Aurelius really like? Hollywood famously fictionalized the emperor in 2000 for Ridley Scott's Oscar-winning epic Gl adiator; ___________, the true life of Marcus Aurelius elicits far more interest than the character portrayed by the late Richard Harris.

(a) nevertheless
(b) thus
(c) likewise
(d) moreover

11. In the midst of wild controversies about the Ministry of Gender Equality, we must keep in mind the ultimate goal they seek. (a) Pursuing harmonious coexistence of work and family, the Ministry strives to develop a tight relationship between family members. (b) In this way, they not only represent the females but fight extensively for peace of society. (c) It is unfortunate to see the traditional values of family and harmony debased and de-emphasized and the Ministry scolded by the media. (d) In response to the rise of individualism and the constant competitive atmosphere, they work to give something special back to social minorities and families.

12. Even though luxuries are exorbitant, people have several reasons to justify their consumption. (a) First, some claim that the luxuries they carry on their body is somewhat a representation of their wealth. (b) Others may derive extreme satisfaction while concentrating on their ostentation. (c) Obviously it has been a long time since the people started to care about what they put on, spending massive amount of money on extravagances. (d) Finally, people who are sensitive to fashion claim that the high price is strongly correlated with fashionable and high-quality items.

13. One of Percival Anthony's bestselling novels, Helen's Mistress, was released in 1926 and instantly became the bestseller across the United States. In many ways, it is a reflection of the author's trauma, an epitaph that commemorated an innocence lost. Together with the pessimistic atmosphere of the time during the Great Depression, its stark portrayal of a dreadful and morbid childhood attracted many sympathetic readers.

Q: What is the main topic of the passage?
(a) The socio-historical context of the success of Helen's Mistress
(b) The factors that contributed to the release of Helen's Mistress
(c) The overall atmosphere of the United States in the 1920s
(d) The common theme of Percival Tumbledoor's novels

14. The 1938 fluoric acid containment breach wiped off 30 different species of plants and animals in the town of San Bronzino, providing the first actual evidence that fluoric acid leakage can cause devastating damage to the regional flora and fauna. "It was a disaster", one witness of the incident said. "The green fields suddenly turned into a lifeless wasteland". Our investigation conducted in the area revealed that the area is still heavily contaminated after nearly a century since the incident, leading to pessimistic predictions on whether the region will ever be able to recover.

Q: What is the best title for the passage?
(a) An Investigation into Catastrophic Chemical Breach in San Bronzino
(b) Preventing Ecological Damage due to Fluoric Acid Containment Breach
(c) The Oldest Evidence of Chemical Breach Causing Ecological Damage
(d) A Drop in Regional Species Count due to Fluoric Acid Breach

15. Holi, also known as the Festival of Colors, is the Hindu religious festival that is widely known for the use of colored powders. Colored powders being thrown at each other represents the celebration of spring and a new beginning. Contrary to recent reports on the usage of chemically produced industrial dyes, people still extract natural pigments from flowers and leaves for the coloration of powder. Due to its religious background, people preserve the old tradition of applying turmeric, sandalwood paste, or extracts of plants. Following the custom of utilizing natural resources adds another reason to why Holi is a sacred religious ritual as well as a festival with joy and excitement

Q: What is the main point of the advertisement?
(a) Holi is celebrated at the start of the new season
(b) Natural colors have been continuously used since the past
(c) Colored powders were labeled as synthetic due to environmental reasons
(d) Flowers and leaves contain color pigments

16. With the advent of New Year, people are determined to follow their New Year's resolutions. From losing twenty pounds to learning a foreign language, various goals are set with a sense of hope and motivation. The plan is somewhat unrealistic, however, if the goal is too broad or not organized in a detailed manner. In epitome, "losing weight" sounds way too vague to achieve, in which a person might be overwhelmed even before the start. To prevent such happenings, one should come up with concrete ideas to materialize the plan. "Going to the gym at 7 A.M." or "eating more vegetables instead of junk foods" is more realistic. It is indeed always better to have details in actualizing the goal.

Q: What is the writer's main advice for achieving a goal?
(a) The importance of objective cannot be highlighted more
(b) Specific details impede an individual's success
(c) Be strict to oneself in keeping personal promises
(d) Detailed plans are necessary to accomplish goals

17. The newest paragliding ride program offered by our camp is beyond imagination. With each ride down the mountainside a rider can experience 10 minutes of total excitement, view nature of all kinds, and gain a greater insight into life. Riders can also choose to fly alone without aid from the professional at the flying camp with additional costs and training hours. Please contact us for further details.

Q. Which of the following is correct according to the advertisement?
(a) It takes less than 10 minutes to finish the flight course
(b) It is hard to view nature during the flight
(c) Flying without a teacher is not an option
(d) Riders can choose to fly alone with additional costs

18. Before enjoying yourself at our amusement park there are many different precautionary measures that riders should pay close attention to. Always keep your arms and feet inside your seats at all times and never attempt physical contact with your friends at any time after takeoff. Also, since many rides include dropping from great heights, riders with health issues related in any way should refrain themselves. It might also be helpful for first time riders to get on the ride with experienced users for guidance along the way.

Q. Which of the following is correct according to the instructions?
(a) There are times when putting your hand out of the ride are tolerated
(b) Health issues do not deter riders from getting on certain rides
(c) There are not many rides that include dropping from great heights
(d) It may be helpful for first time riders to ride with an experienced person

19. The discovery of the United States typically starts with Christopher Columbus's voyage to the Americas in 1492. Even before the arrival of the European colonists, European colonists from England began to settle in the American lands. With the arrival of more than 10,000 settlers, the first successful English colony was established in 1607 at Jamestown. Between 1622 and the Revolution the British government sent more than 50,000 convicts to these American colonies reaching the peak at 1624. In that year, the Native Americans decided to start a bloody war against the English government.

Q. When did the American settlers decide to start a war?
(a) 1492
(b) 1607
(c) 1610
(d) 1624

20. The Green Environment Film Festival (GEFF) is an internationally acclaimed film festival that is held by Green International. As one of the relatively new internationally funded festival, the event gathers many different professionals in the field of environmentalism. On a yearly basis the festival renews its collection of the most recent films or documentaries on environmental protection and presents them to an audience for up to 30 minutes in duration. Those wishing to submit a proposal of their film should submit a two page report with an examination fee of $10 to GEFF headquarters by April 10th.

Q. Which of the following is correct about GEFF?
(a) It is a festival privately subsidized by corporations
(b) It shows movies longer than half an hour in duration
(c) It take place on April 10th
(d) It receives new movies for presenting every year

21. Eskimos or Inuit-Yupiks are indigenous people who have previously inhabited the lands of Eastern Siberia, Alaska, Canada, and Greenland. These people are well known for protecting themselves from the cold weather at all times. Using bricks and sand to build stiff walls, the Inuits were able to keep warm during any type of weather and shield themselves in times of sudden showers and snow. Their households were usually located away from waters. Given the unavailability of technology these house are viewed as a marvel by many.

Q. Which of the following is correct about the Innuit people according to the passage?
(a) Living near water sources kept them warm
(b) Their buildings were able to keep the heat especially during winter
(c) Their living quarters were constructed partly from sand
(d) They were respected for little use of tools in their daily lives

22. Some companies have amazing ideas that should be supported and funded properly, but the company may not be large enough to afford the necessary costs. That is where the National Startup Support Foundation Bank steps in. Through our government-approved subsidies, ambitious new entrepreneurs across the nation can realize their dreams. We provide funding based on potential commercial success and social contribution. Applications are open to all companies and individuals with a net yearly profit of less than 100,000USD.

Q. Which of the following is correct about the foundation according to the passage?
(a) It provides funding for companies of all sizes
(b) It provides amazing business ideas to startup companies
(c) It subsidizes firms from all around the world
(d) It helps relatively small entrepreneurs with financial support

23.

> To Whom It May concern:
>
> As a fan of certain celebrities, I was greatly dejected at the fact that Amanda Williams was harassed the other day at her own residence. These celebrities are victims of intimidation from their own fans! The definition of being a fan does not mean stalking and aggravating the celebrities, but rather enjoying their presence. Because of these psychotic behaviors demonstrated by certain individuals, genuine fans are looked upon in a demeaning manner. In other words, I have fallen victim to the generalization of 'fans' because of a minority. Those people who have harassed celebrities need to be dealt with immediately.

Q. What can be inferred about the author?

(a) The author is an avid fan of Amanda Williams

(b) The author is fully aware that stalkers are an inescapable problem for celebrities

(c) The author thinks that being a fan justifies behaviors similar to a stalker

(d) The author is annoyed at the stereotypes people have acquired about fans

24. Oil prices have shown a gradual increase over the past few years. The reason for this is because the supply of oil is limited while the demand is rising. It does not help that frequent wars in the Middle East have made oil supply inconsistent and volatile. As a result, coming next week, the price of oil is predicted to hit a record $130 per barrel. Given the high level of dependency on oil, the situation is causing a nationwide panic. The nation depends on the government to alleviate this crisis through policies such as new trade agreements and renegotiations with the Middle East.

Q. What can be inferred by the writer?

(a) The writer believes that inflation cannot be dealt with in the current situation

(b) The writer claims there exists an excess supply for oil in the Middle East

(c) The writer is concerned that government inaction could debilitate the nation economy

(d) The writer does not regard oil as a necessity in today's economy

25. Possibility of water in existing in Mars is widely strengthened after the recent photos and samples taken by the satellite, Curiosity. These photos contained topography and matter similar to that of Earth. Further examinations are being taken for more proof on this, but for example, the soil found in Australian grassland has shown identical features to a particular sample of the land on Mars. The similarities of the two match up to as high as 67% regarding texture and quality. Such a high percentage substantiates the fact that there could possibly be water on Mars. Soon we may be able to find a new source of water, an indispensible resource for all of mankind.

Q. What can be inferred about the author of the passage?

(a) The author is an avid believer of scientology

(b) The author knows that there are life forms other than those on Earth in the universe

(c) The author believes mankind should make Mars a new habitat

(d) The author is hopeful that Mars contains water

26~27

Recruiting Skilled Personal Shoppers

Fashion evolves at a breakneck speed and catching up with the trends is harder than ever. At Barneys, we are deeply committed to ensuring consumer satisfaction, and our new Personal Shopping department is an innovative venture in such efforts. As this is a brand-new step, the job will not be an entirely easy one. Nevertheless, we remain firm in our vision for this ambitious launch, as well as the abundance of qualified candidates out there.

If you:

- Love Barneys' bubbly mood and all our little quirks
- Are passionate about shopping and fashion
- Have an eye for would-be trends
- Enjoy giving fashion advice to others
- Are a people person who likes to bond

Then this is the job for you!

26. Q: Which of the following is correct according to the passage?

(a) There are currently many employees working in the Personal Shopping department.
(b) The store doubts there will be a large pool of potential personal shoppers.
(c) The Personal Shopping department aims to facilitate shopping for customers.
(d) The store mostly deals with retro fashion.

27. Q: What can be inferred from the passage?

(a) The store has a negative opinion on fast-changing trends.
(b) The store will only accept candidates who have shopped at Barneys.
(c) Many other stores have already implemented a personal shopping service.
(d) The position may require personnel to establish rapport with customers.

28~29 Are you looking for job experience in marketing, advertising, or public relations? Do you consider yourself to be driven and committed? Prepared to hustle hard for success? Then join us at AEHS Associations for an internship!

This is an ambitious break from AEHS tradition, since previously it was something of a principle that we do not hire employees on a temporary basis. However, we have recently embraced new and more progressive ideas along with our global expansion, including this innovative launch of our very own intern policy. Through this new step forward, we aim to achieve mutual growth for both prospective interns and AEHS. In other words, we offer opportunities to develop for aspiring youths, and we have no doubt that this new blood will be advantageous to the corporation as a whole.

To apply for our internship, please fill out the attached application form. We also enclose an example for a CV, which you may utilize. You are required to submit the two documents along with an optional cover letter by June 15th. Questions should be directed to our human resources department at hraehs@aehs.com.

28. Q: Which of the following is correct according to the announcement?

(a) The company offers internships for all of its departments.
(b) Interviews will take place before June 15th.
(c) It is the first time for the company to recruit interns.
(d) A cover letter is mandatory for application.

29. Q: What can be inferred from the announcement?

(a) The company focuses on marketing as its central department.
(b) The company's human resources department is irrelevant to the internship.
(c) Interns will be assigned to the company's global branches.
(d) The addition of interns to the workforce will be beneficial to the company as well.

30~31 Not many people are aware of the fact that Charlotte Brontë was once known as a man. It was because she used the pen name Currer Bell when publishing her works, so as to be taken as seriously as her male contemporaries. Nevertheless, she did not want to entirely forsake her femininity. This resulted in her gender-ambiguous pseudonym, instead of a positively masculine one like some other woman writers of her time.

Today, Charlotte Brontë is considered one of the greatest British writers in her own right. Although the Victorian era was extremely oppressive of women, Brontë is one of the many females who refused the obfuscation of her identity based on gender. Regardless of gender, Brontë is an excellent role model to many in that her story encompasses both hard work, independence, and dedication. This persona recurs in many of her works. Her most famous novel, *Jane Eyre*, is especially known for its eponymous female protagonist's independence and strong will.

30. Q: What is the passage mainly about?

(a) How Brontë became known as a woman writer

(b) The influence Brontë's gender had on her writing career

(c) Why Victorian women were often successful

(d) The reason for Jane Eyre's popularity

31. Q: What can be inferred about Brontë from the passage?

(a) Jane Eyre is an autobiographical characterization of Brontë's own personality.

(b) She used her own name to publish Jane Eyre.

(c) She only wrote novels, preferring them over any other literary genre.

(d) She was the first to write about female oppression during the Victorian era.

32~33

Growing Concerns Over the Olympic Games in Paris 2024

Paris was recently named as the host of the 2024 Olympic Games. Despite the cheerful atmosphere, there are growing concerns over the games. Mark Antonio, project manager of Greenpeace International emphasized the need to realize that there may be long-lasting environmental harms after the Olympic games. The Saint-Montagne Marie, a forest that has been preserved for over hundreds of years is planned to be partially cut down. "The destruction of the forest may result in aggravation of air pollution and extinction of natural animals", says Antonio. "The short-term economic benefits may actually lead to further expenses in the future because the reconstruction of nature is something that cannot be easily done."

Currently, protests are going on in front of the city hall of Paris but they lack in number to process an official petition. While 3000 signatures are needed to submit an official petition, only 40% of the requisite is fulfilled for now.

32. Q: How many signatures are needed in addition to submit an official petition?

(a) 1000
(b) 1500
(c) 3000
(d) 6000

33. Q: What is NOT a reason for the concerns of Mark Antonio regarding the Olympic games?

(a) It may result in destruction of the eco-system in Saint-Montagne Marie.
(b) The problem of air pollution may become exacerbated.
(c) It may lead to future costs in the future.
(d) The signatures needed to submit an official petition is lacking.

34~35

Hannah:
Hey, Mark.
As I told you at our last lunch, I've turned in my two weeks' notice last week. So, I've been quite busy looking for new career opportunities. I would love to talk to you in person before I leave. Why don't I take you out for lunch at our favorite spot, maybe this Friday?
I do feel torn about leaving XYZ. It was my first job, and I learned a great deal working here. Of course, I know that my time here is over and that I should move on. Still, I'll miss my colleagues, especially you.

Mark:
Hi, Hannah.
How are you doing? I remember you expressed concerns about looking for a new job. Do you know Lucy from Accounting? She used to work here at XYZ but left a few years ago to pursue a completely different career path. I'm sure she'd have useful advice for your circumstances. Let me know if you'd like to consult her on your current situation.
Just the thought of being on the job hunt again is daunting to me. However, I understand that you've been contemplating this career move for a while, and I'm sure you'll find a more fulfilling position. And by the way, I'd love to meet up for lunch this Friday. I'll see you then.

34. Q: Why did Hannah send the message?
(a) She wants to meet Lucy for lunch.
(b) She wants to introduce her favorite restaurant to Mark.
(c) She wants to meet her colleagues on Friday.
(d) She wants to say goodbye to Mark before leaving XYZ.

35. Q: What can be inferred from the conversation?
(a) Hannah and Mark had lunch last week.
(b) Hannah is satisfied with her current career path.
(c) Lucy earns more money at her current job.
(d) Mark will continue to work at XYZ.

제4부
실전 모의고사

독해 실전 세트 #4

연습문제

우선 30~40초동안 문제를 먼저 풀어보세요

1. Freidberger & Parks has always been number one in providing the optimum financing and investing solutions in consulting programs of internationally prominent corporations and organizations. We have an incomparable databank and the utmost consultants to give you the best services and finance solutions for strong- holding your company. Whatever you desire, from professional help forming adroit strategies to financial management of your company, you can count on Freidberger & Parks. Contact us now ______________________.

(a) to make an appointment with our manager
(b) to register for an orientation regarding recruitments at Freidberger & Parks
(c) for unerring tactics on vested interests in operating your corporation
(d) for more information on the international companies and organizations we work with

2. In the 1930s it was difficult for Korean students to learn their own native language. South Korea was colonized by Japan and many students were forced to conceal their Korean identities and embrace Japanese names. Learning their native language was out of the question. Students using Korean would be harshly punished and sometimes expelled. It is no wonder, therefore, that Koreans became very sensitive to learning Japanese these days. They understood ______________________.

(a) the sad history of language use in Korea.
(b) the importance of learning foreign languages.
(c) the history of military conflicts.
(d) the importance of being bilingual.

3. The National Basketball Association is finally getting serious about ______________________. Roy Hibbert of the Indiana Pacers was fined $20,000 the other day for the use of swear words and insults against sports reporters during a press conference. Kobe Bryant was also fined a substantial amount of money by the league last month after belligerently undermining a reporter. The biggest fine in league history, however, was issued when Ron Artest of the Los Angeles Lakers punched a sports reporter for 'crossing the line'. The NBA hopes that the series of fines will somewhat help restore peace to the league.

(a) protecting the reputation and safety of sports reporters
(b) regulating what players say in public
(c) educating its players to have better manners
(d) collecting money from its players

4. Dear Gloria,
Amsterdam has been great so far. There are so many places to see and so many places to take photos that I feel like I never have enough battery left on my phone. By the way, there was one queer experience during my stay at the Hotel of Opera. The name sounded interesting since I have always been a huge fan of opera. However, the reason for its name was because apparently there is a huge opera house adjacent to the hotel, hence the "Hotel of Opera". As a result, I was barely able to sleep from all the loud noises from the venue. Next time, I will make sure ______________________.

(a) learn more about Amsterdam
(b) take more photos when I visit a new city
(c) go to a hostel instead of a hotel
(d) research in advance and never assume

5. It was found in a research that children mingle and interact differently when ____________________ ____________. Children perceive and treat their peers in rather different ways. Conversing and solving problems together is preferred and they also study on their own less frequently in comparison to adults. In addition, because children are less competitive than adults, they see each other as companions rather than competitors.

(a) at night than they do during the day
(b) being taught by an adult
(c) having conversations while studying
(d) studying in groups than adults do

6. I, James White, on behalf of the townspeople, ____.
A recent research conducted by a team of urban engineers revealed that the new construction by I&C Company will greatly affect the local ecosystem. The parking space planned to be built would be placed over an area of Atwood Woods, meaning that the construction will require lumbering of the precious Sequoia trees. These trees are indispensable as they play the most important role in keeping the nearby ecosystem healthy. Anyone who wants to support the petition is asked to please sign it at the city hall before July 25th.

(a) ask for a transfer of the Sequoia Trees
(b) demand that the new trees be planted in town
(c) am joining the I&C Company to help with the construction
(d) appeal an official petition over the new parking lot

7. Andrews, our international law firm ________________. That is because we recognize that our client may have been wrongly discriminated and the future of an individual might depend on our performance in court. Furthermore, our law firm has a very low acceptance rate of clients, only accepting those who are truly innocent yet suffering. When it comes to defending our client and deliberating on what rights have been exploited, our law firm is impeccable. Without doubt, we will continue to endeavor to remain as a global guardian of those in need. Andrews-the law firm for the world.

(a) has been growing upon remarkable winning records
(b) protects rights at a lower expense than competing firms
(c) offers a comfortable environment for clients
(d) is unquestionably the ideal agency for victimized citizens globally

8. Funafuti spear illustration developed among Tuvaluans during the Paleolithic age. Since then, people have engraved the ancient legends of the Tuvaluans on their sacred spears. Therefore, the study of spear art can unfold the anthropological aspects of the Funafuti culture and history. Indeed, a number of recently unearthed spears were useful in drawing clues to the anthropocentric backgrounds. For example, they contain intricate depictions of its major gods that held considerable significance. Because of their distinctive traits, Funafuti spears ________________.

(a) show the number of different tribes present then
(b) stand for people's natural yearning to leave records of their history
(c) represent the importance of spears as weapons
(d) offer some insight into the Tuvaluans' lifestyle

제1부
제2부
제3부
제4부

9. Memories about one's past have a crucial influence on one's present.1) Often, the most painful and crippling memories are those from a person's childhood,2) since that is the time when a person's identity is being formed. Some people may still be haunted by an embarrassing incident that occurred during their school years. __________, a memory of being made fun of as a child can do permanent damage to one's self-image.

(a) Nevertheless
(b) Besides
(c) Indeed
(d) However

10. Recent developments in genetic research have unleashed a world of potential that is simultaneously exciting and disconcerting. As a result of new gene splicing techniques, researchers are now able to create hitherto unknown forms of life. Advocates maintain that gene splicing will one day benefit humans in areas such as agriculture, as it allows for the development of more nutritious grains and more productive livestock. __________, gene splicing remains a contentious practice in scientific circles, as many experts counter its supposed boons to humanity by underscoring its indeterminate liabilities.

(a) That being said
(b) In consequence
(c) That is to say
(d) In summary

11. Throughout the whole year the exhibition that embodies the world's eminent philosopher's ideas into concrete substance is taking place in Seoul. (a) It will be a new challenge for the hosting institution to convey the abstract meanings to the audience. (b) World renowned modern philosophers such as Jirou De Jour, will be present to briefly greet the spectators. (c) In each and every corner, there will be guides who will help people to understand some knotty works. (d) Prominent modern philosophers such as Shin Hyeong Seon, Yurike Siman, Bruno Holy Junior collaborated their concepts in order to elevate the modern philosophy to the next level

12. Working out on a regular basis is likely to decrease the possibility of getting infectious diseases. (a) People who work out periodically somehow get infected by virulence insects or animals. (b) It is scientifically proven that people who work out at least 3 times a week have lower blood pressure compared to the people who do not. (c) The oxygen that an individual inhales while working out annihilates the malignant virus. (d) Deep respiration while exercising is the key factor of getting rid of infectious diseases.

13. Individuals, schools, and societies are gearing toward practicality over true interests or talents. Due to financial reasons in relations to one's future job opportunities, career and income, people choose fields of study that can lead to a "decent, high-paying job". As a result, the studies of engineering, business administration, and medicine are preferred to the fundamental studies of physics, linguistics, and history. The perpetuation of the trend will weaken the cornerstone of all studies and even the research and development of various sectors. Thus, the society will become imbalanced, and ultimately its overall growth and advancement are hindered.

Q: What is the main idea of the passage?
(a) Academic institutions should provide more support for opportunities of advancement
(b) Detrimental societal impacts are expected due to extensive curricular of fundamental studies
(c) The tendency to focus on practicality will result in negative repercussions
(d) Studies that can be easily applied in the real work environment should be emphasized over those that cannot be applied

14. Consumption of animal flesh has been a part of human diet from the dawn of humanity. Consequently, it has become a significant aspect in the establishments of cultures and languages. Religious practices have long since been associated with the consumption of meat, like the Abrahmic tradition of butchering animals in the Halal or Kosher method. The etymology of various types of meat is also entangled with our history. The English words representing the meat of cows, pigs and sheep all correspond to the French terms for the animals themselves, like beef from the French boeuf, pork from porc, and mutton as in mouton.

Q: What is the main topic of the passage?
(a) The influence of meat in human culture
(b) The consumption of meat from early history
(c) The words associated with meat in English
(d) The necessity of protein from animal flesh consumption

15. It is a well-known fact that Tasty Mango Islands will face a drastic increase in their population over the next century or so. However, as UNICEF official Abdul Hassukh pointed out, that is not a fact that we can be optimistic about. The lack of land and social infrastructure in the islands will make the country face a grave challenge handling the increase in population. By 2050, the population of Tasty Mango Island is expected to reach 10 million. In the small landmass of the islands, there would only be 1.44 square meters of space per person. That means the island will literally be full of people, unless the government reacts with appropriate policies to counter the problem.

Q: What is the best title for the passage?
(a) Tasty Mango Islands, the Land of Tranquility
(b) Immigration Problem; What is the government doing?
(c) UNICEF Official Warns of an impending global crisis
(d) Rising Population Causes Concern of Overpopulation

16. Poaching can be an exciting and rewarding career. And there are all kinds of places to go poaching out there, away from the eyes of law. Poachers need to have sharp instincts to find wild animals and approach them without being detected, and also know when the police are coming for you. Do you have what it takes to become a poacher? Are you ready to live the romantic life roaming the African plains? Then, the Latchford Poaching Coaching will provide you with the training to become a professional poacher. Suitable applicants will join us for our trip to Serengeti late this year. Contact us now at 1544-7979 for more information.

Q: What is the main idea of the advertisement?
(a) Latchford Poaching Coaching offers a trip to Serengeti
(b) Poaching is a very dangerous occupation, which entails many difficult tasks
(c) Latchford Poaching Coaching is looking for suitable individuals to train as poachers
(d) Poaching positions open at Latchford Poaching

17. The game of chess is a popular board game played in high schools all around the world. The objective of the game is to command a set of individual pieces that have distinctive functions and capture the opposite player's most important piece - the King. Winning a game of chess takes a well-planned strategy; even a small mistake can jeopardize your chance of winning. In the end, victory comes to whoever can more accurately read the other player's intentions and react accordingly. High schools encourage students to play chess because it helps develop a logical mindset associated with mathematical skills.

Q. Which of the following is correct about the game of chess?
(a) It is a computer game played all around the world.
(b) It is used in some schools to fight Autism.
(c) It teaches students to be artistic and imaginative
(d) It develops students' logical and mathematical thinking

18. A cause of the ice age has been controversial for decades and the debate still remains unresolved. Some scientists have claimed that volcanic eruptions triggered the ice age. However, other experts insist that volcanic eruptions, regardless of their size, can never cause the ice age. They argue that the ice age is instigated by tectonic plates which can be arranged in a position such that warm water flowing from the equator to the two poles is blocked or reduced. Today's ice age, experts assume, resulted when the land bridge between North and South America formed and ended the exchange of tropical water between the Atlantic and Pacific Oceans.

Q. Which of the following is correct about the cause of the ice age according to the passage?
(a) Many experts believe massive earthquake is the cause of the ice age.
(b) The cause of the ice age has already been revealed.
(c) There is few substantial support to the theory that plate tectonics caused the ice age
(d) Plates' blockage of warm water may have resulted in the ice age

19. Dear Mr. Cannon,

I noticed that you have failed to upload your assignment on the student portal before the deadline. Since you have not e-mailed me about giving an extension for the deadline, I cannot accept your assignment anytime from tomorrow. It is really unfortunate that I have no other option but to give you an F grade on this assignment if you fail to meet the deadline. This will obviously be a problem for any graduation plans. Please make sure to submit it by tomorrow

Sincerely,

Cory Koster Professor of Economics, Baker College

Q: According to the letter, what will happen if Mr. Cannon does not submit the assignment tomorrow?

(a) He will fail the assignment
(b) He will not be able to graduate this semester
(c) The deadline will be extended for a few more days
(d) He will need to visit the professor

제1부
제2부
제3부
제4부

20. In 1936, the Berlin Summer Olympics took place. At the time, Nazi propaganda promoted the superiority of the Aryan race and depicted Africans as inferior. To prove this, Adolf Hitler and other Nazi authorities had high hopes that German athletes would dominate the games. However, Jesse Owens, an African-American athlete competing for the United States, took home four gold medals which set a world record that remained unbroken for 25 years. Owens demonstrated to Hitler as well as the German people just how wrong they had been. This incident is still considered as one of the most significant happenings in Olympics history.

Q. Which of the following is correct according to the passage?

(a) Hitler considered Africans to be superior to the Aryan race
(b) Jesse Owens' record was unbroken for a quarter of a century
(c) German athletes beat Jesse Owens in four different categories
(d) Jesse Owens set four world records

21. The proverb "Treat others the way you want to be treated" is sometimes referred to as "The Golden Rule" and can be applied to many real-life scenarios. For example, I had to visit the emergency room at the local hospital last year when I broke my finger. There was a long line at the emergency room and I had been waiting for more than an hour. Suddenly, a man and his young son barged through the doors in a hurry. Evidently, they were on a fishing trip and the fishing hook got stuck deeply in the little boy's arm. Seeing that the boy was in a lot of pain, I told the boy and his father to go in ahead of me. At the moment I think I sympathized with the father and imagined what it would be like to be in the other person's shoe.

Q. Which of the following is correct according to the passage?
(a) The emergency room was vacant when the writer entered
(b) The writer was on a fishing trip when he broke his finger
(c) The writer allowed a little boy to see the doctor first
(d) The little boy's father had to beg to see the doctor first

22. In the past, it was believed that human activities had no effect on the global climate. In the last few decades, however, climate scientists have found that any human activity that emits carbon dioxide may contribute to a gradual change of the world's climate. They claim humans have raised the average temperature of the earth's atmosphere by 1 degree Fahrenheit since the Industrial Revolution. This seemingly miniscule amount was enough to devastate farmlands and even small islands. Such findings have resulted in a change in the public's opinion on how to treat the environment and gave birth to numerous environmental groups, such as Greenpeace.

Q. Which of the following is correct according to the passage?
(a) Human activities and global warming are hardly correlated
(b) Carbon monoxide is the root cause of global climate change
(c) It has come to light that humans are to blame for many recent environmental damages
(d) Groups like Greenpeace are striving to change public opinion about global warming

23. The ironic relationship of wars and economic development has been demonstrated fairly consistently throughout history. In actuality, after a country declares war, job rates, economic development, and the wellbeing of citizens that didn't go to war have been enhanced. In other words, after a country engages in war, many have become more affluent. A well-known example is the United States. During the Great Depression in the US, widespread starvation and a rise of gang activities were rampant. However, after participating in World War II, the USA has become one of the superpowers of the world. Nevertheless, people will always question the legitimacy of war even if the economy develops

Q. What would the writer most likely agree with?
(a) The USA engaged in war in order to end the Great Depression
(b) Consistent historic data proves war is beneficial to a nation
(c) After a war, the economy suffers more than before going into war
(d) Economic development only is not enough to justify war

24. Stem-cell research was a new, but yet highly controversial field of bio-science that brought about much debate about morality and ethics. However, incumbent US president Barack Obama removed the unexplainable ban that former US president George W. Bush placed on stem-cell experimentation, in the name of "promising research". He now funds this new field of bio-science that clones the human embryo and uses the duplication in order to create new, but identical organs for the irreversibly sick.

Q. Which of the following statements would the author most likely agree with?
(a) He is not very enthusiastic about the new policy change
(b) He would like the US to be a leader in bio-science
(c) He is probably for stem-cell research.
(d) He is overly religious

25. A recent study indicates that educational complacency in American schools can be very dangerous. According to the research, only the top quarter of America's kindergarten to 12th grade students are performing on par with the average students in Asian countries. Experts point out that this gap in academic achievement was first found at the beginning of the 21st century, and has been growing larger ever since. Lawmakers now believe that educational reform is of utmost importance. The US has gone too long in being overly confident at its children's academic performance.

Q. What can be inferred from the passage?

(a) America cannot afford to be satisfied with the education they receive
(b) Asian students are gifted with great educational systems and policies
(c) Half of America's students do not receive the education they deserve
(d) Recent findings indicate a severe worldwide problem in education

26~27

Juice of the People, by the People, for the People

Here at Juice for You, we aim to serve our local community to the best of our ability. Having Started out as a little street vendor downtown, we would not be here without the support from all of you. Of course, our primary focus is to serve healthy and nutritious juices to our customers day to day. At the same time, we wanted to support the local farmers and contribute in sustaining our local economy. That is why we stick to using fruits and vegetables sourced straight from the local farms.

Some people criticize that our juices are not for everyone. We acknowledge that everyone leads different lifestyles, and one company cannot satisfy everyone's needs. Furthermore, Juice for You believes in the idea that every little bit helps. Again, our objective is to do the best we can to bring a positive impact to our community. By working directly with the local farmers, we hope to support our wonderful community as it has done for us.

26. Q: Which of the following is correct according to the passage?

(a) Juice for You cannot sell juice on the streets.

(b) Serving the local community is a core value at Juice for You.

(c) Juice for You believes that one person cannot help effectively.

(d) Juice for You has its ingredients delivered from corporate farms.

27. Q: What can be inferred from the passage?

(a) Juice for You regularly hosts community events.

(b) Juice for You buys fruits and vegetables from local markets.

(c) Juice for You knows that its products may be unappealing to some people.

(d) Juice for You is the only beverage shop focused on the local community.

28~29

The Charmington Post
Editorial: Spring Cleaning for City

Comments
Laura Stevens / 6 hours ago
The *Charmington Post* is infamous for its lack of sensitivity in town matters. When the officials decided it was time to get rid of the local stray dog shelter, the one-sided newspaper leapt to defend them, saying that the shelter had been "derogative to the town's overall image."
I can't believe how such a charitable facility could be so depreciated by authorities. What I can infer is that the officials' main interest is the real estate values, and that they think these kinds of establishments negatively impact the local land prices. Although the shelter in question is well out on the outskirts of the town, some people still do not seem to be satisfied.
How can The *Charmington Post* be so cold-hearted on this issue? Has the newspaper decided to abandon all sense of empathy? Is there anything to gain on the newspaper's side if land prices rise?

28. Q: What is the main purpose of the passage?
(a) To criticize the newspaper for miscalculating the losses the stray dog shelter would bring to Charmington
(b) To reproach the newspaper for being unsympathetic of the locals
(c) To stress that general selfishness is overshadowing the town's sympathy
(d) To encourage the newspaper to support charitable issues

29. Q: What can be inferred about Stevens from the passage?
(a) She regularly receives copies of The *Charmington Post*.
(b) She does not think that The *Charmington Post* is compassionate.
(c) She has been ill-disposed towards the town officials since their employment.
(d) She will sell her residence at Charmington shortly.

30~31

Guidelines for Submitting Videos>Deadlines and Submission Fees

Early Deadline: Feb 28, 2018
Election Promotion: Free
Hometown Introduction: $100
Free Topic: $250

Official Deadline: April 6, 2018
Election Promotion: Free
Hometown Introduction: $200
Free Topic: $350
Submission Policy
- Please note that all free topic videos must include an explanation on the chosen topic.
- We will not accept overly violent or controversial content.

Should you have further inquiries, please email Kevin Lindon at kev38@cemc.com.

30. Q: What would be the submission fee if you submit a video of your pet cat on March 30, 2018?
(a) Free
(b) $150
(c) $250
(d) $350

31. Q: What can be inferred from the guidelines?
(a) The guideline suggests that submissions cannot be retracted.
(b) You are eligible for submission regardless of date.
(c) Mr. Lindon will send all inquiries to the host committee.
(d) The host committee hopes to encourage promotion of the upcoming election.

32~33

Changes in Main Library Entrance Permissions

As our school members may already be aware, our main library has and is constantly meeting requests to open up to the public. Many are of a view that the school ought to share its extensive amount of data.
The school understands the need to contribute to the greater good of the community. Then again, securing enough material and space for our own students and faculty members should be the school's foremost objective.
After careful consideration, the school has settled on the following adjustments of rules:

- Visitors who are former staff members with over five years of service to the college can now register for honorary membership, which grants free access to all services of the library.
- Visitors whose family members are currently studying at the college can now receive a 50% discount on public membership fees.
- Visitors whose family members are among the faculty at the college can now receive a 60% discount on public membership fees.
- Visitors whose family members have made a donation of over $1,000 can now register for honorary membership.

32. Q: Which of the following visitors will be charged the most when applying for membership?
(a) Carl, who had worked at the college administrative office for 10 years
(b) Ruth, whose cousin is a professor at the college.
(c) Tylor, whose brother is a student at the college.
(d) Luke, whose grandfather have donated a sum of $1,200 to the library.

33. Q: What can be inferred from the notice?
(a) The college is famed for its insensitivity toward community issues.
(b) The college is particular about preserving their collection of rare documents.
(c) The college has made adjustments in the past.
(d) The public view was that membership fees were excessively high.

34~35

Changes in Bulletin Board Regulations

As you may already know, many students have been complaining that the bulletin boards around the college campus are too crowded and messy. Students are frustrated that they cannot find important announcements because there are simply too many posters and advertisements.

On the one hand, we are aware that individuals should be allowed to comfortably utilise the bulletin boards. On the other hand, our most important goal is to maintain the bulletin boards in organised fashion.

With that in mind, we will be implementing the following regulations regarding the usage of bulletin boards in campus:

- The bulletin board in front of the school gates cannot be used until next month for reconstruction
- Undergraduate students can post notifications on bulletin boards for 2 weeks at maximum.
- Graduate students can post notifications on bulletin boards for 3 weeks at maximum.
- Faculty can post notifications on bulletin boards for 2 months at maximum.
- Visitors can only post notifications approved by the school administrative board for 1 week at maximum.

34. Q: Amongst the following people, who can post notifications on the bulletin board for the longest amount of time?

(a) Connor, who knows a professor at the university
(b) Alyssa, who is a professor of Literature at the university
(c) Tina, whose mother is the mayor of this town
(d) Joan, who is an undergraduate student studying chemistry

35. Q: What can be inferred from the notice?

(a) The university has historically been hostile towards visitors
(b) The main goal of the university is promoting ethnic diversity
(c) University regulations concerning bulletin board usage can be swayed by student opinions
(d) Many students claimed that bulletin boards were too small

제4부
실전 모의고사

독해 실전 세트 # 5

연습문제

우선 30~40초동안 문제를 먼저 풀어보세요

1. Most armadillos ______________________________. When they are first born, their skin is soft and fragile which makes it challenging for them to protect themselves from predators. This makes their survival strenuous when they are young. However, as their bodies grow longer and wider about two or three weeks after birth, the armadillos form plates composed of bone and layered with horns. When a month passes and the plates are fully grown, they play a crucial role in the defense mechanism of many armadillos, and as they escape from predators into patches of thorns, they are protected by their armored plates.

(a) utilize escaping methods when faced with predators
(b) are able to attack the predators with their horns
(c) have no ability to catch prey
(d) lack ways of defense until they mature physically

2. During my stay in Lithuania, people's sensitivity in giving flowers as gifts was bewildering for me. The most idealistic way of giving flowers is sending an odd number of flowers in a wrapping of bright colors such as red and yellow, yet people seldom followed that traditional custom. Nevertheless, there was an incident in which I brought chrysanthemums for a party host and received unpleasant looks from him, which made me baffled. On another occasion, I had brought a bundle of white flowers for my friend's birthday, and only realized afterwards that white flowers are strictly reserved for weddings. Giving flowers as gifts ______________________________.

(a) was very helpful when trying to acquaint with new people
(b) is deemed useful only for wedding occasions.
(c) requires a knowledge of several etiquettes regarding the act
(d) should not be encouraged for health purposes

3. Most people are aware of the fact that 'one-ingredient diet', a dietary plan based on only consuming one ingredient, is often times fatal to health. Luckily, experts in this field have derived a more effective yet healthier diet method that has been named the "penta-ingredient diet". Success stories on this new diet technique are currently sprouting from many different regions in the United States. The main idea of the 'penta-ingredient diet' is that five different food products should be chosen and consumed equally on a daily basis. When following this diet, people should ______________________________. For example, if a person chooses apples as one of their five ingredients, bananas should be disregarded as being another food product.

(a) focus on choosing the most filling ingredient
(b) understand how tiresome it is to start a strict diet
(c) give priority to fruits over others when choosing the five food products
(d) find each food product from different food criteria

4.

> Dear Sebastian,
>
> Why do couples always have to celebrate petty events like New Years Day or Valentines Day? I have a girlfriend that I have been in a relationship with for 2 years already, and I feel that such events do not truly reflect the love I have for the other person. In fact, those events are artificial, and do not demonstrate true affection. Never have I in the past celebrated such events with my girlfriend. It still upsets me when ______________.
> Is there a problem in thinking this way?
> Sincerely, Jack

(a) my girlfriend agrees with me
(b) my friends criticize me for not celebrating those events
(c) my friends say that Valentine's Day is artificial
(d) I receive presents from my girlfriend

5. ______________________________ has resulted from a chronological observation of different countries around the world. Social scientists have concluded that industrialization first began in Great Britain. During the next decade, usage of machines, which ignited the process of industrialization, spread to other European countries such as France, Italy, and Poland. Gradually, Asian and North American countries began to be industrialized as well, as they became colonized by European countries that had prospered and grown through industrialization. Today, most countries around the world are industrialized.

(a) The understanding of the development of industrialization
(b) Proof of increase in globalization
(c) The information cycle of industrialization
(d) Evidence that industrialization didn't occur in Asia

6. The article above summarizes the progress made in the United States to resolve the national problem of obesity. Some states have attempted to reduce obesity by introducing state-wide policies to implement low-calorie lunch programs in schools, which has successfully lowered obesity rates. However, smaller and low-budgeted states have found it too costly to introduce state-wide low-calorie lunch programs. Therefore, ______________________________.

(a) more research is no longer necessary for a solution
(b) high school and middle school students must cooperate
(c) funding is required in order to reduce obesity nationwide
(d) progress in decreasing obesity rates has been outstanding

7. Last year my Labrador was involved in a car crash that left his forelegs broken. Despite taking him to the veterinarian immediately, the damage was proven to be much too severe for treatment, leading to an amputation of both legs. We tried to make life as comfortable as possible for him, but it was simply too devastating to see him unable to walk. Therefore, after several weeks, we decided to euthanize him. Fortunately, we were told upon arrival that a new medical procedure could give him prosthetic legs. Although very costly and exhausting, the procedure was successful and now ______________________.

(a) our Labrador has been put to sleep
(b) our Labrador still has trouble walking
(c) our Labrador is enjoying his new legs, running around happily
(d) we have been compensated for the crash

8. Hats were a fundamental feature of male fashion for several decades in the Victorian Age, during which men had to wear chadors that covered the entire body except for the eyes. Hats acted as more than just a necessary item, however. Although men during this time were prohibited from expressing themselves because it would violate social principles, they could express emotions by wearing different colors of hats. In other words, men ______________________.

(a) wore only one type of hat
(b) who had no hats had only one way of expressing themselves
(c) from the Victorian Age wore colored hats
(d) utilized hats as a way of unique communication

9. Although the use of cell phones has exploded across the world, not all parts of the world use the technology in the same way. This is particularly true of text messaging. In Asia, __________, text messaging is being used for everything from sending and receiving payments to receiving medical advice. In North America, however, text messaging is still in its infancy.

(a) nevertheless
(b) for instance
(c) moreover
(d) in contrast

10. It has been a foregone conclusion for weeks that national high school basketball player of the year, Brandon Knight, would choose to attend the University of Kentucky. __________, it was no surprise when Knight donned a Kentucky cap on Monday, the first day of the spring signing period. Knight, a 6-foot-3 point guard who averaged 31.9 points and 8.6 rebounds per game for Pine Crest High School in Florida, chose Kentucky over Kansas, Syracuse, Connecticut, and Florida.

(a) Hence
(b) Granted
(c) Furthermore
(d) Meanwhile

11. Judith Butler's famous article about Rodney Uith, the Hispanic person who was beaten to death, was truly a sensational thing at the time. (a) Back in the 1870's Hispanics were never welcomed to America, and were frequent victims of persecution. (b) Right after the Rodney Uith case took place the atmosphere was cold-hearted toward the powerless Hispanics. (c) Sometimes history repeats itself making the wrong decision never able to restore the old glorified days. (d) However, Judith Butler's courage to publicize the unjustifiable atrocity was a monumental step in converting the prevailing atmosphere into a new phase.

12. Whenever a sports player gets injured during a game, certain protocols are to be strictly followed. (a) Immediately after an injury the first aid agents are urgently deployed into the field to examine the injured player on-site. (b) The abilities and stardom of the injured player is an important factor to decide the necessary treatment. (c) Severely injured players are carried out of the field or the court and carried to the emergency doctor room, which is in the stadium, for more detailed diagnoses. (d) After quick analysis, if the player is able to return to the game, the agents escort them to the field or the court

13.

> Dear Mrs. Thompson,
>
> With accordance to the Calculus class rules, I left my last Calculus exam paper on your desk for a correction. The syllabus said to leave the test in your office for any questions or mistakes. I have not altered any answers and it is in the same state as you handed out yesterday. My answer for question number 9 seems to pass as an alternative solution according to what the textbook elaborates on the equation. It seems that other students got partial credit for the alternative answer in which, for some reason, I was not able to receive. I would appreciate it if you would take a look at the problem and let me know if I could receive the credit.
>
> Sincerely, Tim Jackson

Q: What is the email mainly about?
(a) A request for full credit on the question
(b) A mistake made on question number 9
(c) An appeal for a re-scoring of the calculus exam
(d) A calculus test having intricate equations

14. Renowned psychologists and linguists have continuously researched the correlation of the human mind and language. Widely known as "The Power of Words," scientists have been proving how a simple change of words could lead to tremendous or unexpected transitions. In epitome, people simply ignored and passed by a blind man holding a sign of "Changes Appreciated" on the subway. However, as the blind man held up a new sign that says, "It is a beautiful day, but I cannot see it", people were moved by the inspiring phrase, donating their change and even large amounts of money to help the blind man.

Q: What is the passage mainly about?
(a) How the relationship between language and human psychology has led to a mishap
(b) The experiment done to a blind man on the subway
(c) The profound influence of donation on a person
(d) The display of Power of Words and its effect

15. Library and Information Science (LIS) is the combination of two fields of studies: library science and information science. It has first started as a professional training program then developed into a university-level academic institution amid the mid-20th century. Information, especially nowadays, is a crucial asset. Thus, the education of LIS cannot be highlighted any further. However, many scholars question the core concept of the field, some emphasizing computing and internetworking concepts and skills while others claiming that LIS is a social science requiring a mix of practical skills in ethnography and interviewing. The domain still seems open to debate.

Q: What is the best title for the passage?
(a) The importance of educating students with computing skills
(b) How interviewing affects the study of LIS
(c) The questionable nature of the LIS field
(d) The rise of information in the mid-20th century

16. Mitochondrion is undoubtedly the energy factory of all cells, including for both animal and plant cells. It has a tremendous influence on the cell growth and the control of the cell cycle. The process of respiration, using the oxygen to generate energy, produces adenosine triphosphate (ATP), a key element of the mitochondrion. Then, ATP is used as the source of chemical energy in which it enables the mitochondria to supply important cellular energy. Mitochondrion is also involved in other cellular activities, such as cellular differentiation, signaling, and cell death.

Q: What does mitochondrion mainly do?
(a) It helps ATP to produce oxygen
(b) It produces ATP, which is where energy comes from
(c) It has a tremendous influence on the birth and death of a cell
(d) It controls the cell cycle

17. Many nation economies around the world are suffering from the rise in stock prices. As a result, great fluctuations of imports and exports on both national level and transnational trades on an international level have been found. More specifically many multinational corporations are seeing a shift in power structures especially between trades between strong economies. Unable to reach a point of compromise in achieving advantageous trade, strong economies are increasingly moving in to developing countries in an attempt exploit their human labor and natural resources. Such attempts have seriously harmed not only the environment but also the standards of living in various developing countries around the world.

Q. Which of the following claims is made in the passage?

(a) The fall in interests has brought about many changes
(b) Strong economies are liable for some problems that are arising in developing countries
(c) Multinational corporations have not changed ways in which they are operating
(d) Developing countries have a way of defending exploitations of any kind

18. Paying close attention to the recent controversy of reverse discrimination of men, the story of Kim Il Dong in "Man's Rights" reveals how privileges offered to women such as women parking lots and lounges can be the driving force behind social inequality. The story is a single event that is interconnected with various events leading up to the death of Kim Il Dong. Told in first person narrative, the speaker is a fictional character who is a close acquaintance of Il Dong. Because of this setting, readers are able to closely relate with his views.

Q. Which of the following is correct about "Man's Rights" according to the passage?

(a) It illustrates the arguments behind women's rights
(b) It is based on the life of a women activist
(c) It is told from a first point narrative
(d) Its stories contain many different acquaintances of Il Dong throughout the story

19. Dear whoever it may concern, I am hoping to file an official complaint regarding one of my recent visits to your restaurant about a few days ago. A week before visiting your restaurant, the staff were fully informed of a marriage proposal that I was planning to make that evening. I was assured that everything would be set on order like clockwork. Despite another confirmation right before entry, the employees that followed soon after were not aware of such pre-orders and did not follow through with my plans. I hope future requests, something as important and serious as this one can be met with much attention and care by the restaurant staff in the future.
Sincerely, Joe Friedman

Q. Which of the following is correct according to the letter?
(a) The writer did not make his orders clearly to the restaurant manager
(b) The writer's intentions were not satisfactorily met by the restaurant staff
(c) The writer confirmed his request three times with management before dining
(d) The writer's marriage proposal later on was a success

20. The university Career Planning Center is inviting students of all majors to join us at the annual conference for young career planners. Seating at the conference is only available upon registration at the center's office. The university will be working cooperatively with the local government especially to provide insight into many jobs related to government and public administration. Attending students will also be offered the chance to directly converse with assigned mentors, employees of these institutions.

Q. Which of the following is correct about the advertisement?
(a) Only students of selected majors are able to attend this conference
(b) The seats are allotted on a first-come-first-served basis
(c) The conference provides practical job training and seminars
(d) The conference will be closely working with institutions of the public sector

21. The migration of American rock-raccoons is expected to cause great damage to the wheat farms this summer. The National Ministry of Agriculture (NAMA) claims that the newly distributed species of wheat has proven to repel harmful animals, but according to anecdotes of many farmers, it isn't as effective as they say. One farmer in Wheatfield County complained that about a quarter of his 200-acre farm was ravaged by raccoons, putting his expected harvest down to 400 tons this year. There are doubts, however, that the ministry will do anything to further counter the problem, as their budget this year was cut half by the Senate.

Q. Which of the following is correct according to the passage?
(a) NAMA has promised to issue the vermin problem
(b) The harvest last year was at 1600 tons of wheat
(c) Vermin damage has decreased significantly thanks to the new species of wheat
(d) NAMA has insufficient funds to do anything more about this problem now

22. The health of the city's residents is greatly influenced by the presence of small clinics, surprisingly more than large hospitals. Each small clinic contributes tremendously to the health of nearby residents by providing easy-access and friendly health checks, even when the clinics can only do so much for really sick patients. In the northern suburbs of Bedford, where there is one clinic per 50 people, only one in 4000 people have any severe illness. In the east downtown area, where there is no clinic within reach, there is a drastically higher number of sick people, even despite the fact that there is a huge hospital nearby.

Q. Which of the following is correct according to the passage?
(a) Large hospitals are less effective in preventing health issues
(b) Small clinics are distributed throughout the city of Cropsford
(c) The outskirts of the city has the least number of clinics within reach
(d) Small clinics are even capable of treating patients who are seriously ill

23. An examination was in need to assess the quality of the students wanting to participate in the internship program of a multinational corporation. The interviewers administered a test of two students that passed the initial assessment. The two students were extremely alike on paper, in terms of grades, experience and recommendation. In the final test, the perseverance and tenacity in handling pressure from customer sales was assessed. A notable psychological difference was discovered between the two participants, with one not being able to handle the pressure, while the other proficiently dealing with obstacles calmly.

Q. What can be inferred from the passage?
(a) The people who passed the initial test both possess experience as an intern before
(b) Only one spot was offered in the whole internship program
(c) Internship at the company is highly competitive amongst students
(d) Mental strength is a characteristic not well represented on paper alone

24. James Banks, the multi-billionaire, had lately donated $300 million for brain research to the Allen Institute for Brain Science. Such a huge donation enabled researchers to finally initiate the 10 year research plan to examine questions about Alzheimer's disease. The research is aimed at ultimately developing an effective cure. Already the Institute has made remarkable progress, unveiling some new technology for mapping the brain. The world's attention is focused on the long-term results from this funding by Banks.

Q. What can be inferred from the passage?
(a) Without the donation, the research plan could not have been established at this time
(b) The Allen Institute for Brain Science has been focusing on Alzheimer's
(c) Banks has donated the money with plans to take over the institution
(d) Even with some new discoveries, the world is skeptical about the donation

25. Canadian actor and director, Ray Maynard is most loved for his outstanding performance as "The Cop" in the movie: Life and Death. However, not many outside the United States know that the blockbuster movie was released six months after Maynard's death. As a prominent figure in the film industry, his death seems most unfortunate, having left the world many masterpieces even at a young age. Who knows what he would have accomplished if he were still alive today?

Q. What does the writer suggest about Ray Maynard?

(a) That Maynard's character was respected by many in the movie industry
(b) Maynard's directing was most noticeable in the movie Life and Death
(c) Maynard's death was from a tragic accident
(d) He left many potential legacies untold by his premature death

26~27 Dear Professor Hartmann:

I must first start out by mentioning how enlightening your lecture about philosophical discourses was. Humbled I was, when I noticed how shallow and petty my understanding of philosophical quotes and statements was. Although philosophy may not be my major, I am putting in full effort to catch up with other students. Philosophy really has its attractive aspects, in that it searches for the answers to deep questions like "What makes a human, human?" Some might call it a less-practical subject, but I have discovered the beauty in it.

As I mentioned above, your course "Philosophy and Me" had an immense impact on my perception of philosophy. All your lectures left me mesmerized, except your most recent one on last Monday. I whole-heartedly understand that the comparison between "practical" subjects and liberal arts tires you. However, I do not think that devaluing business and economics, calling them less-noble academia, was an appropriate way to respond to such accusations. Especially, since I am a student majoring in economics, I was very devastated due to the ever-occurring conflict and division between the two fields of study. Therefore, it would be much appreciated if you could formally address this issue and tend to the like-minded students.

Please try to understand the pain that us social-science major students would have had to experience sitting there throughout your lecture.

Sincerely yours,

Emily Kher

Economics major

West High University

26. Q: What is the main purpose of the letter?

(a) To express enthusiasm and admiration towards philosophy

(b) To notify her dropping out of class

(c) To congratulate professor Hartmann on opening the course "Philosophy and me"

(d) To express discontent regarding a statement mentioned in-class by the professor

27. Q: Which statement would the author most likely agree with?

(a) Philosophy is more valuable than other practical academia

(b) The professor should never teach philosophy again

(c) The professor should officially apologize and correct his words

(d) Economics is better than philosophy

28~29

Video Review

Invitation to the collaboration of photography and video

Chloe Antasiou is holding her third exhibition with the slogan "Floral Mystique." Chloe has already held two photo exhibitions prior to the upcoming event, each with different themes such as "Art of Stones" and "Illusion of Light." Although Chloe has been pursuing a prestigious career in the field of photography, she has always advocated the beauty of non-stationary media. Chloe is aware of the biggest limitation of photographs, which is that they cannot include details of the whole scene. That is why she actively participates in activities such as video-projects that focus on "movement".

Although specializing in photography, Chloe found a way to utilize her proficiency in the video industry. She made several videos using a technique called "Panorama". It is a method of assembling multiple images into one wide picture. A combination of these photo-compilations results in a panoramic video. Ms. Antasiou is sharing her talent and knowledge by collaborating with public advertisements, donation PR videos, and etc.

Her videos inspired a lot of people, and lead to a boom in the photography/ video-making major. Anyone interested in exploring more about photography and its different uses, should take time to watch Chloe's contribution.

28. Q: According to the passage, what is a Panoramic Video?

(a) An accumulation of Panoramic photos
(b) A sum of many stationary images
(c) Video taken by a photographer
(d) A video taken non-stop

29. Q: What can be inferred from the review?

(a) Chloe converted from photography to videography, thinking that the latter is superior
(b) Ms. Antasiou is a master of videography, and Chloe specializes in photography
(c) Chloe is the owner of a big video company
(d) Chloe acknowledges that photos are not enough to collect detailed portrayal of the world

30~31 Dear Mr. and Mrs. Carew:

Thank you for coming to the Parent-Teacher conference last Friday. I could see how much concern both of you have for your son Jeremy. As her advisor, I will always give my best in helping him construct his academic career. I am sure he will perform well throughout the school year. Not only is he capable of excelling his schoolwork, he is keen to help those around him and share his ideas.

I would like to once again stress that Jeremy is an exceptional student. He is on top of almost all of his classes, except mathematics. He seems to think that the subject is all about memorizing the various solutions to problems. However, one cannot truly understand math unless fully aware of the patterns and developmental logistics of concepts. Unfortunately, due to time constraints, I cannot force him to start understanding such relationships in mathematics. Therefore, I recommend that he start organizing the concepts he learns during class and then practice using them to solve problem sets.

If you wish to ask any questions regarding his education, feel free to email me at katherineg@catholichhigh.org.

Sincerely yours,

Katherine Gertrude

Mathematics Teacher

Catholic High School

30. Q: What is the main purpose of the letter?

(a) To show gratitude to Mr. and Mrs. Carew for helping in organizing the school's annual conference.

(b) To praise Mr. and Mrs. Carew for assisting Jeremy through his school year

(c) To thank the two for sending such a bright student to Catholic High School

(d) To give advice to Jeremy's parents on how to help him understand Mathematics better

31. Q: Which statement would the author most likely agree with?

(a) Jeremy's proficiency in his studies is curbing his efforts of making friends.

(b) The Carews must be aware of Jeremy's extreme potential in his schoolwork.

(c) Math cannot be understood just by memorizing solutions to problems.

(d) The teacher wants to have a second appointment since e-mail exchanges are not as effective.

32~33 Hi Emma,

Thank you for your email and yes, I'd be happy to give you feedback on your final essay. Overall, it was an excellent piece of work that examined the issues of gender, race, and class in the assigned material. You did a great job of reading the play A Streetcar Named Desire through the lens of the masculinity theory.

With that being said, I felt the direction of the essay strayed away from the requirements, which were to illustrate your understanding of the production, circulation, and consumption of American culture as commodity. And this is where points were taken off in the essay. For example, one way to do this could be to view the play as a cultural commodity and how it was received by different audience groups (such as race or class), or how it has been marketed in America vs. other countries. A closer reading and understanding of the prompt would have helped your essay.

If you have any further questions, please let me know. And keep up the hard work!

Best regards,

Karen J. Martinez, Ph.D.

Adjunct faculty at University of Texas, Austin

32. Q: According to the email, why have points been deducted?

(a) Because her analysis focused exclusively on the play's marketing strategy.

(b) Because it failed to be sufficiently analytical regarding the masculinity theory.

(c) Because her analysis of race and class was not what the professor required.

(d) Because it did not follow the guidelines of the prompt.

33. Q: What can be inferred from the email?

(a) Emma will probably revise her essay to receive a better grade.

(b) The professor directed her students to discuss A Streetcar Named Desire in their essays.

(c) Masculinity theory is a central aspect from which to study American culture.

(d) Plays cannot be considered as a cultural commodity.

34~35

Invitation to the 13th Annual Chicago Auto Show!

They say that finding your true destiny is one of the most important things in the world. As for men, we can say that finding the perfect car for ourselves is a lifelong goal. So, for all the men out there waiting for their long-destined 'babe'. we invite you to the 13th Chicago Auto Show!

The Chicago Auto Show, first staged in 1997, is one of the largest auto shows in the entire continent. We feature more than 1500 vehicles to suit all budgets ranging from the Morning to the Bentley. Starting from this Wednesday through Friday, everyone is invited to attend this fabulous event!

Tickets are available both at our website and show box offices. We offer the tickets on a great deal, only $14 for adults and $10 for children 8-11. For children under 8, when accompanied by a legal guardian, fees are fully granted.

For further information, contact us at chicagoauto@auto.com

34. Q: Which is correct according to the announcement?

(a) Children under 8 can enjoy the show on their own.
(b) The Chicago Auto Show is the biggest auto show in the world.
(c) Tickets can be bought only through online routes.
(d) Affordable cars are also featured on the show.

35. Q: What cannot be inferred from the announcement?

(a) It is not the first time for the Chicago Auto Show to take place.
(b) The Auto Show lasts for more than a day.
(c) There are no special discounts for seniors.
(d) Children under 8 has to pay for the ticket, but only partially.

정 답 표

해석본

제1부	Q1	Q2	Q3	Q4	Q5
1	B	C	C	B	D
2	D	A	B	A	A
3	B	A	D	A	C
4	D	C	C	C	A
5	D	C	A	B	–
6	B	B	A	C	D
7	B	A	D	C	C
8	D	B	C	C	B
9	A	B	A	D	C
10	B	C	A	D	B
11	D	C	B	–	–
12	D	C	A	D	C
13	B	A	D	C	D
14	A	A	C	C	B
15	A	C	A	B	D
16	C	D	B	D	A
17	D	D	A	B	D
18	C	D	D	A	C
19	D	D	D	C	B

제2부	Q1	Q2	Q3	Q4	Q5
빈칸	D	D	B	A	D
연결어	A	C	C	C	–
흐름상	C	B	B	D	–
주제	D	C	D	C	D
코렉트	Q1	Q2	Q3	Q4	Q5
	A	B	A	C	D
	Q6	Q7	Q8	Q9	
	A	C	D	C	

추론	Q1	Q2	Q3	Q3	Q5
	C	C	D	D	B
	Q6				
	D				
세트 문제	Q1	Q2	Q3	Q4	
	C	D	D	D	

제3부	Q1	Q2	Q3	Q4	Q5
지엽성	D	C	B	A	C
	Q6	Q7			
	B	D			
일반화	D	D	A	D	D
극단적	C	D	D	C	B
정반대	D	A	D	D	C
논리 전개	B	A	A	B	–
디테일	D	C	B	A	B
부정 내용	C	D	D	B	C

제4부 독해 실전 세트 #1

Q1	Q2	Q3	Q4	Q5	Q6	Q7	Q8	Q9	Q10
A	A	B	C	B	A	B	B	A	C
Q11	Q12	Q13	Q14	Q15	Q16	Q17	Q18	Q19	Q20
B	D	B	A	D	B	D	B	C	D
Q21	Q22	Q23	Q24	Q25	Q26	Q27	Q28	Q29	Q30
C	C	D	D	D	A	D	D	B	A
Q31	Q32	Q33	Q34	Q35					
B	B	C	B	D					

제4부 독해 실전 세트 #2

Q1	Q2	Q3	Q4	Q5	Q6	Q7	Q8	Q9	Q10
C	D	C	A	B	A	A	C	D	C
Q11	Q12	Q13	Q14	Q15	Q16	Q17	Q18	Q19	Q20
D	C	D	C	A	D	C	C	B	D
Q21	Q22	Q23	Q24	Q25	Q26	Q27	Q28	Q29	Q30
D	B	D	C	A	B	C	A	B	A
Q31	Q32	Q33	Q34	Q35					
C	B	B	D	A					

제4부 실전 세트 #3

Q1	Q2	Q3	Q4	Q5	Q6	Q7	Q8	Q9	Q10
D	D	D	B	D	A	B	A	B	A
Q11	Q12	Q13	Q14	Q15	Q16	Q17	Q18	Q19	Q20
C	C	A	A	B	D	D	D	D	D
Q21	Q22	Q23	Q24	Q25	Q26	Q27	Q28	Q29	Q30
C	D	D	C	D	C	D	C	D	B
Q31	Q32	Q33	Q34	Q35					
A	C	D	D	D					

제4부 독해 실전 세트 #4

Q1	Q2	Q3	Q4	Q5	Q6	Q7	Q8	Q9	Q10
C	A	A	D	D	D	D	D	C	A
Q11	Q12	Q13	Q14	Q15	Q16	Q17	Q18	Q19	Q20
D	A	C	A	D	C	D	D	A	B
Q21	Q22	Q23	Q24	Q25	Q26	Q27	Q28	Q29	Q30
C	C	D	C	A	B	C	B	B	D
Q31	Q32	Q33	Q34	Q35					
D	C	C	B	C					

제4부 독해 실전 세트 #5

Q1	Q2	Q3	Q4	Q5	Q6	Q7	Q8	Q9	Q10
D	C	D	B	A	C	C	D	B	A
Q11	Q12	Q13	Q14	Q15	Q16	Q17	Q18	Q19	Q20
C	B	C	D	C	B	B	C	B	D
Q21	Q22	Q23	Q24	Q25	Q26	Q27	Q28	Q29	Q30
D	A	D	B	D	D	C	A	D	D
Q31	Q32	Q33	Q34	Q35					
C	D	B	D	D					

전체 지문 해석

빈칸정답

패턴#2 통념뒤집기

원리 설명 p. 26 – 27

Nowadays, These days

Scientists

첫째는 시간 개념으로 뒤집히는 방식이고

둘째는 대중, 다수 vs 전문가 로 뒤집히는 방식

무조건 바로 주제

문제 푸는 방법 p. 27

뒤집힌 통념인지 뒤집히고 나서의 통념인지 파악해서 빈칸을 채워넣기

패턴#3 예시, 나열

쏘아보기 단서 p. 34

쉼표의 연속

원리 설명 p. 34

such. 뒤쪽이 중요

such as. 앞쪽이 중요

문제 푸는 방법 p. 35

쉼표가 연속해서 나오면 나열이다. 나열된 것은 읽지 않고 main idea를 파악하면 끝.

그 앞 / 그 뒤

패턴#4 빈칸 위치 접근법

원리 설명 p. 43

마지막 문장 읽는다

패턴#6 편지글

쏘아보기 단서 p. 58

i'm afraid that, unfortunately

please, would appreciate it if

패턴#8 문장 기호

원리 설명 및 문제풀이 방법 p. 74 - 75

질문에 대한 답이 정답

읽지 않는다.

무조건 읽는다.

강조, 인용, 인용 / 강조

쉼표가 여럿이 나열된 경우는 나열(예시 나열 단원 참고)

코렉트문제풀이

패턴#9 양괄식

문제풀이 p. 83

Thus, Therefore, consequently, So

연결어

패턴#11 부정 후엔 긍정

원리 설명 p. 98

A is C

A is C

A is C

패턴#12 연구내용/결과

p. 104

연구 내용

연구 결과

원리 설명 p. 104

연구 내용

연구 결과

원리 설명 p. 105

연구 내용

연구 결과

패턴#15 인과 관계

쏘아보기 단서 p. 128

As a result, consequently, initially, due to, factor, so, then

문제풀이 p. 129

지문 전체에 인과관계 쏘아보기 단서가 하나 더 있을 때

패턴#16 시간 흐름

쏘아보기 단서 p. 136

연도

변화를 나타내는 동사 (become, increase, decrease)

문제풀이 p. 137

2개

패턴#17 트윈타워

원리 설명 p. 144

둘의 관계

관계